Definiteness: A Linguistic Study (Volume 2)

Definiteness: A Linguistic Study (Volume 2)

Edited by
Sylvester Carey

MURPHY & MOORE

www.murphy-moorepublishing.com

Published by Murphy & Moore Publishing,
1 Rockefeller Plaza,
New York City, NY 10020, USA

ISBN: 978-1-63987-153-7

Cataloging-in-Publication Data

Definiteness : a linguistic study. Volume 2 / edited by Sylvester Carey.
    p. cm.
Includes bibliographical references and index.
ISBN 978-1-63987-153-7
1. Definiteness (Linguistics). 2. Linguistics. 3. Grammar, Comparative and general--Determiners. I. Carey, Sylvester.
P299.D43 D44 2022
415--dc23

For information on all Murphy & Moore Publications
visit our website at www.murphy-moorepublishing.com

Contents

Preface

The main aim of this book is to educate learners and enhance their research focus by presenting diverse topics covering this vast field. This is an advanced book which compiles significant studies by distinguished experts in the area of analysis. This book addresses successive solutions to the challenges arising in the area of application, along with it; the book provides scope for future developments.

Definiteness is a semantic feature of noun phrases that distinguishes between entities that are specific and identifiable in a given context, and others which are not. The typical noun phrase picks out a unique, familiar, specific referent. The expression of definiteness varies considerably across languages. Definiteness is usually marked in the English language by the selection of determiners, such as articles. Certain determiners like 'a', 'an', 'many', and 'some', along with numbers mark indefinite noun phrases, while others like 'the', 'that', etc., mark definite noun phrases. Definiteness is also marked morphologically in a few languages. Some languages like Japanese do not express definiteness at all. This book is a compilation of chapters that discuss the most vital concepts and emerging trends in the study of definiteness. Different approaches, evaluations, methodologies and advanced studies on this topic have been included herein. A number of latest researches have been included to keep the readers up-to-date with the global concepts in this area of linguistics.

It was a great honour to edit this book, though there were challenges, as it involved a lot of communication and networking between me and the editorial team. However, the end result was this all-inclusive book covering diverse themes in the field.

Finally, it is important to acknowledge the efforts of the contributors for their excellent chapters, through which a wide variety of issues have been addressed. I would also like to thank my colleagues for their valuable feedback during the making of this book.

Editor

A morpho-semantic account of weak definites and bare institutional singulars in English

Adina Williams

New York University

Weak definites in English have been widely studied as an example of when the definite article doesn't contribute uniqueness (Aguilar-Guevara & Zwarts 2011; Aguilar-Guevara et al. 2014, among others). I take *uniqueness* to stem from the interaction between definiteness and number within the noun phrase. From this perspective, weak definites should be seen as a data point situated in the larger cross-literature on number. One particular phenomenon from the literature on number, the understudied class of the English bare institutional singulars (BISs), has been discovered to share several semantic properties with weak definiteness, namely number neutrality, referential deficiency, and lexical idiosyncrasy. In this chapter, I postulate a shared account of English weak definites and BISs that utilizes semantic root ambiguity (Rappaport Hovav & Levin 1998; Levinson 2014) as a way to account for these facts. This account has syntactic consequences that resonate with recent morphosyntactic accounts of number phenomena that argue NumP is the host of number interpretation and marking (Ritter 1991; 1992; 1995) in languages like Amharic, (Kramer 2009), Halkomelem Salish (Wiltschko 2008), and Haitian Creole (Déprez 2005).

1 Introduction

Noun phrase constructions called *weak definites* (Birner & Ward 1994; Poesio 1994) have been heavily studied in English (Carlson & Sussman 2005; Carlson et al. 2006; Aguilar-Guevara & Zwarts 2011; Aguilar-Guevara 2014) and other languages (Schwarz 2009; 2013; 2014). They pose a problem for classical accounts of definite noun phrases (Frege 1892; Russell 1905; Hawkins 1978; Sharvy 1980; Heim 1982) which require them to be referential and denote unique individuals in the discourse, as is evidenced by (1) below.

(1) *Bob went to **the store** and Mary did too.* (Carlson 2006: 19)
     (Different stores OK.)

(2) *Bob is in **jail** and Fred is too.* (Carlson 2006: 18)
     (Different jails OK.)

Interestingly, English has yet another noun phrase construction – the BARE INSTITUTIONAL SINGULAR (BIS), as in (2) – that is not marked for definiteness, but shares many semantic properties with the weak definite, including number neutrality, diminished referential capacity, and lexical idiosyncrasy. Although it has been noted that not all lexical items can participate in weak definite and BIS constructions (Carlson 2006; Carlson et al. 2006; Aguilar-Guevara & Zwarts 2011; Aguilar-Guevara et al. 2014; Aguilar-Guevara & Schulpen 2014), very few accounts have used this fact as fundamental in their analysis of weak definites (but see Baldwin et al. 2006). In this chapter, I propose a shared account for both weak definite and BIS constructions that accounts for both their interpretive similarities and their lexical idiosyncrasy.

I propose that interpretive similarities between weak definite and BIS constructions can be derived via root semantic type ambiguity (see Rappaport Hovav & Levin 1998), parallel to Levinson (2014) on verbal argument structure alternations. The lexical items that can occur in weak definite or BIS constructions have a many-to-one mapping between their syntactic roots and potential denotations of those roots, unlike most lexical items (e.g. the *strong definites*[1]) that have a one-to-one mapping. Interestingly, no lexical item can participate in both weak definite and BIS constructions, suggesting that, although roots from both classes are special in that they are semantically ambiguous, the two subclasses of roots are associated with different pairs of possible denotations. Furthermore, the root denotation interacts with whether a definite determiner can be merged later in the derivation, and determines which of two versions of the determiner can be merged.

---

[1]I use the term *strong* to mean definites that are unique and referring, which is slightly different from the use of the term in Schwarz (2009; 2013).

I restrict my focus to weak nominal constructions[2] utilizing directional predicates with location/institution nouns, because they provide a unique testing ground for investigating the relationship between number and definiteness. Representative sentences of the three types are given below in (3–5):

(3)   *Ron went to **the store**.*   WEAK DEFINITE SINGULAR

(4)   *Ron went to **school**.*   BARE INSTITUTIONAL SINGULAR

(5)   *Ron went to **the castle**.*   STRONG DEFINITE SINGULAR

In my examples, I hold the main verb and preposition constant, because altering either has been shown to affect the availability of the number neutral interpretation (Aguilar-Guevara 2014: 18–19). Although other verbal predicates can be used in sentences that get weak readings, I use the light verb *to go* because it is compatible with all three sentence types (3–5). Because of their restricted syntactic distribution, weak definites are often cited as having an "idiomatic" flavor (Nunberg et al. 1994) – a property they share with BISs. I chose to use lexical items from the location/institution class of weak definites (Stvan 1998) and BISs, because they are the most freely combining (Baldwin et al. 2006), making them a good class to work with.

This chapter is organized as follows. §2 argues in favor of interpretive similarities between weak definites and BISs. §3 discusses the lexical idiosyncrasy of roots that participate in weak definite and BIS constructions. §4 discusses syntactic consequences of adopting a root semantic type ambiguity account of weakness in English nominals. §5 provides a morpho-syntactic analysis that builds on work on cross-linguistic number that suggests number neutrality has a syntactic reflex, i.e. a lack of a Num projection (as in languages with *general number*). I also show that the denotation of roots affects which interpretations and syntactic structures are possible. Finally, §6 concludes.

---

[2]The term *weak definite* does not necessarily correspond to a single, uniform class in either the syntactic or semantic sense, and thus, different subtypes of weak definites have been given a wide range of theoretical and experimental treatments (see, for example, Barker 2005; Klein et al. 2009; Aguilar-Guevara & Zwarts 2011; Klein 2011; Aguilar-Guevara & Schulpen 2014; Schwarz 2014), and extending this account to other subtypes (e.g. those given in Stvan 1998) is left for future work.

2 Weak definite singulars and bare institutional singulars share semantic properties

Weak definite singulars and BISs share interpretive similarities with each other, to the exclusion of strong, referring definite singulars. There are multiple diagnostics for weakness (see Carlson & Sussman 2005), all of which indicate that BISs and weak definites do not have to refer to a singular entity: they can be used in contexts where multiple entities can satisfy the descriptive content of the definite, they can receive sloppy identity under VP ellipsis, their behavior differs from that of referring definites under a type of sluice (under a novel diagnostic test), and they have an impaired ability to antecede pronouns in the following discourse.

Before I present the diagnostic tests, it is important to caution the reader that some weak definite Det-N strings are ambiguous between weak and strong interpretations. Therefore, I use a subset of lexical items for each class of nominals to help readers access the appropriate readings throughout this section (these lexical items are provided in the footnotes to Table 1 for reference).

Table 1: Classes of lexical items

	+Definite marked	−Definite marked
Weak interpretation	WEAK DEFINITE[a]	BARE INSTITUTIONAL SINGULAR[b]
Strong interpretation	STRONG DEFINITE[c]	*[d]

[a]Relevant lexical items: e.g. *the store, the bank, the hospital* (potentially ambiguous between weak and strong definite interpretations).
[b]Relevant lexical items: e.g. *school, church, prison, jail* (unambiguously weak).
[c]Relevant lexical items: e.g. *the castle, the stadium, the restaurant* (unambiguously strong).
[d]I assume this cell is empty due to the Blocking Principle discussed in Chierchia (1998: 360), and Deal & Nee (2016). The Blocking Principle states that bare nominals cannot be interpreted as definite, because there is a lexically specified type shifter present in the language that performs this function.

2.1 Multiple entities satisfying descriptive content

Weak definites and BISs can be used in contexts where multiple entities satisfy the descriptive content of the noun phrase, suggesting that they don't uniquely refer (Carlson & Sussman 2005). In (6–8) below, each of the bolded noun phrases fails to require a single unique referent:

(6)   *Don went to **the zoo**.*

(7)   *Sue took her nephew to **the hospital/the store/the beach**.* (Carlson et al. 2006: 2)

(8)   *Please take **the elevator** to the second floor.* (Aguilar-Guevara 2014: 14)

Although the examples above can be used to refer to identifiable, unique referents in the discourse, one can also utter (6) in cities where there are multiple zoos, (7) in towns where there are multiple hospitals, stores or beaches, and (8) when standing before a bay of elevators. Furthermore, weak definites can also be used in situations with multiple potential referents in the discourse, allowing the weak definite noun phrase to stand for a plurality of entities:[3]

(9)   Context: Ron has been looking for Don, who was supposed to help him set up a party, but then went missing for a while.
Ron: *Hey Don! Where have you been? The party starts in an hour!*
Don: *I went to **the store** to buy balloons. I had to go to **four of them** because the first three were all sold out!*

In the mini-discourse in (9), the bolded definite marked noun phrase *the store* does not impose a restriction that there only be a single, unique store in the context, because immediately following the definite, Don mentions that he went to *four of them*. If the definite noun phrase in (9) did impose this restriction, we would predict the mini-discourse to be infelicitous. Similarly, the bare singular, as in (10), can also be used felicitiously in situations where multiple entities satisfy the BIS's descriptive content.

(10)   Context: Ron just met up with Don at their ten-year high school reunion.
Ron: *Hey Don! Wow, you look great! What have you been up to for the last ten years?*
Don: *Funny you should ask... Actually I went to **prison** for five years after high school. I spent the first three years on Riker's Island, and the last two, in Alcatraz.*

Since BISs and singular weak definite noun phrases both lack the uniqueness required for strong definite descriptions under this diagnostic, one would hope that the two types of weak nominal should have some grammatical similarities. Compare the two discourses above with the one below:

---

[3]The interpretation of the following examples is not exhaustive; they are infelicitous in situations where there are only e.g. four stores, as in (9).

(11)   Context: Ron and Don are on a vacation in Britain. They split up for a few days and are just meeting up again to continue on their adventure. The two had discussed their travel plans before splitting up.
Ron: *Hey Don! How did your weekend go? See anything interesting?*
Don: *Yeah, I had a really great weekend. I went to* **the castle** *and got some great pictures.* ??*On Saturday, I went to Windsor Castle, then took a train over to Dover Castle on Sunday.*

In this case, because Don's response is unnatural, I conclude that the definite noun phrase *the castle* requires a single, unique referent in the discourse. The incompatibility of (11) suggests that the lexical item conditions whether the uniqueness presupposition is present, since it is unacceptable to use the singular definite noun phrase *the castle* in a context where there are multiple castles.

2.2 Sloppy readings under VP ellipsis

Singular weak definites and BISs differ from strong definites in that they do not require that the elided noun and the overt one refer to the same exact individual; they merely require that the individual(s) they refer to satisfy the descriptive content of their shared noun phrase. This loose identity requirement on noun phrases under VP ellipsis is called SLOPPY IDENTITY.

(12)   *Bob went to* **the store** *and Mary did too.* (Carlson 2006: 19)
(Different stores OK.)

(13)   *Bob is in* **jail** *and Fred is too.* (Carlson 2006: 18)
(Different jails OK.)

If the noun phrases in the antecedent VP in (12) and (13) are still faithfully duplicated in the ellipsis site, then presumably they cannot be strong definite noun phrases. Under VP ellipsis, they only need to match in the syntactic material that is present. Since the syntactic material present does not introduce a unique noun phrase, strict coreference is not required. In other cases, the noun in the elided phrase is required to be coreferential with the unique singular individual in the antecedent VP, as in (14):

(14)   *Ron went to* **the castle** *and Don did too.*   (strong reading only)
(Must be the same castle.)

In (14), there is a full strong noun phrase present in the ellipsis site. We only get a felicitous interpretation if the overt noun phrase and elided one refer to the same individual. In (15) below, we can see that *the store* is interpreted as a weak definite based on this diagnostic from above:

(15)   *Ron went to **the store** and Don did too. Ron went to Krogers, and Don went to Meijers.*

We can see that *the store* in (15) can be used felicitiously in VP ellipsis contexts, where multiple locations satisfy the descriptive content of the noun phrase.

2.3 Sluicing

One final diagnostic, which is novel, comes from another ellipsis phenomenon, sluicing (Ross 1967; 1969). Sluicing separates strong definites from weak definites and BISs, as the latter two are acceptable under a sluice, and the former is not:

(16)   *I know Ron went to **church** as a kid, but I don't know which one/church.*

(17)   *I know Don went to **the store** after work, but I don't know which one/store.*

(18)   *?? I know Don went to **the castle** after work, but I don't know which one/castle.*

In (18), one must have a referent in mind to felicitiously use the definite marked noun phrase, which explains the unnaturalness of the sluice. Since (16) and (17) are acceptable under the sluice, one particular referent is not required. Thus, like the ellipsis diagnostic above in §2.3, sluicing allows us to argue for the lack of referentiality present in weak nominals.

2.4 Limited capacity to establish discourse referents

Following Aguilar-Guevara & Zwarts (2011: 182), I note that weak definites and BISs have a limited ability to establish discourse referents, which results in them being worse than strong definites at anteceding pronominal *it*. I assume that anaphorically linked noun phrases, like *it*, must match their antecedent in as many features (such as number specification and referentiality) as possible. If *it* is taken to be (generally) referring, and specified for singular, then it will have trouble matching its features with weak nominals that are neither referring nor specified as being singular (see §2.1). If there is only one nominal in the context, and it is referential and singular, *it* can be anaphorically linked to it, as in (19) and (20):

(19)   *Ron went to **the store** and Don went to **it** too. They both went to Krogers.*

(20)   *Ron went to* **the castle** *and Don went to* **it** *too. They both went to Neu-schwanstein Castle.*

However, if we have pronominal *it* – which is referring (in this case), and wants to match its number features with its antecedent – in a context with multiple potential referents (as in 21), the sentence becomes less felicitious.

(21)   *Ron went to* **the store** *and Don went to* **it** *too. ?Ron went to Krogers, and Don went to Meijers.*

Despite the fact that lexical items like *store* can participate in weak definite constructions, by establishing coreference with *it* in (21), the noun phrase *the store* can only receive a strong, referring interpretation. One way to encode this difference would be to say that some singular definite noun phrases (like *the store*) are actually ambiguous between noun phrases that are un-marked for number, and those that are marked for singular. In English, these two options will be string identical. When a pronoun tries to establish coreference with a definite noun phrase that is un-marked for number, the result is degraded, as in (21).

If pronouns must match features with their antecedents, non-referring noun phrases like BISs should not have enough features to match with the pronoun, and thus should be even more degraded. This prediction is borne out:

(22)   *Don went to* **church**$_i$ *and Ron went to* **it**$_{*i,j}$ *too.*

Establishing an anaphoric link with a referring pronoun is less acceptable for weak definites, but the BISs are unable to establish coreference with the pronoun at all. Therefore, one could assume that there are two missing features that make BISs unable to set up coreference, while for weak definites, there is only one (i.e. the number feature is missing). I claim that NumP is the crucial projection that is missing in both types of weak nominals; see §4 for further discussion.

2.5 Summary

In this section, I described the interpretive similarities that weak definites and BISs share to the exclusion of strong definites; weak nominals can be used in situations where multiple entities satisfy the descriptive content (§2.1), can receive sloppy readings under VP ellipsis (§2.3), are compatible with sluicing (§2.3), and have limited capacity to establish discourse referents (§2.4).

3 Lexical idiosyncrasy

As discussed in the introduction, not all lexical items are equally able to participate in weak constructions (see Table 1). Weak definite and BIS interpretations
are particularly sensitive to the identity of the lexical item:

(23)   *Don went to **the zoo/#the conservatory**.*

(24)   *Please take **the elevator/#the forklift** to the second floor.*

(25)   *Sue took her nephew to **the hospital/#the hospice**.*

Even roots with comparable meanings (e.g. *hospital* and *hospice*) are unable to
receive weak interpretations. It has been widely noted that weak interpretations
for nominals are only available for certain lexical items, but few works other
than Baldwin et al. (2006) discuss this explicitly. Certain lexical items, e.g. *store*,
from the WEAK-STRONG AMBIGUOUS class can be interpreted as weak or as strong,
while others, e.g. *castle*, from the STRONG-ONLY class can never be interpreted
weakly (repeated from above, 12 and 14).

(26)   *Ron went to **the store** and Don did too.*
       (Can be the same store.)

(27)   *Ron went to **the castle** and Don did too.*
       (Must be the same castle.)

Because root identity seems to condition whether the weak reading is available, perhaps a lexical ambiguity is present. This could mean that there are two
denotations paired with the root, *store*, but only one denotation for the root, *castle*. I argue that this lexical ambiguity manifests itself in the semantic type of
the root (a lá Levinson 2014), as opposed to being a restriction on the type of
elements that are present in the extension of the noun phrase.

The choice of root has consequences for the syntax. One piece of evidence
in favor of a root-level semantic ambiguity that affects syntax is that the weak
interpretation disappears when the root appears outside of constrained syntactic
frames compatible with the weak interpretation. For example, *store* cannot be
interpreted weakly in subject position:[4]

---

[4]If the noun is present in the subject position of a "characterizing sentence" in the sense of
Carlson (1977) and subsequent work, the definite noun phrase can receive a kind interpretation:

   (i)   ***The store** is a miraculous and entertaining place to visit.*

I take kind-referring noun phrases to be constructed differently than the definites I account
for here, and leave an account comparing the two for future work.

(28)   ***The store*** *is closed today* (**but I don't know which*).
       (Must be a strong reading.)

Similarly, lexical items from the BIS class cannot receive a weak interpretation in subject position, see (29). However, when they occur with a definite article, they must receive a strong, referring interpretation; the weak interpretation is not allowed, see (30):

(29)   ***School*** *is closed today.*
       ('School' here is a proper name referring to the speaker's school, or to the maximal set of all relevant schools.)

(30)   *Ron went to* ***the school*** *and Don did too.*
       (Must be the same school.)

Thus, lexical items from each of the three classes can receive a referring interpretation when they are in definite marked noun phrases, but only a subset can receive a weak interpretation when definite marked or bare. Some roots can only receive strong interpretations (STRONG ONLY). Some (roots from the WEAK-STRONG AMBIGUOUS class) can receive either. Yet, a third class of lexical items can be unmarked for plurality or definiteness, and also when they have definite marking, they can only receive a strong interpretation (BIS). The behavior of these classes of roots is summarized in Table 2.[5]

Table 2: Three lexical classes of roots

	STRONG ONLY	STRONG-WEAK AMBIG.	BIS
the+NP can be strong	Y	Y	Y
the+NP can be weak	N	Y	N
can be bare/incorporated	N	N	Y

3.1 Root semantic type ambiguity is not homophony

I've argued that weakness starts at the root as a type difference, which then percolates up to affect higher syntactic projections. However, what sort of semantic

---

[5]A lexical item that cannot get a strong or a weak interpretation, and cannot be bare, is unlikely to exist. What would be its distribution? Would it only be present in indefinite noun phrases with *a*? This doesn't seem very plausible. I leave the task of extending my lexical account to indefinites to future work.

ambiguity do we have in this case? I argue that this is a case of true ambiguity, and not simple homophony. Under a homophony account, the roots have no inherent connection to each other. This would mean that we would have two lexical items that are both pronounced, e.g. *store*, and that their interpretive similarity is accidental.

One way to test for homophony was put forth in the general number literature (Rullmann & You 2006; Wilhelm 2008). In this diagnostic, homophonous lexical items receive parallel interpretations under VP ellipsis. I assume the following denotations[6] for the two homophonous lexical items:

(31) $[\![\text{pen}_{\text{enclosure}}]\!] := \lambda x.pen_{enclosure}(x)$

(32) $[\![\text{pen}_{\text{implement}}]\!] := \lambda x.pen_{implement}(x)$

(33) *Lee saw a pen, and Sam did, too.*

    a.   *Lee saw an animal enclosure and Sam saw an animal enclosure too.*

    b.   *Lee saw a writing implement and Sam saw a writing implement too.*

    c. * *Lee saw a writing implement and Sam saw an animal enclosure.*

    d. * *Lee saw an animal enclosure and Lee saw a writing implement.*

In the example above, the word *pen* must receive the same lexical interpretation across the two seeing events; either it always has to be interpreted as an animal enclosure (as in 33a, with denotation as in 31), or always interpreted as a writing implement (as in 33b, with denotation as in 32). Thus, if singular weak definites and BISs were lexically ambiguous, we should not expect them to have readings where the number interpretation of the noun phrase differed between the main clause and the elided one. However, the two phrases are allowed to differ in number interpretation:

(34) *Lee went to **the school**/school in Boston and Sam did too.*

    a. *Lee went to only one school/store in Boston and Sam went to only one too.*

    b. *Lee went to multiple schools/stores in Boston and Sam went to multiple too.*

    c. *Lee went to only one school/store in Boston and Sam went to multiple.*

    d. *Lee went to multiple schools/stores in Boston and Sam went to only one.*

---

[6]Type conventions are as follows: x, y, z are from the domain of individuals and are type e; e', e'', e''' are from the domain of events and are type v; m, n are from the domain of numbers and are type n; j, k are from the domain of kinds and are type k; type t is for truth values; types can be combinatory; P, Q are used for higher types, and their types are specified via subscript.

Thus, we can conclude that the ambiguity associated with certain lexical items is not an ambiguity in the interpretation of the lexical item that merely prunes the elements in the extension. Instead, I argue for a semantic lexical ambiguity that affects higher structure (i.e. a type ambiguity), paired with a structural ambiguity that is higher.

3.2 Root denotations for weak definites, BISs, and strong definites

Now that we know no single lexical root can participate in both weak definite and BIS constructions, I postulate semantic types for the three classes of roots. Across all classes, roots with type $\langle n, \langle e, t \rangle \rangle$ are "countable"; and for the strong determiner to be present, there must be a countable root present in the tree. This accords with the intuition that if one knows the referent of a noun phrase, one also knows the number specification of that referent. Otherwise, the weak version of the determiner is inserted, resulting in a weak, non-uniquely referring interpretation for the noun phrase.

Each of the three classes of lexical item has different sets of potential denotations for their roots; STRONG-ONLY lexical items have only one potential meaning, and can only be of type $\langle n, \langle e, t \rangle \rangle$, STRONG-WEAK AMBIGUOUS lexical items are semantically ambiguous and can be of type $\langle n, \langle e, t \rangle \rangle$, or type $\langle e, t \rangle$, and BIS lexical items can have roots of type $\langle n, \langle e, t \rangle \rangle$ or type $\langle k, t \rangle$. Furthermore, I postulate two versions of the definite determiner, one that encodes the "strong", uniquely referring interpretation of the definite, and another that does not.

4 Syntactic consequences of root semantic ambiguity

The interpretive similarities discussed in §2 align with cross-linguistic analyses of non-inflectional number phenomena in Haitian Creole (Déprez 2005) and Halkomelem Salish (Wiltschko 2008); these accounts argue that these properties correspond to number neutrality which is syntactically cashed out as the absence of NumP. Additionally, recent work on Russian nominal agreement (Landau 2016) also points to NumP as necessary for both cardinality and anaphoricity. Bringing together semantic work on definiteness and cross-linguistic work on number neutrality, this analysis splits the semantic contribution to definiteness across two heads, D and Num, with Num contributing to number interpretation, and D contributing referentiality.

Following this cross-linguistic literature on number, I assume this I assume that both weak definites and BISs lack a NumP, which is the projection that contributes singular or plural interpretation (Ritter 1991; 1992; 1995). I build towards the structures in (35–37), which correspond to (3–5).

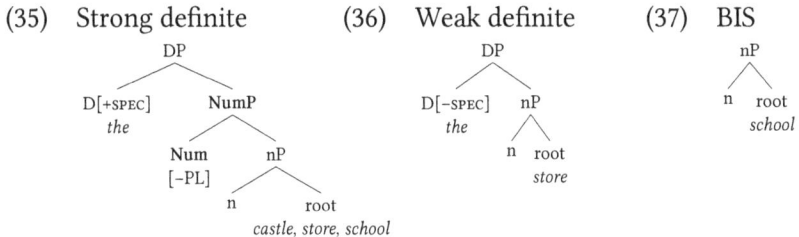

(35) Strong definite   (36) Weak definite   (37) BIS

In (35–37), we see that all three classes of roots can appear in the strong construction (35), but only certain roots can appear in the weak construction (36) and the BIS construction (37). This accords with the data provided in §3. Moreover, (36) and (37) differ from (35) in that they lack a Num projection. I argue that this syntactic difference results from the semantic type of the root. While BIS and the weak definite are syntactically similar in lacking a NumP, they differ in whether they have a DP layer. This analysis takes BISs to be pseudo-incorporated noun phrases, following Carlson (2006: 9–10), who has argued for such an account in English and for languages like Greek (Gehrke & Lekakou 2013), as well as Niuean and Turkish (Massam 2001; 2009). Thus, weak definites and BISs are both smaller than strong, uniquely referring definites; weak definites are missing one projection, NumP, while BISs are missing two, NumP and DP. This "small" size interacts with an aspect of the interpretation of weak definites and BISs: the so-called semantic enrichment of weak definites and BISs follows from their super-local relationships in a manner that is reminiscent of many idiomatic constructions across languages (Marantz 1995). This is discussed in more detail in the next section.

If the account is correct in correlating root ambiguity with syntactic consequences, we might expect syntactic structure to affect the weak, number neutral interpretation. This prediction is borne out in two ways: changing the morphological number marking on these nominals or modifying them with structurally high adjectives bleeds the weak number-neutral interpretation. If we assume that the locus of number marking and interpretation is NumP (Ritter 1991; 1992; 1995), then these syntactic effects suggest that this projection cannot be present in noun phrases that receive the weak interpretation. Other preliminary evidence of the importance of NumP for interpretation comes from the domain of semantic agreement; Landau (2016) adduces additional evidence that NumP may be an important boundary for referential interpretation within the nominal domain from Hebrew attributive adjectival agreement.

4.1 Enrichment of weak nominals

Another often discussed fact about weak definites is that they receive semantically enriched interpretations. Following Aguilar-Guevara & Zwarts (2011: 182), weak definites display "enrichment [that] is stereotypical in the sense that it invokes the most common circumstances under which the event referred to by the sentence could happen". Furthermore, Aguilar-Guevara & Zwarts note that if the presence of the weak reading tends to co-occur with the presence of the semantic enrichment (below examples copied from Aguilar-Guevara & Zwarts 2011: 182, ex. 10b, 11b):

(38)   *Lola went to the store. = Lola went to the store. + Lola did shopping.*

(39)   *?? Lola went to the store to pick up a friend.*

Under the weak reading, (39) is anomalous, because the stereotypical enrichment is not present. Like weak definites, BISs require enrichment:

(40)   *The janitor went to school. = The janitor went to a school + attended it.*

(41)   *?? The janitor went to school to clean.*[7]

Parallel to (38–39), (40–41) show that the weak reading generally disappears when the extra enrichment is blocked. Extra enrichment is reminiscent of idiomatic expressions, where lexical items can get special meanings based on the contexts they are found in. Following (Marantz 1997: 208), I take idiomatic interpretations of lexical items to crucially depend on their local syntactic context. Given my claim in earlier sections that weak definites and BISs are syntactically smaller than strong definites (see 35–37), the root is closer to the definite or the preposition in weak definite and BIS constructions, creating the perfect local environment for idiom-like enrichment of meaning.

4.2 Bleeding weakness

Now that we have seen some preliminary data compatible with the idea that weak nominals (i.e. singular weak definites and BISs) could be analyzed differently from their strong counterparts, I motivate my claim that this correlates with a syntactic difference at NumP. What evidence can we adduce that strings like *the store* can have weak or strong interpretations depending on whether NumP is

---

[7]This sentence can receive an interpretation that is full referential. Under this interpretation, the speaker claims that the janitor is going to the speaker's school to clean. For a similar example and more discussion, please see (28).

syntactically present? There are a few syntactic tests that suggest the difference between weak and strong nominals is below the level of DP. In the rest of this section, I discuss two syntactic modifications that block weak interpretations: plural marking and modification by high adjectives.

Following Carlson & Sussman (2005) and Aguilar-Guevara (2014), I use sloppy identity under VP ellipsis as the standard accepted diagnostic for weak interpretations of definites for the remainder of this section. Thus, when I use # for a sentence under the weak interpretation, I mean that it cannot be read as sloppy under VP ellipsis.

4.2.1 Plural marking bleeds weak interpretations

One test for this fact is that changing the apparent number marking on the definite description bleeds the weak reading (Aguilar-Guevara 2014: 19):[8]

(42) *Don went to **the bank** and Ron did too. Don went to First National Bank, and Ron went to CitiBank.* (copied from (15) above)

(43) *Don went to **the banks** and Ron did too. #Don went to First National Bank and CitiBank, while Don went to Chase and Bank of America.*

(44) *Don went to **the banks** and Ron did too. They both visited First National Bank and CitiBank.*

If we compare (42) and (43), the only difference is the plural marking. While (42) can receive sloppy readings under ellipsis and patterns as weak nominals do with respect to the diagnostics in §2, (44) cannot, because the noun phrase *the banks* must be interpreted as uniquely referring to a salient plurality of banks.

---

[8]Examples of plural-marked weak definites do exist:

(i) *Lola went to **the mountains** and Alice did too. Lola went to the Alps and Alice visited the Appalachians.* (Based on Aguilar-Guevara 2014: 20, ex. 42)

(ii) *Ron washed **the dishes** and Don did too. Ron washed 20 dishes, but Don only washed one.*

Crucially, these readings are also only allowed for certain lexical items. For examples like these, I would assume that the plural marker has a different meaning, and perhaps, a different syntactic height. This is not entirely implausible in light of (i), because one has the intuition that the plural marker is talking about a number of mountain peaks which all contribute to a single mountain range. One potential way to go would be to follow Kramer (2015) in taking some plural markers to be merged low on the little n head, following the intuition that lower projections are more likely to get idiosyncratic meaning and condition contextual allosemy (Romanova 2004; Svenonius 2005; Marantz 2013).

In (44), adding plural marking causes the definite-marked noun phrase to lose its weak interpretation, and can only be taken to refer to a unique and salient plural set of bank locations. If weak readings are derived from kind property-denoting roots (i.e. they are not countable), and the addition of NumP requires a countable root, then plural marking hosted on NumP will be incompatible with weak readings. In (46) below, we have further evidence that adding plural marking bleeds the weak interpretation because the enrichment we see with the weak interpretation is suddenly no longer available.

(45) *Don went to **school** and Ron did too. Don went to Pioneer and Ron went to Huron.*

(46) *Don went to **schools** and Ron did too.*

For (46) the two boys both physically went to multiple institutions for whatever purpose (i.e. it doesn't have to be to attend school); this is in contrast to (45), where the enrichment is present, and each boy had to attend his respective school. Thus, if one varies the number specification on the noun phrase in a weak definite or BIS construction, the weak reading disappears, as is evidenced by the loss of the semantic enrichment. If it is true that number specification falls on NumP then adding a NumP bleeds the weak reading.

4.2.2 High adjectival modification bleeds weak interpretations

Another source of evidence comes from the fact that certain modifiers can bleed the weak interpretations of definite noun phrases (Aguilar-Guevara 2014). Certain modifiers (e.g. canonical property adjectives) are base-generated higher (Cinque 2010) than NumP, while others, classificatory or kind-referring ones (e.g. noun-noun compounds) are lower (see e.g. Laenzlinger 2005). The height differences between these subtypes of modifiers is straightforwardly visible from ordering facts:

(47)   *the expensive grocery store*

(48)   * *the grocery expensive store*

High modifiers force strong interpretations of definite marked noun phrases, suggesting that certain modifiers require countable nominals, while others don't.

(49)   *Don went to the [grocery, pet, drug, #good, #red, #expensive] store.*
       (Weak reading)

(50) *Don went to* [*boarding, nursing, catholic,* **good,* **red,* *expensive] *school.*
(Bare institutional singular)

(51) *Don went to the* [*good, red, expensive*] *school.*

In (49), the definite noun phrase is unable to receive a weak reading if there is a high adjective merged in the DP. Similarly, because BISs are structurally small, they also cannot host high modifiers, as in (50). These differences could be cashed out as the trees below in (52–54), which build upon (35–37).

(52) Strong definite   (53) Weak definite   (54) BIS

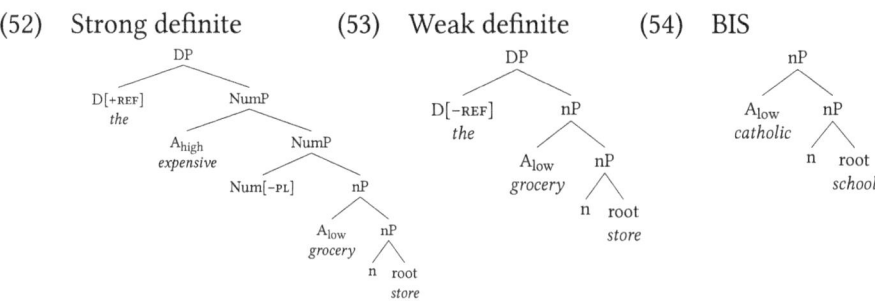

hus, high adjectives[9] select for a NumP. he presence of a NumP requires that the root be countable (i.e. type $\langle n, \langle e, t \rangle \rangle$), and countable roots require that the strong D be merged above it (or else there is a type clash). If there is no NumP present, a D could be merged or it could not be, depending on the identity of the root; this is the distinction between weak interpretations of definites and BISs.

4.3 Summary

In sum, this section has argued that a root semantic type ambiguity account has several syntactic consequences. Such an account predicts that semantic enrichment and idioms are similar, based on locality, and that the weak readings can be bled by several syntactic alterations within the DP, including plural marking and modification by high adjectives.

---

[9] The modifiers that preserve the weak readings, i.e. *grocery, pet* and *drug* do not seem to be run-of-the-mill modifiers (e.g. it appears that they're nominal and not adjectival). Thus, you could say that a syntactically low derivation process like noun-noun compounding could be happening here, perhaps at the little n level. I leave the question of how the syntax of compounding interacts with weakness to future work.

5 Analysis

Now that we have determined what sorts of semantic interpretation are required for weak readings of noun phrases, and that there are syntactic consequences, this section presents a compositional semantic fragment for strong definites, weak definites, and BISs, showing how root semantic type interacts with the interpretation of the definite article. I lay out my assumptions, then list lexical items, and finally provide a working fragment that derives the three separate interpretations, based on the syntactic structures I've advocated in §4.

First, I assume that countable nouns have atoms in their extensions, thus, I need to take an atomizer function; I take this one:

(55)   ATOMS(x) = $\{y|y \leq x \& \forall z \leq x[z \not\leq y]\}$ (Ouwayda 2014)

Starting at the root, we need different types of lexical items to capture the differences in potential interpretations each lexical item can receive. My three classes of roots have the following sets of denotations:

(56)   STRONG-ONLY: e.g. *castle, graveyard, stadium, restaurant.*
   a. Countable noun: $[\![castle]\!]_{\langle n, \langle e, t\rangle\rangle}$:= $\lambda n.\lambda x.castle(x)$ & $|$ATOMS$(x)|$ = n
      & $\forall y \in$ ATOMS$(x)[castle(y)]$

(57)   STRONG-WEAK AMBIGUOUS: e.g. *store, bank, hospital.*
   a. Countable noun: $[\![store_1]\!]_{\langle n, \langle e, t\rangle\rangle}$:= $\lambda n.\lambda x.store(x)$ & $|$ATOMS$(x)|$ = n
      & $\forall y \in$ ATOMS$(x)[store(y)]$
   b. Property: $[\![store_2]\!]_{\langle e, t\rangle}$:= $\lambda x.store(x)$

(58)   BIS: e.g. *school, jail, prison, church.*
   a. Countable noun: $[\![school_1]\!]_{\langle n, \langle e, t\rangle\rangle}$:= $\lambda n.\lambda x.school(x)$ & $|$ATOMS$(x)|$ =
      n & $\forall y \in$ ATOMS$(x)[school(y)]$
   b. Kind property: $[\![school_2]\!]_{\langle k, t\rangle}$:= $\lambda k.school(k)$

Next, I assume that the syntax requires a null categorizing head, n, which has the denotation of the polymorphic identity function; alternatively, it could have no semantic interpretation, and merely be a syntactically (and potentially phonologically) realized functional element.

Continuing up the tree, the insertion of Num depends on whether the noun phrase will be interpreted as plural or singular.[10] I assume three potential options.

---

[10]This is somewhat similar to Sauerland (2003) in that it assumes a binary specification for number, but unlike his system, my denotation for the plural does not include atoms in its extension.

If the noun phrase is specified for number, a contentful Num (as in 60 and 61) merges, otherwise, no lexical item[11] will be inserted.

(59)	∅ : No lexical item inserted

(60)	$[\![\text{Num}_{[+\text{PL}]}]\!] := \lambda P_{\langle n, \langle e, t \rangle \rangle}.\lambda y.\lambda m_{\langle n \rangle}.[P(m)(y) \;\&\; m > 1]$

(61)	$[\![\text{Num}_{[-\text{PL}]}]\!] := \lambda P_{\langle n, \langle e, t \rangle \rangle}.\lambda y.\lambda m_{\langle n \rangle}.[P(m)(y) \;\&\; m = 1]$

The choice of which option is possible is determined by the meaning of the root. First, if the root is not countable, no Num can be inserted; if it were, there would be a type-clash. If the root is countable, a Num is merged,[12] and it could either be a plural or a singular.

Finally, a $D_{[+\text{Def}]}$ can be inserted, depending on the type. There are two potential interpretations for the definite article.[13] The first is roughly Sharvy's (1980) denotation for *the* updated to take a higher type, $\langle n, \langle e, t \rangle \rangle$, to account for the countability of roots; this dentotation confers referentiality. The second is a kindifying definite article that takes a property and returns its corresponding kind if that kind is well-established (see Chierchia 1998 for details):

(62)	$[\![D_{[+\text{REF}]}]\!] := \lambda P_{\langle n, \langle e, t \rangle \rangle} : \exists x.\exists n.\forall y[\text{MAX}(P)(n)(y) \leftrightarrow x = y].\iota x.\exists n.$
	$[\text{MAX}(P)(n)(x)]$

(63)	$\text{MAX}(P)(n) := \lambda x.P(n)(x) \& \neg \exists y.[P(n)(y) \& x < y]$

(64)	$[\![D_{[-\text{REF}]}]\!] := \lambda P_{\langle e, t \rangle}.\lambda k.^{\cap}P = k$

If we have a STRONG-WEAK AMBIGUOUS lexical item, (64) will be inserted after the little n head, but if we have a BIS lexical item, (64) cannot be inserted or else there would be a type clash.

Next, we merge the preposition. I take prepositions that can facilitate weak readings to be ambiguous between normal (e.g. to_2) and incorporating variants

---

[11]For the moment, nothing relies on whether no Num is merged or whether a vacuous, or "expletive" version is merged, along the lines of Wood (2012), Myler (2014), among others.

[12]For this work, one could say that Num is privative and has the value PL and it would not affect the analysis. In this case, the singular would merely be a Num without any features. In this work, I follow Harbour (2007) and others in assuming a binary specification for Num.

[13]These two denotations for the definite article are not lexically connected under the present account. For the moment, these are merely homophones. This is not a desirable result, since the intuition is that there is something universally shared between a kindifying definite and a regular strong definite. In fact, there is no language known by this author that has a kindifying determiner that is not homophonous with the definite article. In future, it would be better to find an account which unifies the two, either by constructing one out of the other, or by finding a single denotation that can yield both interpretations.

(e.g. to_2),[14] since the weak interpretation can only occur when the definite is in certain syntactic configurations (e.g. when it is the complement of *to*). I also assume, following Aguilar-Guevara (2014), among others, that weak definites do not make explicit reference to individual atoms, and take Chierchia's (1998) type-shifters, DOWN and UP; DOWN takes one from a property to a kind, while UP takes one from a kind to a property.

(65) $[\![to_1]\!]_{\langle e, \langle v, t \rangle\rangle} := \lambda x.\lambda e.\text{GOAL}(e) = x$

(66) $[\![to_2]\!]_{\langle\langle k, t \rangle, \langle e, \langle v, t \rangle\rangle\rangle} := \lambda P_{\langle k,t\rangle}.\lambda e.\exists x.\exists k.[P(k) \& ^{\cup}k(x) \& \text{GOAL}(e) = x]$

The denotation for to_1 is the classical one for directional prepositions from event semantics (see Champollion 2017: 57, for one formulation). The denotation for to_1 is more unique, since it is an incorporating adposition.[15] It takes a kind property and tells you that there is a kind that satisfies the property and that one of its instantiations is the GOAL of an event.

The structure of a strong definite such as (5) is exemplified below as in (67). The main difference between this singular strong noun phrase and a strong plural one would be the specification on NumP:

(67)

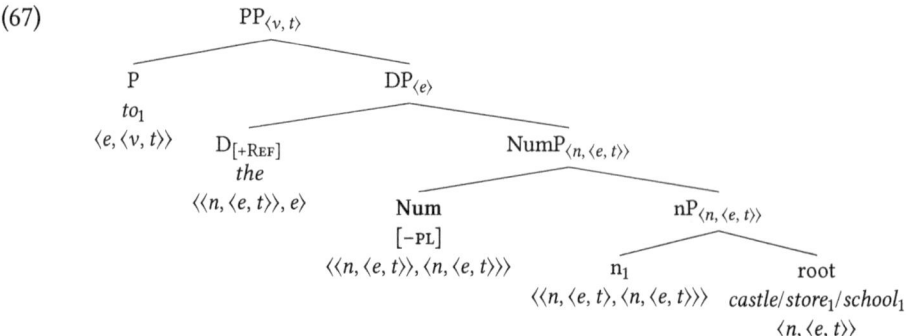

We combine the categorizing head with the countable root, which passes up the interpretation of the root. Next, we add in the number specification, which restricts the extension of the noun to singletons. Finally, the type requires that

---

[14] I use the lower types for simplicity, but, if you prefer a continuations-style denotation, the preposition could have an additional argument for the main event predicate. This has no consequences for my account of weakness.

(i) $[\![to_{1\text{high-type}}]\!]_{\langle\langle v, t \rangle, \langle e, \langle v, t \rangle\rangle\rangle} := \lambda P_{<v,t>}\lambda x.\lambda e.P(e) \& \text{GOAL}(e) = x$

[15] Another potential way to avoid this ambiguity would be to use an explicit incorporating element that constructs to_2 from to_1.

we add the updated Sharvy definite (as in 62, and then the regular directional preposition, as in 65), resulting in the following derivation:

(68) $[\![n_1\ castle]\!]$
$= \lambda n.\lambda y.castle\,(y)\&\,\big|\text{ATOMS}(y)\big| = n\&\forall z \in \text{ATOMS}(y)[castle\,(z)]$

(69) $[\![\text{Num}_{[-\text{PL}]}\ n_1\ castle]\!]$
$= \lambda m.\lambda y.castle\,(y)\&\,\big|\text{ATOMS}(y)\big| = m\&\forall z \in \text{ATOMS}(y)[castle\,(z)]\&m = 1$

(70) $[\![D_{[+\text{SPEC}]}\ \text{Num}_{[-\text{PL}]}\ n_1\ castle]]$
$= \iota x.\exists m.[(castle\,(x)\&\,\big|\text{ATOMS}(x)\big| = m\&\forall z \in \text{ATOMS}(x)[castle\,(z)]$
$\&m = 1)\&\neg\exists y.[castle\,(y)\&\,\big|\text{ATOMS}(y)\big| = m\&\forall x' \in \text{ATOMS}(y)[castle\,(y)]$
$\&m = 1\&x < y\,]$

(71) $[\![to_1\ D_{[+\text{SPEC}]}\ \text{Num}_{[-\text{PL}]}\ n_1\ castle]\!]$
$= \lambda e.\text{GOAL}(e) = \iota x.\exists m.[(castle\,(x)\&\,\big|\text{ATOMS}(x)\big| = m\&\forall z \in \text{ATOMS}(x)[castle\,(z)]$
$\&m = 1)\&\neg\exists y.[castle\,(y)\&\,\big|\text{ATOMS}(y)\big| = m\&\forall x' \in \text{ATOMS}(y)[castle\,(y)]$
$\&m = 1\&x < y\,]$

The denotation in (71) gives a set of events whose GOAL is a unique castle. Some number of atoms is in the extension of *castle* and each of them are also castles, and their cardinality is one (i.e. there is only one of them). Additionally, it asserts that there isn't any other entity (which is a castle that has a number of atoms, which are also castles, and whose cardinality is one) that has the original castle as one of its proper subparts. This is indeed the interpretation we get for the strong definite noun phrase.

Compared to a strong definite, a weak definite, such as in (3), differs in at least two ways. First, the denotation of the root is different, resulting in the weak definite article (66) being merged. Second, these two choices conspire to combine with the incorporating adposition. These combinations are required based on the type of the root.

(72)

```
                    PP⟨v, t⟩
              ┌───────────┴───────────┐
              P                      DP⟨k, t⟩
             to₂                ┌──────┴──────┐
      ⟨⟨k, t⟩, ⟨v, t⟩⟩     D[−REF]          nP⟨e, t⟩
                             the          ┌────┴────┐
                      ⟨⟨e, t⟩, ⟨k, t⟩⟩   n₂        root
                                    ⟨⟨e, t⟩, ⟨e, t⟩⟩  store₂
                                                    ⟨e, t⟩
```

(73) $[\![n_2\ store_2]\!]$
$= \lambda x.store\,(x)$

(74) $[\![D_{[-\text{SPEC}]} \; n_2 \; store_2]\!]$
     $= \lambda k.^{\cap} store = k$

(75) $[\![to_2 \; D_{[-\text{SPEC}]} \; n_2 \; store_2]\!]$
     $= \lambda e.\exists y.\exists k.[^{\cap} store = k \&^{\cup} k(y) \text{GOAL}(e) = y]$

Finally, we take the BIS, as in (4). Roots that can be bare have the denotation of a kind-property (see 58b). This root merges with a categorizing head, which passes up the type and denotation of the root, and then with the incorporating preposition.

(76)

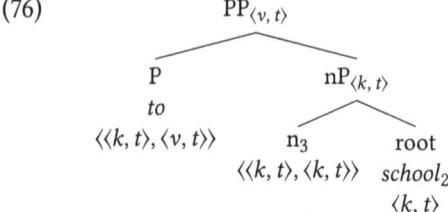

(77) $[\![n_3 \; store_2]\!]$
     $= \lambda k.school(k)$

(78) $[\![to_2 \; D_{[-\text{SPEC}]} \; n_2 \; school_2]\!]$
     $= \lambda e.\exists y.\exists k.[school(k) \&^{\cup} k(y) \& \text{GOAL}(e) = y]$

The derivation for the BIS reflects their similarity with weak definites. More specifically, both derivations lack a Num projection, and combine with the incorporating adposition.

6 Conclusion

I have argued that weak definites and bare singulars mean similar things (both are number neutral), and share comparable morphosyntactic structure (both lack a Num projection, and merge with an incorporating adposition). Roots that participate in weak nominal constructions divide into two lexical classes; one participates in weak definite constructions and the other participates in BIS constructions. These two classes are distinct, with no single lexical item can participate in both weak definite and BIS constructions. Lexical items from these classes are semantically type ambiguous at the root level, with two denotations each. This semantic ambiguity affects whether the root can appear in particular syntactic configurations (e.g. whether it requires an overt strong determiner to be merged).

Interpretive differences between strong and weak nominals correspond to differences at two syntactic positions: first, at the root-level, semantic type ambiguity determines which interpretation(s) is/are possible, and second, at the determiner-level, the semantic type of the root conditions which of two versions of the definite determiner will be chosen. Using these two ingredients, this account explains why weak definites and bare singulars receive number neutral interpretations, while simultaneously explaining their lexical idiosyncrasies.

Acknowledgements

Special thanks to Ruth Kramer and the students in her Seminar on the Syntax of Number (NYU, Spring 2015); to Curt Anderson, David Beaver, Hagen Blix, Dylan Bumford, Lucas Champollion, Simon Charlow, Chris Collins, Masha Esipova, Paloma Jeretič, Maria Kouneli, Marcin Morzycki, Alan Munn, Neil Myler, Rob Pasternak, Sarah Phillips, and Anna Szabolcsi for advice, skepticism, criticism, proofreading, and/or encouragement; to the members of Rutgers' SURGE and New York University's MorphBeer; the audiences, organizers, and reviewers for Definiteness across Languages; and finally, to attendees of SYNC 2013 and SWAMP 2012 for comments on much earlier versions of this work.

Abbreviations

BIS	Bare institutional singular	PL	Plural
NUM	Number	REF	Referential

References

Aguilar-Guevara, Ana. 2014. *Weak definites: Semantics, lexicon and pragmatics* (LOT Dissertation Series 360). Utrecht: LOT.

Aguilar-Guevara, Ana, Bert Le Bruyn & Joost Zwarts (eds.). 2014. *Weak referentiality* (Linguistik Aktuell/Linguistics Today 219). Amsterdam: John Benjamins.

Aguilar-Guevara, Ana & Maartje Schulpen. 2014. Modified weak definites. In Ana Aguilar-Guevara, Bert Le Bruyn & Joost Zwarts (eds.), *Weak referentiality* (Linguistik Aktuell/Linguistics Today 219), 237–264. Amsterdam: John Benjamins.

Aguilar-Guevara, Ana & Joost Zwarts. 2011. Weak definites and reference to kinds. *Proceedings of SALT* 20. 179–196.

Baldwin, Timothy, John Beavers, Leonoor van der Beek, Francis Bond, Dan Flickinger & Ivan A. Sag. 2006. In search of a systematic treatment of determinerless PPs. In Patrick Saint-Dizier (ed.), *Syntax and semantics of prepositions* (Text, Speech and Language Technology 29), 163–179. Berlin: Springer.

Barker, Chris. 2005. Possessive weak definites. In Ji-Yung Kim, Barbara Hall Partee & Yury A. Lander (eds.), *Possessives and beyond: Semantics and syntax* (University of Massachusetts Ocassional Papers in Linguistics 29), 89–113. Amherst: GSLA, University of Massachusetts.

Birner, Betty & Gregory Ward. 1994. Uniqueness, familiarity, and the definite article in English. In *Proceedings of the Twentieth Annual Meeting of the Berkeley Linguistics Society*, vol. 1, 93–102. Berkeley: Berkeley Linguistics Society.

Carlson, Greg N. 1977. *Reference to kinds in English*. Amherst: University of Massachusetts. (Doctoral dissertation).

Carlson, Greg N. 2006. The meaningful bounds of incorporation. In Svetlana Vogeleer & Liliane Tasmowski (eds.), *Non-definiteness and plurality* (Linguistik Aktuell/Linguistics Today 95), 35–50. Amsterdam: John Benjamins.

Carlson, Greg N. & Rachel Shirley Sussman. 2005. Seemingly indefinite definites. In Stephan Kepser & Marga Reis (eds.), *Linguistic evidence: Empirical, theoretical and computational perspectives* (Studies in Generative Grammar 85), 71–86. Berlin: Mouton de Gruyter.

Carlson, Greg N., Rachel Shirley Sussman, Natalie M. Klein & Michael K. Tanenhaus. 2006. Weak definite noun phrases. *Proceedings of NELS* 36(1). 179–196.

Champollion, Lucas. 2017. *Parts of a whole: Distributivity as a bridge between aspect and measurement* (Oxford Studies in Theoretical Linguistics). Oxford: Oxford University Press.

Chierchia, Gennaro. 1998. Reference to kinds across languages. *Natural Language Semantics* 6(4). 339–405.

Cinque, Guglielmo. 2010. *The syntax of adjectives: A comparative study* (Linguistic Inquiry Monographs 57). Cambridge: MIT Press.

Deal, Amy Rose & Julia Nee. 2016. Number marking and the definite interpretation of bare nouns in Teotitlán del Valle Zapotec. (Talk presented at the workshop Definiteness across Languages, Mexico City, 22–24 June 2016).

Déprez, Viviane. 2005. Morphological number, semantic number and bare nouns. *Lingua* 115(6). 857–883.

Frege, Gottlob. 1892. Über Sinn und Bedeutung. *Zeitschrift für Philosophie und Philosophische Kritik* 100. 25–50.

Gehrke, Berit & Marika Lekakou. 2013. Preposition drop in Greek: A case for pseudo-incorporation. (Talk presented at Sinn und Bedeutung 17, École normale supérieure, Paris, September 2013).

Harbour, Daniel. 2007. *Morphosemantic number: From Kiowa noun classes to UG number features* (Studies in Natural Language and Linguistic Theory 69). Springer.

Hawkins, John A. 1978. *Definiteness and indefiniteness: A study in reference and grammaticality prediction.* London: Croon Helm.

Heim, Irene. 1982. *The semantics of definite and indefinite noun phrases.* Amherst: University of Massachusetts. (Doctoral dissertation).

Klein, Natalie M. 2011. *Convention and cognition: Weak definite noun phrases.* Rochester: University of Rochester. (Doctoral dissertation).

Klein, Natalie M., Whitney Gegg-Harrison, Greg N. Carlson & Michael K. Tanenhaus. 2009. Special but not unique: Weak definite noun phrases. In Uli Sauerland & Kazuko Yatsushiro (eds.), *Semantics and pragmatics: From experiment to theory* (Palgrave Studies in Pragmatics, Language and Cognition), 175–264. London: Palgrave.

Kramer, Ruth. 2009. *Definite markers, phi features and agreement: A morphosyntactic investigation of the Amharic DP.* Santa Cruz: University of California. (Doctoral dissertation).

Kramer, Ruth. 2015. General number in Amharic. (Talk presented at the 8th World Congress of African Linguistics, Kyoto, August 2015).

Laenzlinger, Christopher. 2005. French adjective ordering: Perspectives on DP-internal movement types. *Lingua* 115(5). 645–689.

Landau, Idan. 2016. DP-internal semantic agreement: A configurational analysis. *Natural Language & Linguistic Theory* 34(3). 1–46.

Levinson, Lisa. 2014. The ontology of roots and verbs. In Artemis Alexiadou, Hagit Borer & Florian Schäfer (eds.), *The syntax of roots and the roots of syntax* (Oxford Studies in Theoretical Linguistics). Oxford: Oxford University Press.

Marantz, Alec. 1995. Cat as a phrasal idiom: Consequences of late insertion in Distributed Morphology. (Cambridge: Massachusetts Institute of Technology. Manuscript).

Marantz, Alec. 1997. No escape from syntax: Don't try morphological analysis in the privacy of your own lexicon. *University of Pennsylvania Working Papers in Linguistics* 4(2). 14.

Marantz, Alec. 2013. Locality domains for contextual allomorphy across the interfaces. In Ora Matushansky & Alec Marantz (eds.), *Distributed Morphology today: Morphemes for Morris Halle*, 95–115. Cambridge: MIT Press.

Massam, Diane. 2001. Pseudo noun incorporation in Niuean. *Natural Language & Linguistic Theory* 19(1). 153–197.

Massam, Diane. 2009. Noun incorporation: Essentials and extensions. *Language and Linguistics Compass* 3. 1076–1096.

Myler, Neil. 2014. *Building and interpreting possession sentences*. New York: New York University. (Doctoral dissertation).

Nunberg, Geoffrey, Ivan A. Sag & Thomas Wasow. 1994. Idioms. *Language* 70(3). 491–538.

Ouwayda, Sarah. 2014. *Where number lies: Plural marking, numerals, and the collective-distributive distinction*. Los Angeles: University of Southern California. (Doctoral dissertation).

Poesio, Massimo. 1994. Weak definites. *Proceedings of SALT* 4. 282–299.

Rappaport Hovav, Malka & Beth Levin. 1998. Building verb meanings. In Miriam Butt & Wilhelm Geuder (eds.), *The projection of arguments: Lexical and compositional factors*, 97–134. Stanford: CSLI Publications.

Ritter, Elizabeth. 1991. Two functional categories in noun phrases: Evidence from Modern Hebrew. *Syntax and semantics* 25. 37–62.

Ritter, Elizabeth. 1992. Cross-linguistic evidence for number phrase. *Canadian Journal of Linguistics* 37(2). 197–218.

Ritter, Elizabeth. 1995. On the syntactic category of pronouns and agreement. *Natural Language & Linguistic Theory* 13(3). 405–443.

Romanova, Eugenia. 2004. Superlexical versus lexical prefixes. *Nordlyd* 32(2). 255–278.

Ross, John Robert. 1967. *Constraints on variables in syntax*. Cambridge: Massachusetts Institute of Technology. (Doctoral dissertation).

Ross, John Robert. 1969. Guess who. In Robert I. Binnick, Alice Davidson, Georgia M. Green & Jerry L. Morgan (eds.), *Papers from the Fifth Regional Meeting of the Chicago Linguistic Society*, 252–286. Chicago: Chicago Linguistic Society, University of Chicago.

Rullmann, Hotze & Aili You. 2006. General number and the semantics and pragmatics of indefinite bare nouns in Mandarin Chinese. In Klaus von Heusinger & Ken Turner (eds.), *Where semantics meetes pragmatics* (Current Research in the Semantics / Pragmatics Interface 16), 175–196. Elsevier.

Russell, Bertrand. 1905. On denoting. *Mind* 14(56). 479–493.

Sauerland, Uli. 2003. A new semantics for number. *Proceedings of SALT* 13. 258–275.

Schwarz, Florian. 2009. *Two types of definites in natural language*. Amherst: University of Massachusetts. (Doctoral dissertation).

Schwarz, Florian. 2013. Two kinds of definites cross-linguistically. *Language and Linguistics Compass* 7(10). 534–559.

Schwarz, Florian. 2014. How weak and how definite are weak definites? In Ana Aguilar-Guevara, Bert Le Bruyn & Joost Zwarts (eds.), *Weak referentiality* (Linguistik Aktuell/Linguistics Today 219), 213–235. Amsterdam: John Benjamins.

Sharvy, Richard. 1980. A more general theory of definite descriptions. *The Philosophical Review* 89(4). 607–624.

Stvan, Laurel Smith. 1998. *The semantics and pragmatics of bare singular noun phrases*. Evanston: Northwestern University. (Doctoral dissertation).

Svenonius, Peter. 2005. Slavic prefixes inside and outside VP. *Nordlyd* 32(2). 205–253.

Wilhelm, Andrea. 2008. Bare nouns and number in Dëne Sųłiné. *Natural Language Semantics* 16(1). 39–68.

Wiltschko, Martina. 2008. The syntax of non-inflectional plural marking. *Natural Language & Linguistic Theory* 26(3). 639–694.

Wood, Jim. 2012. *Icelandic morphosyntax and argument structure* (Studies in Natural Language and Linguistic Theory 90). Berlin: Springer.

Definiteness, partitivity, and domain restriction: A fresh look at definite reduplication

Urtzi Etxeberria
CNRS-IKER

Anastasia Giannakidou
University of Chicago

We propose that the phenomenon of definite reduplication in Greek involves using the definite determiner D as domain restrictor in the sense of Etxeberria & Giannakidou (2009). The use of D as a domain-restricting function with quantifiers has been well documented for European languages such as Greek, Basque, Bulgarian and Hungarian – and typically results in a partitive-like interpretation of the QP. We propose a unifying analysis that treats domain restriction and D-reduplication as the same phenomenon; and in our analysis, D-reduplication emerges semantically as similar to a partitive structure, a result resonating with earlier claims to this end by Kolliakou (2004). None of the existing accounts of definites can capture the correlations in the use of D with quantifiers and in reduplication that we establish here.

1 Quantifiers, domain restriction, and D

One of the most fruitful ideas in the formal semantics tradition has been the thesis that quantifier phrases (QPs) denote generalized quantifiers (GQs; see Montague 1974; Barwise & Cooper 1981; Westerståhl 1984; Partee 1986; Zwarts 1986; Keenan 1987; 1996; Keenan & Westerståhl 1997; among many others). Classical GQ theory posits that there is a natural class of expressions in language, called quantificational determiners (Qs), which combine with a nominal constituent (an

NP of type *et*, a first order predicate) to form a quantifier nominal (QP). This QP denotes a GQ, a set of sets. In a language like English, the syntax of a QP like *every woman* is as follows:

(1)   a. $[\![every\ woman]\!] = \lambda Q.\ \forall x.\ \text{woman}(x) \rightarrow Q(x)$

     b. $[\![every]\!] = \lambda P.\ \lambda Q.\ \forall x.\ P(x) \rightarrow Q(x)$

     c.

          QP *ett*

           ⟋‾‾⟍

   Q *et,ett*   NP *et*

     | |

   every   *woman*

The Q *every* combines first with the NP argument *woman*, and this is what we have come to think of as the "standard" QP-internal syntax. The NP argument provides the domain of the Q, and the Q expresses a relation between this domain and the set denoted by the VP. Qs like *every, most*, etc. are known as STRONG, and they contrast with the so-called WEAK quantifiers like e.g. *some, few, three, many* (Milsark 1977).

It has also long been noted that the domain of strong quantifiers is contextually (explicitly or implicitly) restricted (see *inter alia* Reuland & ter Meulen 1989). Contemporary work agrees that we need to encode contextual restriction in the QP, but opinions vary as to whether contextual restriction is part of the syntax/semantics (Partee 1986; von Fintel 1994; 1998; Stanley & Szabó 2000; Stanley 2002; Matthewson 2001; Martí 2003; Giannakidou 2004; Etxeberria 2005; 2008; 2009; Gillon 2006; 2009; Etxeberria & Giannakidou 2009; 2014; Giannakidou & Rathert 2009), or not (Recanati 1996; 2004; 2007 and others in the strong contextualism tradition). In the syntax-semantics approach, it is assumed that the domains of Qs are contextually restricted by covert domain variables at LF (which are usually free, but can also be bound, and they can be either atomic, e.g. *C*, or complex of the form $f(x)$, corresponding to selection functions; see von Fintel 1998; Stanley 2002; Martí 2003). Below, we employ C:

(2)   *Many people came to the concert last night; every student got drunk.*

(3) $\forall x\ [\ \text{student}\ (x) \cap C(x)\ ] \rightarrow \text{got drunk}\ (x).$

Here, the nominal argument of the universal quantifier *every*, i.e. *student*, is the set of students who came to the concert last night, not the students in the whole world. This is achieved by the domain variable C, which is an anaphor and will look back in the discourse for a salient property, in this case the set of people who came to the concert last night. *Every student* then will draw values from the intersection of *student* with C.

Another element that combines with a domain to give a nominal argument is the definite determiner, i.e. the English *the* and its equivalents (including demonstratives), designated as D (Abney 1987; see Alexiadou et al. 2008 for an extensive overview). The demonstrative is generated in English under the same head (thus *this the book*). The DP has a structure parallel to (1c), only we have D, and the constituent is called DP (though some authors call the Q uniformly D; see Matthewson 1998; Gillon 2009). As indicated below, the DP produces a referential expression, a (maximal or unique) individual, indicated here with *iota*:

(4)   DP*e*: $\iota(\lambda x.\text{woman}(x))$

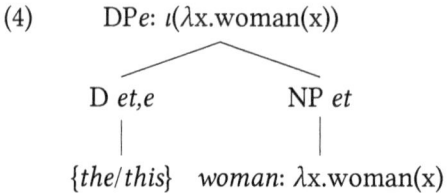

D *et,e*   NP *et*
   | |
{*the/this*}   *woman*: $\lambda x.\text{woman}(x)$

(5)   a.   *the/this woman* = ι ($\lambda x.\text{woman}$ (x))
      b.   *the/these women* = max ($\lambda x.\text{woman}$ (x))

The DP produces the most basic argument *e* which can be lifted up to the GQ type when necessary. Both D and Q are functions that need a domain, and it is the NP that provides this domain. Contextual presuppositions are indicated above in the indexing with C. The DP denotes the unique or maximal individual presupposed to exist in the common ground. Coppock & Beaver (2015) use θ-notation to capture the presupposition of uniqueness as the argument of the θ operator:

(6)   Lexical entry: *the*
      the $\rightarrow \lambda P.\lambda x [\theta(|P| \leq 1) \wedge P(x)]$

Notice that, contrary to all other approaches, for Coppock & Beaver (2015) *the* is a non-saturated constituent in the referential use. We come back to this assumption later. We take it here that the use of D creates a morphologically definite argument, it is thus the core of what can be understood as "definiteness".

DP has been argued to exhibit different types of referentiality. For one thing, a DP can be generic and refer to a kind which is itself a very different "object" than a concrete unique entity in the world. Observe, in addition, the following:

(7) a. *John got these data from* **the student of a linguist.**
  b. *John went* **to the store.**
  c. *I read* **the newspaper** *every day.*
  d. *I raised* **my hand.**

In the examples here the DPs do not make reference to unique entities: the linguist in (7a) possibly has more than one student; in (7b) the particular identity of the store to which John has gone is not important, and the store is certainly not unique; (7c) can be used in a context in which no newspaper has been mentioned or in which multiple newspapers are read; in (7d) *my hand* is used to make reference to one of my two hands. Poesio (1994) introduced the term "weak definite" to refer to such "non-uniquely referential" uses of D (see among others Carlson & Sussman 2005; Schwarz 2009; Aguilar-Guevara & Zwarts 2011; Corblin 2013). More recent relevant work identifies "sloppy" identity, narrow scope interpretation, lexical restrictions (*John took the bus* vs #*John took the coach*), restrictions on modification, number restrictions, and meaning enrichment (*John went to the store* means that John went to a store to do some shopping) for such non-unique DPs (see Carlson & Sussman 2005; Aguilar-Guevara et al. 2014).

In some languages, the referential strength of DP is reflected in a difference between weak and strong forms of D itself (Cieschinger 2006; Puig Waldmüller 2008; Schwarz 2009). In Standard German, for example, a preposition and the definite article can be contracted (*zum* vs. *zu dem*). Schwarz (2009) proposes that the strong/non-contracted D is used when the noun phrase is anaphoric (a pragmatic definite) and it picks up a unique/given referent from the discourse; the weak/contracted article is used when the noun phrase has unique reference on the basis of its own description.

In the present paper, we discuss two puzzles of D in Greek and Basque that cannot be described by the existing approaches in terms of non-uniqueness or weak/strong D. The D in the case we focus on appears in a non-canonical position: (a) on a quantificational determiner; and (b) multiple D structures. Let us illustrate the first, which holds also in Salish languages, Hungarian and Bulgarian. D can be an independent head (Greek, St'át'imcets),[1] or suffixal D (Basque, Bulgarian):

---

[1] The St'át'imcets D has a proclitic part (*ti* for singulars; *i* for plurals) encoding deictic and number morphology, and an enclitic part ...*a* adding to the first lexical item in the DP (Matthewson 1998).

(8)   Greek (Giannakidou 2004: 121)

    a.   *o*   *kathe fititis*

        DET.SG every student

        'each student'

    b.   * *kathe o*   *fititis*

        every DET.SG student

        ('each student')

(9)   Basque (Etxeberria 2005: 41–42)

    a.   *mutil guzti-ak*

        boy   all-DET.PL

        'all the students'

    b.   *mutil bakoitz-a*

        boy   each-DET.SG

        'each student'

    c.   * *mutil guzti* / * *mutil bakoitz*

        boy   all   /   boy   each

        ('all students / each student')

    d.   * *mutil-ak*   *guzti*

        boy-DET.PL all

        ('all the students')

    e.   * *mutil-a*   *bakoitz*

        boy-DET.SG each

        ('each boy')

(10)   St'át'imcets Salish (Matthewson 1999; 2001)

    a.   *i*   *tákem-a sm'ulhats*

        DET.PL all-DET   woman

        'all of the women'

    b.   *i*   *zí7zeg'-a sk'wemk'úk'wm'it*

        DET.PL each-DET child(PL)

        'each of the children'

(11) Hungarian (Szabolcsi 2010)

    a.   *minden diák*
        every   student
        'every student'

    b.   *az összes diák*
        the all   student
        'all the students'

    c. * *összes az diák*
        all   the student
        ('all the students')

(12) Bulgarian (Schürcks et al. 2014)

    a. *vsjako momče*
        every boy
        'every boy'

    b. *vsički-te   momčeta*
        every-DET.PL boy.PL
        'all the boys'

These data, where the D combines with a Q are unexpected under the standard analysis of DP because D combines with a Q and not an NP. Hence D above does not have the proper input *et*, and instead combines with the wrong type, a Q (type *et,ett*). That should be ruled out, as it indeed happens in English **the every boy*. In Greek, Basque, St'át'imcets, Hungarian, or Bulgarian the mismatch is "salvaged", we argued in earlier work, by the ability of D to function as a domain restrictor (Giannakidou 2004; Etxeberria 2005; Etxeberria & Giannakidou 2009; 2014).

In the present paper, we will argue that the domain restriction function of D is key to understand the phenomenon of definite reduplication in Greek. This phenomenon includes multiple occurrences of D within the same DP:

(13) Greek

    a. *to kalo to paidi*
        the good the child
        'the good child'

    b. *to kalo paidi*
        the good child
        'the good child'

The D-reduplicated structure is puzzling because there is only one referent (just like with the simple definite *to kalo paidi* 'the good child'); and, just like with D on Q, one of the two Ds combines with an adjective, a *prima facie* non-canonical combination. Definite reduplication occurs in other languages, e.g. Swedish (but not in Danish, a related language), although in this paper we will only concentrate on Greek D-reduplication:

(14)   Swedish
       den gamla mus-en
       the old   mouse-DEF
       'the old mouse'

Although Greek definite reduplications, or polydefinites, as Kolliakou (2004) calls them, have received lots of attention in the literature (see Alexiadou & Wilder 1998; Campos & Stavrou 2004; Kolliakou 2004; Ioannidou & den Dikken 2006; Lekakou & Szendroi 2007), there is no consensus on what exactly the proper treatment is, with accounts ranging from vacuity of D to close apposition. In addition, polydefinites have never been linked to the use of D with quantifiers.

In our paper, we will connect the two phenomena and argue that they are both manifestations of the function of D as domain restriction. The only difference between the two is that in one case D applies on Q, but with polydefinites D applies on a predicate. At the same time, it is important to note that neither of the two phenomena can be captured by the concepts of "weak definiteness" or "determinacy" (Coppock & Beaver 2015) used in the literature. Importantly, our analysis of the two phenomena renders them akin to partitives semantically, and from this it follows that partitive structures, domain restriction, and definite reduplication are different, but related strategies for partitivity.

The discussion proceeds as follows. We illustrate first, in §2, the theory of D as domain restrictor developed in our earlier work, specifically when D applies to Q. In §3, we present the option of D as domain restriction on the NP, an option observed in Salish languages. We point out that this option is a direct equivalent to a partitive semantically, and then focus on multiple definites (§4). We suggest here that multiple definites are the Greek equivalent to the Salish strategy. Our analysis is most related to Kolliakou (2004), and predicts a number of behaviors consistent with partitivity.

Our overall conclusion is that "definiteness" is a family of phenomena revealing the following functions of D:

(15) Types for D

- Saturating:
  - *et* → *e* (*iota*); intensionalized version (generic)
- Non-saturating:
  - *et,ett* → *et,ett* (D_{DR} on Q)
  - *et* → *et* (D_{DR} on NP or AP)

"Weak definiteness" D, in contrast to domain restriction, is a saturating function, and determinacy (Coppock & Beaver 2015) only relates to the b-version of non-saturating D.

2 D as a domain restrictor

In recent work, Giannakidou (2004), Etxeberria (2005), and Etxeberria & Giannakidou (2009; 2014) proposed that supplying C is a function that D heads can perform cross-linguistically. We based this idea on Westerståhl (1984; 1985), who argued that the definite article supplies a context set C; our proposal was that supplying C actually happens as an overt syntactic strategy in some languages. Domain restricting D is a non-saturating, type-preserving (i.e. modifier) function that applies to the Q and adds the C variable to the nominal argument of Q. This is akin to property anaphora, since C is anaphoric to a property present in the context, as we said earlier. Domain restricting D comes in two forms: as a Q modifier or as a predicate modifier, found in St'át'imcets and similar languages (Matthewson 2001; Gillon 2006; 2009). Definite reduplication, we will argue, is the manifestation of the predicate modifier strategy in Greek.

2.1 D on Q and property anaphora

Recall the examples mentioned in the introduction. We repeat here only the Greek and Basque data for simplicity. Etxeberria & Giannakidou (2009; 2014) propose that D here is a modifier function D_{DR}, defined it as in (18):

(16) Greek (Giannakidou 2004)

    a.   *o*   *kathe fititis*

          DET.SG every student

          'each student'

    b. * *kathe o*   *fititis*

          every DET.SG student

          ('each student')

(17)   Basque (Etxeberria 2005)

    a.   *mutil guzti-ak* // *mutil bakoitz-a*
       boy   all-DET.PL // boy   each-DET.SG

       'all the students // each student'

    b.   * *mutil guzti/bakoitz;* *mutil-ak guzti;* *mutil-a bakoitz*
       boy   all/each   boy-DET.PL all   boy-DET.SG each

       ('all students / each student; all the students; each student')

(18)   D to D_{DR} type-shifting:

     1. D_{DR} rule: When D composes with Q, use D_{DR}.

     2. $D_{DR} = \lambda Z_{et,ett}\ \lambda P_{et}\ \lambda Q_{et}\ Z\ (P \cap C)\ (Q)$;
        Z is the relation denoted by Q

D_{DR} is a non-saturating function that definite heads can type-shift to. Above, we formulate it as a combinatorial rule D_{DR}. When D functions as D_{DR} it introduces the context set variable C. D_{DR} does not create a referential expression, but is simply a modifier of Q, apparently emerging to fix the mismatch since D is fed the wrong type of argument. By supplying C, which is an anaphor, D_{DR} triggers the presupposition that the common ground contains a property to be picked as the value for C. Application of D_{DR}, in other words, creates a presuppositional, anaphoric domain for Q, necessitating a discourse familiar property to be anchored to. This renders the interpretation of the QP akin to a partitive, although it is not morphologically a partitive (for more details, see Etxeberria & Giannakidou 2009; 2014).

Syntactically, we assume that D attaches to Q, so the result is a QP with the following structure:

(19)   a.   [$_{QP}$ o$_D$ + kathe$_Q$ [$_{NP}$ fititis$_N$]]

      b.   *o kathe fititis* = [(C) kathe] (student)   'each student'

(20)   a.

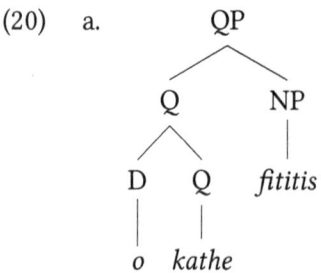

   b. Greek: *o kathe fititis* = [(C) kathe] (fititis)

   c. Basque: *ikasle guzti-ak* = (ikasle) [guzti (C)]

   d. $[\![Q]\!] = \lambda P \lambda R. \forall x \, P(x) \rightarrow R(x)$

   e. $[\![D]\!] = \lambda Z_{et,ett} \, \lambda P_{et} \, \lambda R_{et} \, Z \, (P \cap C) \, (R);$
      Z is the relation denoted by Q

   f. $[\![D(Q)]\!] = \lambda P \lambda R. \forall x \, (P(x) \cap C(x)) \rightarrow R(x)$

O kathe 'each' and *guzti-ak* 'all' end up being presuppositional Qs since their domain will always be anaphoric to C, as a consequence of them being D-restricted. Crucially, Etxeberria and Giannakidou argue that the composition of *each* (and similar D-universals cross-linguistically) involves a structure parallel to the Greek/Basque: [D-every]; only, in contrast to Greek/Basque, with *each*, D is covert. Typologically, D with Qs in Greek, Basque, Hungarian, Bulgarian, and St'át'imcents shifts to D_{DR}, but English *the* does not, so whether D can function as D_{DR} in a given language is subject to parametrization.[2] In a language lacking a definite article, the shift to D_{DR} will be done by the closest approximant of definiteness, e.g. Chinese *dou* (Cheng 2009), and Korean *ku* which is a morphological demonstrative (Kang 2015).

In introducing D_{DR}, we enrich definiteness to include this possibility of D not saturating its argument. NPs preceded by the definite article (definite descriptions) are referential expressions, which, since the classical treatments of Russell (1905), Strawson (1952), and Heim (1982) are known to denote familiar unique entities. In many accounts, reference and familiarity are considered the core properties of a definite description, while uniqueness is a derived one (informational uniqueness in Roberts 2003; see also Ward & Birner 1995; Elbourne 2005; Ludlow 2007 for counterexamples to uniqueness, and Schwarz 2009 suggesting that in German familiarity and uniqueness can be distinguished). In other theories, uniqueness is the core, as in the account by Coppock & Beaver (2015) who argue that "definiteness is a morphological category which, in English, marks a (weak) uniqueness presupposition, while determinacy consists in denoting an individual" (Coppock & Beaver 2015: 377).

Like us, Coppock & Beaver (2015) propose a non-saturating denotation for *the*, with the uniqueness presupposition designated by the θ operator:

---

[2]But why do we have this contrast in the ability of D to perform D_{DR}? Could it be a random fact about Ds across languages? Could it relate to availability of repair strategies more generally? Clearly, whether a D can perform D_{DR} cannot be due to the morphological status of D since, as shown earlier, Greek *o* and English *the* are similar, independent heads and monosyllabic. Greek *o*, however, is phonologically weaker than English *the*, so perhaps phonological weakness is a factor. Suffixal Ds like the Basque D are phonologically weaker too, clitic-like Ds.

(21)   Lexical entry: *the*
       the → $\lambda P.\lambda x\ [\theta(|P| \leq 1) \wedge P(x)]$

(22) $\lambda x[\theta(|\text{MOON}|{\leq}1)\wedge\text{MOON}(x)]$

       $\lambda P\lambda x[\theta(|P|{\leq}1)\wedge P(x)]$ $\lambda x\text{MOON}(x)$
                  | |
                the   *moon*

   The moon denotes the property of being a moon, defined only if there is no more than one moon. This analysis, like our D_{DR}, does not saturate the NP argument, and referential closure happens on top of that, by a covert type shifter. This amounts to saying that D itself is not referential in this basic use. Our D plus Q data remain mysterious under this analysis. (Also mysterious remain weak definite data where uniqueness appears to be systematically violated). Roberts's theory of definiteness, on the other hand, seems to provide a more appropriate frame for domain restriction.

   Roberts (2003) argues that definites conventionally trigger two presuppositions: one of weak familiarity, and a second one called INFORMATIONAL UNIQUENESS. These are the informational counterparts of Russellian existence and uniqueness, respectively.

   Roberts (2004) argues that the same presuppositions characterize the meaning of pronouns and demonstratives (Roberts 2002). In more recent work (Roberts 2010) a Gricean view is developed which permits a simplification of her earlier theory in that the uniqueness effect observed in certain contexts follows from retrievability, with no need to stipulate even informational uniqueness. The resulting theory stands in contrast to a number of other recent treatments of definites (Neale 1990, as well as those that treat definites as E-type or D-type implicit descriptions Heim 1990; Elbourne 2005; *inter alia*; Coppock & Beaver 2015, see also Fara 2001). For the purposes of this paper, it is not necessary to dwell in the details of this discussion; we will concentrate on the main theses of Roberts's theory that are essential to our analysis of D_{DR}:

(23)   a. English Definite NPs: definite descriptions, personal pronouns, demonstrative descriptions and pronouns, proper names.

       b. Semantic Definiteness: A DP is definite if it carries an anaphoric presupposition of weak familiarity.

c. Weak familiarity: Weak familiarity requires that the existence of the relevant entity be entailed in the common ground. Existence entailments alone are sufficient to license introduction of a discourse referent into the context. Weak familiarity does not mean previous mention. Previous mention is strong familiarity.

d. The antecedent of an anaphoric expression is the discourse referent which satisfies its anaphoric presupposition.

e. Anaphora and weak familiarity do not presuppose a linguistic antecedent.

f. Pronouns, unlike definite descriptions, carry the additional presupposition that the discourse referent which satisfies their presupposition is maximally salient at that point in the discourse. This explains why uniqueness effects do not arise with pronouns.

In other words,

> The notion of familiarity involved [in definites] is not that more commonly assumed, which I will call strong familiarity, where this usually involves explicit previous mention of the entity in question. Rather, I define a new notion, that of weak familiarity wherein the existence of the entity in question need only be entailed by the (local) context of interpretation. [...] Gricean principles and the epistemic features of particular types of context are invoked to explain the uniqueness effects observed by Russell and others. (Roberts 2003: 288)

The notions of *hearer old* versus *discourse old* have also been used (Prince 1981; Ward & Birner 1995) to distinguish different "shades" of familiarity.

The definiteness criterion is thus the anaphoric presupposition of weak familiarity, and some definites will further need prior mention (strong familiarity). Our idea that D in D_{DR} supplies a context set C, renders D_{DR} a case of property anaphora, since C targets a familiar property in the common ground. In D_{DR}, D is a signal that such a property exists in the common ground. This renders the D-restricted QP similar to a partitive (*every one of the students*), since this is the typical structure where the NP domain is presupposed.

We move on now to provide some syntactic arguments for our direct composition of D with Q.

2.2 D_{DR} does not produce a syntactic DP

The application of D_{DR}, as we envision it, is a type shifting rule; but we could also think of it as a lexical modification of Q. In either case, a type shifting or lexical rule would not make us expect that the product will alter the category of Q: we have a QP and not a DP. However, one could ask: how do we know that Greek *o kathe* or Basque *guzti-ak* (and the rest of Basque strong Qs that can be modified by D; Etxeberria 2005; 2009) do not create DPs? These are certainly attested structures:

(24)   a. Greek
       [*I*   [*tris*   *fitites*   *pu*   *irthan sto*   *parti*]], *itan   endelos*
       [the [three students that came to.the party]] were completely
       methismeni.
       drunk

       'The three students that came to the party were completely drunk.'

   b. Basque
       [*Festara*   *etorri ziren*   *hiru*   *ikasle*]   -ak]   *erabat*
       [to.the.party came AUX.PL three student] -DET.PL] completely
       mozkortuta zeuden.
       drunk   were

       'The three students that came to the party were completely drunk.'

These are referential DPs. The output is of type *e*, and not a GQ, which is the output of the D_{DR} structure, as we argued. What are the arguments that our D_{DR} structure is not a DP of this kind? Etxeberria & Giannakidou (2014) offer a number of arguments which we summarize here.[3]

Apart from the obvious fact that *to kathe agori* 'each boy' is a quantificational expression, evidence that D in *o-kathe* does not create a DP comes from two facts. First, [*o-kathe* NP] cannot co-occur with the demonstrative pronoun (*aftos* 'this', *ekinos* 'that') – which in Greek, like in many other languages, must embed DPs (Stavrou 1983; Stavrou & Horrock 1989; Alexiadou et al. 2008):[4]

---

[3]Etxeberria (2005; 2009) excludes the hypothesis that Basque Qs that combine with the D are adjectives. The reader is referred to these works for extensive discussion on this point.

[4]The Greek test on the impossibility of demonstratives and the D-restricted *o kathe* Greek cannot be used in Basque because the D and the demonstratives appear in the same syntactic position D (we exemplify in (i) only with the singular).

(25) Greek

    a. *aftos *(o) fititis*
       this   the student

       'this student'

    b. *ekinos *(o) fititis*
       that   the student

       'that student'

(26) Greek

    a. *afti / ekini i tris fitites*
       these / those the three students

       'these / those three students'

    b. *aftos / ekinos o enas fititis*
       this / that   the one student

       'this / that one student'

(27) Greek
    *aftos / *ekinos o kathe fititis
    this / that   the every student
    (Lit. 'This / that each student')

The demonstratives *aftos/ekinos* are not D heads in Greek, but phrases in [Spec, DP] (Stavrou & Horrock 1989). Since the demonstrative cannot occur with *o kathe*, we must conclude that the phrase headed by the D-*kathe* is not a DP.

(i)   Basque

    a.   *ikasle-a*
       student-DET.SG

       'the student'

    b.   *ikasle hau/hori/hura*
       student DEM.SG.PROXIMAL/MEDIAL/DISTAL

       'this/that/that student'

    c. * *ikasle-a   hau/hori/hura*
       student-DET.SG DEM.SG.PROXIMAL/MEDIAL/DISTAL

       ('this/that/that student')

The second piece of evidence that *o kathe* NP does not behave syntactically as a DP comes from the fact that it cannot reduplicate. Polydefinites, as we mentioned in §1, are pervasive in Greek (see Alexiadou & Wilder 1998; Campos & Stavrou 2004; Kolliakou 2004; Ioannidou & den Dikken 2006; Lekakou & Szendroi 2007):

(28) Greek
      o   kokinos o   tixos
      the red.NOM the wall.NOM
      'the wall that is red'

Reduplication is not possible with *o kathe*, but it is with a numeral:

(29) Greek

      a. * *o   kathe o   fititis*
         the each the student
         ('each student')

      b.   *o   enas o   fititis*
         the one the student
         'the one student'

      c.   *i   tris i   fitites*
         the three the students
         'the three students'

These are, in fact, equivalent semantically to partitives, a point to which we return:

(30) Greek

      a. *enas apo tus fitites*
          one of the students
          'one of the students'

      b. *tris apo tous fitites*
          three of the students
          'three of the students'

In a language where DPs duplicate easily, the impossibility of reduplication with *o kathe* suggests again that *o kathe* is not a DP.

A third argument against the DP analysis comes from Basque, where it is possible to conjoin two NPs or two APs under the same single D, as shown as shown in (31) and (32) (in Greek this is not possible, so we cannot apply this test).

(31)   Basque: NP conjunction
[DP [NP *Ikasle*]   *eta* [NP *irakasle*] -*ak*]   *azterket-a garai-a-n*
[[student] and [teacher] -D.PL.ABS] exam-D.SG period-D.SG-IN
daude.
AUX.PL
'The students and teachers are in exams period.'

(32)   Basque: AdjP conjunction
Maiak   [DP [AdjP *zaldi haundi*] *eta* [AdjP *elefante txiki*] -*ak*]
Maia.erg [[horse big]   and [elephant small] -DET.PL.ABS]
ikusi ditu.
see   AUX.PL
'Maia has seen the big horses and small elephants.'

If Basque strong Qs created DPs, we predict that we should be able to conjoin two strong Qs under the same D; but this is impossible as shown by the following examples:

(33)   Basque

a.   *[DP [QP *Ikasle   gehien*] *eta* [QP *irakasle guzti*] -*ak*]   *goiz*
[[student most]   and [teacher all]   -DET.PL.ABS] early
iritsi   ziren.
arrive AUX.PL
Intended: 'Most of the students and all of the teachers arrived early.'

b.   *[DP [QP *Neska bakoitz*] *eta* [QP *mutil guzti*] -*ek*]   *sari   bat*
[[girl   each]   and [boy   all]   -DET.PL.ERG] prize one
irabazi zuten.
win   AUX.PL
Intended: 'Each girl and all of the boys won a prize.'

These sentences show that Basque strong Qs create QPs and not DPs headed by D (see Etxeberria 2005; 2009 for extensive discussion; for Greek *o-kathe*, more recent discussions are found in Lazaridou-Chatzigoga 2012, Margariti 2014).

We thus conclude that D-restricted Qs do not create referential DPs, unlike the combination of D with a weak numeral. Since D in D_{DR} is a modifier and a head, the simplest thing to assume is, as we do, that D adjoins to Q. Recall that, as we said, we can envision this as a lexical or morphological operation. Another option would be to move D from a lower position and adjoin it to Q in a structure like [QP[DP[NP]]]:

(34)   QP

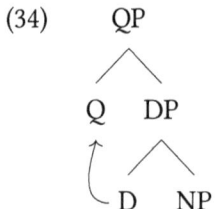

In this case, we get again a QP since Q would be in a structurally higher position; hence both movement of D from a lower to a higher position and our direct adjunction analysis allow D to function as a Q-modifier. In definite reduplication, as we shall see, we clearly observe instances of D in lower position. In this analysis, therefore, a structural parallelism with partitivity is more observable. Given that the lower D position is indeed for D_{DR} in Greek, as we will argue next, it seems reasonable to keep it as an analytical option.

We move on now to the St'át'imcets Salish data which illustrate the other incarnation of D_{DR} applying to a predicate. This is a lower D, and will be the variant needed for Greek D reduplication, we will argue.

3 D_{DR} on the NP: Partitive meaning

St'át'imcets Salish does not have a definite article, but possesses a morphologically deictic D (Matthewson 1998; 2008; see Gillon 2006; 2009 for Squamish, another Salish language). This D, Etxeberria & Giannakidou (2009; 2014) argue, functions as the Greek and Basque D in D_{DR}, but can also function as D_{DR} when applied to the NP argument. The result is again introducing the anaphoric variable C, yielding a contextually salient set of individuals characterized by the [NP∩C] property:

(35)   D to D_{DR} type-shifting:

     1. D_{DR} rule: When D composes with NP under Q, use D_{DR}.

     2. $[\![D_{DR}]\!] = \lambda P_{et} \, \lambda x \, (P(x) \cap C(x))$

(36)   *i...a* in D_{DR}
     $[\![i...a]\!] = \lambda P_{et} \, \lambda x \, (P(x) \cap C(x))$

As noted in Giannakidou (2004), D_{DR} works in this case like Chung & Ladusaw (2003)'s Restrict: it does not saturate the NP argument (i.e. it does not close it under *iota*), but only restricts it via C. It works like a modifier, as in D_{DR} on the Q:

(37)   St'át'imcets Salish

    a.   *Léxlex*   [*tákem-a i*   *smelhmúlhats-a*].
       intelligent [all   DET.PL woman.PL-DET]
       'All of the women are intelligent.'

    b.   * *Léxlex*   [*tákem-a smelhmúlhats*].
       intelligent [all   woman.PL]
       ('All of the women are intelligent.')

(38)   * *every the woman*

(39)   Greek
    * *kathe i   gynaika*
    every the woman
    ('every woman')

Having D_{DR} as an NP modifier is consistent with the idea of a lower DP layer, as we mentioned earlier (see Szabolcsi 1987; 2010, and works cited in Alexiadou et al. 2008). If St'át'imcets D is D_{DR}, the Salish structures are not as peculiar as initially appearing, but illustrate a systematic grammaticalization of domain restriction via D. However, D on NP is generally not allowed in English, Greek and Basque:

(40)   a.   * *every the boy*
    b.   * *most the boys*
    c.   * *many the boys*
    d.   * *three the boys*

(41)   Greek

    a.   * *kathe to   aghori*
       every the boy
       ('every boy')

b. * *merika ta aghoria*
    several the boys

    ('several boys')

c. * *tria   ta aghoria*
    three the boys

    ('three boys')

When D is fed an NP, it functions referentially in European languages; hence the need for the partitive preposition (Greek *apo*, Basque ablative *-tik*, etc.) to give back the right input (*et*) for composition with Q, e.g. *ikasle-eta-tik asko*, lit.: students-D-of many; 'many of the students':

(42) Greek

a. *merika apo ta   aghoria*
    several of   the boys

    'several of the boys'

b. *tria   apo ta aghoria*
    three of   the boys

    'three of the boys'

As Matthewson notes, the Salish DP structures are equivalent to the partitive PPs semantically. In Greek (and Basque) then, the morphological partitive is the way to do domain restriction on the NP argument (inside quantifier phrases); and we correlated this in our earlier work with the observation that St'át'imcets lacks partitive constructions. In European languages, we argued, the partitive is the analogue of the St'át'imcets Q with the D_{DR} restricted NP. This correlation between partitivity and D_{DR} is key, as we show in the next section, to understanding the nature of multiple definites.

We close this section with a few typological remarks. We have added D_{DR} as a possible functions of definites. DEFINITENESS thus emerges as a family of functions of D:

(43) Types for D

- Saturating:
  - $et \rightarrow e$ (iota); intensionalized version (generic)
- Non-saturating:
  - $et,ett \rightarrow et,ett$ (D_{DR} on Q)
  - $et \rightarrow et$ (D_{DR} on NP or AP)

The main division is between saturating (referential) and non-saturating types. D_{DR} belongs to the later, as shown. WEAK DEFINITES discussed in the literature are saturated thus referential, and determinacy, as understood in Coppock & Beaver (2015) only relates to the b-version of non-saturating D. Our point about D_{DR} is that D functions as a generalized modifier, applying not to just nouns but also quantifiers and, as we will show with D reduplication, adjectives.

Finally, it is not even necessary in our analysis that D_{DR} be performed strictly speaking by the definite article. Greek, Basque, Bulgarian and Hungarian, are all languages that have a definite article and employ it for D_{DR}. Why the definite article and not a demonstrative? Because the definite article is phonologically weak (a suffix in Basque and Bulgarian, and monosyllabic in Greek, Hungarian), whereas the demonstrative is typically a strong head (it is heavier lexically, it can stand alone as a phrase, compare *the* and *this*: **read the* versus *read this*). In languages like St'át'imcets and Korean (Kang 2015) that have deictic D but no article distinction, the demonstrative performs D_{DR} (see more arguments in Etxeberria & Giannakidou 2014 that St'át'imcets D is deictic). In case, finally, that a language lacks D altogether, if there is some element that encodes familiarity, that element will function as D_{DR}. The data reported in Cheng (2009) about Chinese *dou* confirm this prediction: *dou* is not a D, but according to Cheng it functions as D_{DR}, while also functioning as the *iota* operator when used with free choice items (Giannakidou & Cheng 2006).

4 Definite reduplication as involving D_{DR}

4.1 Multiple Ds with single reference

The phenomenon of definite reduplication is pervasive in Greek (Alexiadou & Wilder 1998; Campos & Stavrou 2004; Kolliakou 2004; Ioannidou & den Dikken 2006; Lekakou & Szendroi 2007):

(44)   Greek

    a.   *to   kalo paidi*
        the good child
        'the good child'

    b. * *to   paidi kalo*
        the child good
        ('the good child')

    c.   *to kalo to paidi*
       the good the child
       'the good child'

    d.   *to paidi to kalo*
       the child the good
       'the good child'

    e.   * *paidi to kalo*
       child the good
       ('the good child')

In the simple monadic definite, the adjective must precede the noun; this is the canonical structure. In the polydefinite construction, one D appears combined with the noun whereas a second D combines with the adjective. The order now is free, as we see. The major puzzle posed by these [DP+DP] structures is: why have them if they are equivalent to simple definites? We will argue here that they are not.

The polydefinite structures are sometimes thought to express a predication relation between the two DPs, and the sentence would be translated as something like 'the child who/that is good' (Alexiadou & Wilder 1998; Campos & Stavrou 2004). But it has generally been quite difficult in the literature to disentangle the pragmatic differences between monadic and polydefinites.

The order of the elements inside these polydefinites is quite free as we saw, and observe further the following examples:

(45)   Greek

    a. *to palio to spiti to petrino*
       the old   the house the stone-made
       'the old house made of stone'

    b. *to palio to petrino   to spiti*
       the old   the stone-made the house
       'the old house made of stone'

    c. *to spiti   to palio to petrino*
       the house the old   the stone-made
       'the old house made of stone'

The definite reduplication phenomenon only happens with D; the indefinite article results in ungrammaticality:

(46)   Greek

    a. * *ena kalo ena paidi*
         a   good a   child
        ('a good child')

    b. * *ena palio ena spiti   ena petrino*
         a   old a   stone-made a   house
        ('an old house made of stone')

The D with the noun seems to form the referential core of the structure, i.e. the DP that refers to an object. The combinations of D with the additional adjectives are non-referring, and perform D_{DR}, we will claim. Crucially, the phenomenon cannot be reduced to weak definiteness as we know it from the literature.

4.2 Multi-D structures, partitives, and D_{DR}

Our analysis will be that the secondary, adjectival uses of D are applications of D_{DR} on a predicate, with the ensuing partitive interpretation. Kolliakou (2004), as far as we know, is the first to make a clear connection between definite reduplication and partitive interpretation:

> Though in both *to kokino podilato* [the red bike] and *to kokino to podilato* [the red the bike] the same property 'red bike' is uniquely instantiable [in the resource situation], *only in the latter case is the index anchored to an entity that is a proper subset of a previously introduced set.* (Kolliakou 2004: 308, emphasis ours)

Kolliakou continues that:

> The polydefinite *to kokino to podilato*, is, therefore, semantically identical to the monadic *to kokino podilato*, whereas *the special pragmatic import of the former originates from an additional contextual restriction on the anchoring of the index* that interacts with the common morphosyntactic and semantic basis. (Kolliakou 2004: 265, emphasis ours).

Our take of this idea is that one D is referential, the other(s) perform D_{DR}. While the D plus NP introduces a referent, the additional D combining with adjectives performs domain restriction, and the multi-D structure is akin to a partitive.

To understand that the multi-D structure picks out a proper subset of a set introduced in discourse, consider a uniqueness context where there is only one bike and it is red. In this context, reduplication is odd:

(47)   Greek

    a. # *To kokkino to podhilato mou aresei   poli!*
        the red   the bike   me   like.3SG much

        'I like the red bike a lot!'

    b. *To kokkino podhilato mou aresei   poli!*
        the red   bike   me   like.3SG much

        'I like the red bike a lot!'

Consider now maximal contexts where there is no subset:

(48)   Greek (Kolliakou 2004)
    Idame   tis dilitiriodis (#tis) kobres.
    saw.1PL the poisonous   the cobras

    'We saw the poisonous cobras.'

(49)   Greek (Campos & Stavrou 2004)
    # *Tous epikindinous tous kakopious prepi na   tous apofevgeis.*
    the dangerous   the criminals must SUBJ them avoid

    'You must avoid the dangerous criminals.'

The polydefinites are odd because all cobras are poisonous and all criminals are dangerous. In both the unique and the maximal context partitive readings are impossible, and reduplication is impossible too.

Campos & Stavrou (2004) suggest that polydefinites only have intersective readings, see (50b). Compare them with regular DPs in (50a):

(50)   Greek

    a. *Gnorises tin orea   tragoudistria?*
        met.2SG the beautiful singer

        'Did you meet the beautiful singer?'
        P the singer who sings beautifully
        P the singer who is beautiful

    b. *Gnorises tin orea   tin tragoudistria?*
        met.2SG the beautiful the singer

        'Did you meet the beautiful singer?'
        * the singer who sings beautifully
        P the singer who is beautiful

This fact can be interpreted as further supporting the partitive interpretation because the non-intersective reading requires either intensionalization or quantification over events, in either case going beyond the set of physically beautiful singers.

Finally, consider that partitives with adjectives in Greek are generally quite odd. Compare the adjectival partitives with the numeral partitive (which we encountered before). It is fair to generalize that adjectival partitives are odd in English too:

(51) Greek
      Context: In front of us there are red, blue and yellow bikes.

      a. *Dyo / Merika apo ta   podhilata einai gallika.*
          two / several of   the bikes   are   French

          'Two / several of the bikes are French.'

      b. ?? *Ta kokkina   apo ta   podhilata einai gallika.*
             the red (ones) of   the bikes   are   French

          'The red ones of the bikes are French.'

      c. *Ta kokkina ta   podhilata einai gallika.*
          the red   the bikes   are   French.

          'The red bikes are French.'

The definite reduplication looks like a strategy in Greek to try to form a partitive with an adjective, an option not available with the partitive preposition. The inability of (51b), which holds in English too, is in fact quite interesting, indicating that an adjective, unlike a numeral, is not a very good device to establish the part-of relation. Notice that Greek licenses nominal ellipsis with adjectives (*ta kokkina* = 'the red ones', see Giannakidou & Merchant 1997; Giannakidou & Stavrou 1999), and the *ones* version is still odd in English. Hence, the problem with potential adjectival partitives seems to be not with ellipsis or its equivalents; it is rather of a semantic nature. An adjective is not a good device to be used in the partitive structure because it is not a quantity expression and therefore cannot designate a proper subset (as required by partitivity). Quantity expressions such as numerals and quantifiers are the best devices because they are indeed quantity expressions.

Our proposal is that definite reduplication involves the D_{DR} function on a predicate, just like in Salish. And given that with adjectives there is no partitive alternative, the structural parallel is exactly the same (recall the Salish lacks partitives). The structure is as follows:

(52)   Greek

    a. *to kokkino to podhilato*
       the red   the bike

    b. $DP[\iota(\lambda x(bike(x)) \cap C(x) \cap red(x))]$

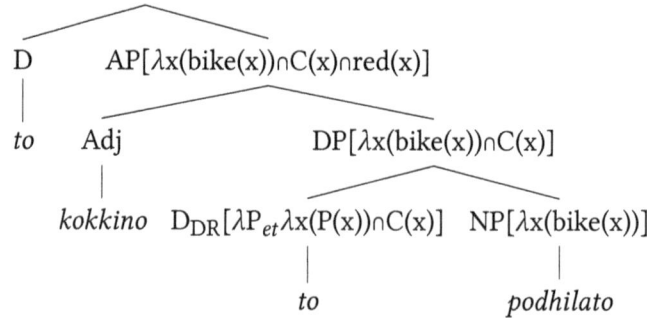

As we see, the top D functions referentially, to saturate the predicate, now domain restricted via D_{DR} coming from below. Since the order permutates syntactically, and since intersection is commutative, it doesn't matter which predicate (the adjective or the noun) undergoes D_{DR}. In fact, the free permutability of the structure can be seen as an argument in favour of the modifier analysis. The top D saturates, while any lower Ds perform D_{DR}. If we have more than two DP layers (as in *to spiti to palio to petrino* (lit. 'the house the old the stone-made')) we assume that there will be an identity relation between the Cs contributed by each application of D_{DR}. C, finally, as is typically the case, will have to refer to a non-singleton set, hence the partitivity effect.

The simple monadic definite, on the other hand, lacks C and there is no partitive effect.

(53)   *to kokkino podhilato* ('the red bike') = ι (red(x) $\cap$ bike (x)).

The partitive effect can be reinforced by focus as discussed further in Kolliakou (2004), e.g. in contrastive contexts: *to kokkino to podhilato, oxi to ble* 'the red bike not the blue one'.

What we are suggesting here, namely application of D_{DR} at the lower level(s), renders, as we said, the reduplication structure of Greek akin to the Salish DP strategy. Crucially, as in Salish, the structure of reduplication is not that of a partitive, i.e. it does not involve a PP, just like in Salish. There must be agreement in case and number, just like with all nominals in Greek (we thank a reviewer for asking this question).

D_DR has been suggested further for certain D+adjective combinations found in Slavic (Schürcks et al. 2014, Marušič & Žaucer 2014). In Slavic languages, so-called long-adjectives are usually interpreted as definites with D *i* combining only with the adjective, not the noun:

(54)   Serbian

    a.   *lep   grad*
        beautiful town

        'a beautiful town'

    b.   *lep-i-   grad*
        beautiful-DEF town

        'the beautiful town'

    c. * *lep   grad-i*
        beautiful town-DEF

        ('the beautiful town')

In Slovenian, there are similar phenomena. We will not delve into more detail here, but simply want to note that the strategy of D_DR on the adjective is possible in other Balkan Sprachbund languages.

4.3 Comparison with other approaches

The D_DR analysis we proposed seems to be an adequate and simple enough analysis of the polydefinite structure. Other alternatives such as for instance the close apposition analysis proposed by Lekakou & Szendroi (2007) cannot capture some of the key properties of the structure:

(55)   Greek

    a. *o aetos o puli*
       the eagle the bird

    b.

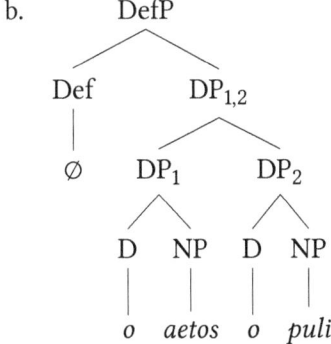

Reduplication as close apposition:

(56)   Greek

    a. *o spiti to petrino*
      the house the stone

    b.

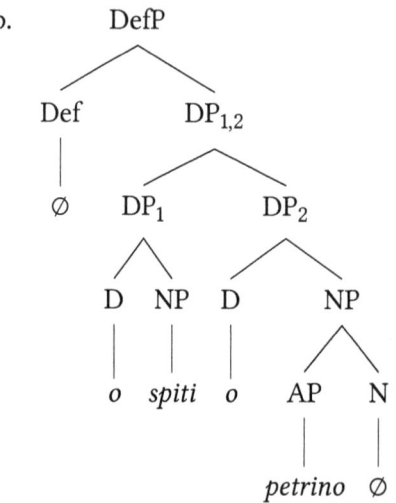

For this analysis to work, a number of assumptions must be made. First, we need to assume definiteness "concord" (*à la* Zeijlstra 2004); but there is no explanation why reduplication is optional whereas concord is obligatory. And a concord analysis would render the difference between a monadic definite and a polydefinite semantically vacuous, missing the partitive and anti-uniqueness effects observed, as well as the correlation with the impossibility of the partitive with adjectives that we noted. The concord/apposition account, finally, fails to unify reduplication with the D on Q.

Our analysis does precisely that. It unifies definite reduplication with the D_{DR} strategy on a predicate and says that polydefinites fall under the phenomenon of domain restriction, which involves a modifier function of D. It turns out, then, very interestingly, that Greek has both options of D_{DR}. Two open questions are: (a) why Basque doesn't exhibit the D-reduplication strategy, and (b) whether our D_{DR} analysis can extend to capture D-reduplication in other languages (e.g. in Swedish, noted earlier). We will leave the latter as a prediction of our theory, to be tested in future research.

5 Conclusions

As a summary of our discussion, we proposed here a modifier analysis D_{DR} of D heads cross-linguistically that includes the following two options:

(57)   D to D_{DR} type-shifting:

1. D_{DR} rule: When D composes with Q, use D_{DR}.

2. $D_{DR} = \lambda Z_{et,ett} \, \lambda P_{et} \, \lambda Q_{et} \, Z \, (P \cap C) \, (Q)$;
     Z is the relation denoted by Q

The domain restricting function is a non-saturating use of D as a modifier (D_{DR}); and if our analysis of Greek definite reduplication is correct, Greek also has the option of D_{DR} on the predicate, just like Salish.

Clearly, given the data from Greek, Basque and Salish languages in contrast to English, a fair question to ask is what determines, in each language, whether the available D will have the option to function as a modifier or not. As we suggested already, the difference doesn't follow from the morphological status of D since Greek *o* and English *the* are both independent heads and monosyllabic. Greek *o*, however, is phonologically weaker than *the*, therefore phonological weakness may be a factor, as we noted earlier. Suffixal Ds are phonologically weaker too since they are clitic Ds; hence, if phonological weakness is a decisive factor, we expect to find more D_{DR} in languages with suffixal Ds.

Finally, our analysis of D reduplication as D_{DR} strengthens our initial link between D_{DR} and partitivity, and suggests that it is actually quite general. By introducing C, D_{DR} creates partitivity in all cases, since NP intersected with C will be as subset of NP. The domain after D_{DR} is therefore always a subset of a larger domain. Hence, partitivity is present even in the case of application of D_{DR} to Q.

Acknowledgements

We thank Alda Mari and Marika Lekakou for their comments on earlier material related to this paper. We also want to thank Klaus von Heusinger for his insightful comments, most of which we will continue thinking about. Thanks also to the audiences of *New Ideas in Semantics and Modeling* (NISM) 2016 as well as the *Linguistics Seminar* of the University of Hamburg. We would also like to thank the two anonymous reviewers for all their insightful comments. And last, but not least, thanks a lot to Ana Aguilar-Guevara, Julia Pozas Loyo, and

Violeta Vázquez-Rojas Maldonado for their careful comments, and for their patience through the writing process. This piece of research is supported by the *Humanities Visiting Committee* at The University of Chicago, and by the following grants: IT769-13 (Basque Government), EC FP7/SSH-2013-1 AThEME 613465 (European Commission), FFI2014-51878-P, FFI2014-52015-P, and FFI2017-82547-P (Spanish MINECO).

References

Abney, Steven P. 1987. *The English noun phrase in its sentential aspect.* Cambridge: Massachusetts Institute of Technology. (Doctoral dissertation).

Aguilar-Guevara, Ana, Bert Le Bruyn & Joost Zwarts (eds.). 2014. *Weak referentiality* (Linguistik Aktuell/Linguistics Today 219). Amsterdam: John Benjamins.

Aguilar-Guevara, Ana & Joost Zwarts. 2011. Weak definites and reference to kinds. *Proceedings of SALT* 20. 179–196.

Alexiadou, Artemis, Liliane Haegeman & Melita Stavrou. 2008. *Noun phrase in the generative perspective* (Studies in Generative Grammar 71). Berlin: De Gruyter Mouton.

Alexiadou, Artemis & Chris Wilder (eds.). 1998. *Possessors, predicates and movement in the determiner phrase* (Linguistik Aktuell/Linguistics Today 22). Amsterdam: John Benjamins.

Barwise, Jon & Robin Cooper. 1981. Generalized quantifiers and natural language. *Linguistics and Philosophy* 4(2). 159–219.

Campos, Héctor & Melita Stavrou. 2004. Polydefinites in Modern Greek and Aromanian. In Olga Mišeska Tomić (ed.), *Balkan syntax and semantics* (Linguistik Aktuell/Linguistics Today 67), 137–173. Amsterdam: John Benjamins.

Carlson, Greg N. & Rachel Shirley Sussman. 2005. Seemingly indefinite definites. In Stephan Kepser & Marga Reis (eds.), *Linguistic evidence: Empirical, theoretical and computational perspectives* (Studies in Generative Grammar 85), 71–86. Berlin: Mouton de Gruyter.

Cheng, Lisa Lai-Shen. 2009. On *every* type of quantificational expression in Chinese. In Anastasia Giannakidou & Monika Rathert (eds.), *Quantification, definiteness and nominalization* (Oxford Studies in Theoretical Linguistics 24), 53–75. Oxford University Press.

Chung, Sandra & William A. Ladusaw. 2003. *Restriction and saturation* (Linguistic Inquiry Monographs 42). Cambridge: MIT Press.

Cieschinger, Maria. 2006. *Constraints on the contraction of preposition and definite article in German*. Osnabrück: University of Osnabrück. (BA Thesis).

Coppock, Elizabeth & David Beaver. 2015. Definiteness and determinacy. *Linguistics and Philosophy* 38(5). 377–435.

Corblin, Francis. 2013. Weak definites as bound relational definites. *Recherches linguistiques de Vincennes* 42. 91–122.

Elbourne, Paul D. 2005. *Situations and individuals* (Current Studies in Linguistics 41). Cambridge: MIT Press.

Etxeberria, Urtzi. 2005. *Quantification and domain restriction in Basque*. Vitoria-Gasteiz: University of the Basque Country. (Doctoral dissertation).

Etxeberria, Urtzi. 2008. On Basque quantification and on how some languages restrict their quantificational domain overtly. In Lisa Matthewson (ed.), *Quantification: A cross-linguistic perspective* (Linguistic Variations 64), 225–276. Bingley: Emerald.

Etxeberria, Urtzi. 2009. Contextually restricted quantification in Basque. In Anastasia Giannakidou & Monica Rathert (eds.), *Quantification, definiteness, and nominalization* (Oxford Studies in Theoretical Linguistics), 76–107. Oxford: Oxford University Press.

Etxeberria, Urtzi & Anastasia Giannakidou. 2009. Contextual domain restriction and the definite determiner. In François Recanati, Isidora Stojanovic & Neftali Villanueva (eds.), *Context-dependence, perspective and relativity* (Mouton Series in Pragmatics 6), 6–93. Berlin: De Gruyter Mouton.

Etxeberria, Urtzi & Anastasia Giannakidou. 2014. Illusory specificity effects with Spanish 'algunos'. (Talk presented at Universidad Autónoma de Madrid, Madrid).

Fara, Delia Graff. 2001. Descriptions as predicates. *Philosophical Studies* 102(1). 1–42.

Giannakidou, Anastasia. 2004. Domain restriction and the arguments of quantificational determiners. *Proceedings of SALT* 14. 110–126.

Giannakidou, Anastasia & Lisa Lai-Shen Cheng. 2006. (In)definiteness, polarity, and the role of wh-morphology in free choice. *Journal of Semantics* 23. 135–183.

Giannakidou, Anastasia & Jason Merchant. 1997. On the interpretation of null indefinite objects in Greek. *Studies in Greek Linguistics* 18. 141–154.

Giannakidou, Anastasia & Monika Rathert. 2009. *Quantification, definiteness, and nominalization*. Anastasia Giannakidou & Monika Rathert (eds.) (Oxford Studies in Theoretical Linguistics). Oxford: Oxford University Press.

Giannakidou, Anastasia & Melita Stavrou. 1999. Nominalization and ellipsis in the Greek DP. *The Linguistic Review* 16(4). 295–332.

Gillon, Carrie. 2006. *The semantics of determiner: Domain restriction in Skwxwú7mesh*. Vancouver: University of British Columbia. (Doctoral dissertation).

Gillon, Carrie. 2009. The semantic core of determiners: Evidence from Skwxwú7mesh. In Jila Ghomeshi, Ileana Paul & Martina Wiltschko (eds.), *Determiners: Universals and variation* (Linguistik Aktuell/Linguistics Today 147), 177–214. Amsterdam: John Benjamins.

Heim, Irene. 1982. *The semantics of definite and indefinite noun phrases*. Amherst: University of Massachusetts. (Doctoral dissertation).

Heim, Irene. 1990. E-type pronouns and donkey anaphora. *Linguistics and Philosophy* 13(2). 137–177.

Ioannidou, Alexandra & Marcel den Dikken. 2006. P-drop, D-drop D-spread. (Talk provided at Syracuse University, 2006).

Kang, Aarum. 2015. *(In)definiteness, disjunction and anti-specificity in Korean: A study in the semantics-pragmatics interface*. Chicago: University of Chicago. (Doctoral dissertation).

Keenan, Edward L. 1987. A semantic definition of "indefinite NP". In Eric Reuland & Alice G. B. ter Meulen (eds.), *The representation of (in)definiteness* (Current Studies in Linguistics 14), 286–317. Cambridge: MIT Press.

Keenan, Edward L. 1996. The semantics of determiners. In Shalom Lappin (ed.), *The handbook of contemporary semantics theory* (Blackwell Handbooks in Linguistics), 41–63. Oxford: Blackwell.

Keenan, Edward L. & Dag Westerståhl. 1997. Generalized quantifiers in linguistics and logic. In Johan van Benthem & Alice G. B. ter Meulen (eds.), *Handbook of logic and language*, 839–893. Amsterdam: North Holland.

Kolliakou, Dimitra. 2004. Monadic definites and polydefinites: Their form, meaning and use. *Journal of Linguistics* 40(2). 263–323.

Lazaridou-Chatzigoga, Dimitra. 2012. The universal distributive quantifier *kathe* with the definite article. *Studies in Greek Linguistics* 32. 235–246.

Lekakou, Marika & Kriszta Szendroi. 2007. Polydefinites in Greek: Ellipsis, close apposition and expletive determiners. *Journal of Linguistics* 48(1). 107–149.

Ludlow, Peter. 2007. Descriptions. In Edward N. Zalta (ed.), *The Stanford Encyclopedia of Philosophy*. Stanford: Metaphysics Research Lab, CSLI, Stanford University. https://plato.stanford.edu/archives/fall2007/entries/descriptions/.

Margariti, Anna-Maria. 2014. *Quantification at the syntax-semantics interface: Greek 'every' NPs*. Patras: University of Patras. (Doctoral dissertation).

Martí, Luisa. 2003. *Contextual variables*. Storrs: University of Connecticut. (Doctoral dissertation).

Marušič, Franc & Rok Žaucer. 2014. A definite article in the AP – Evidence from colloquial Slovenian. In Lilia Schürcks, Anastasia Giannakidou & Urtzi Etxeberria (eds.), *The nominal structure in Slavic and beyond* (Studies in Generative Grammar 116), 184–208. Berlin: De Gruyter Mouton.

Matthewson, Lisa. 1998. *Determiner systems and quantificational strategies: Evidence from Salish* (World Theses 1). The Hague: Holland Academic Graphics.

Matthewson, Lisa. 1999. On the interpretation of wide-scope indefinites. *Natural Language Semantics* 7(1). 79–134.

Matthewson, Lisa. 2001. Quantification and the nature of crosslinguistic variation. *Natural Language Semantics* 9(2). 145–189.

Matthewson, Lisa. 2008. Pronouns, presuppositions, and semantic variation. *Proceedings of SALT* 18. 527–550.

Milsark, Gary L. 1977. Towards the explanation of certain peculiarities of existential sentences in English. *Linguistic Analysis* 3. 1–29.

Montague, Richard. 1974. The proper treatment of quantification in ordinary English. In Jack Kulas, James H. Fetzer & Terry L. Rankin (eds.), *Philosophy, language, and artificial intelligence: Resources for processing natural language* (Studies in Cognitive Systems 2). Dordrecht: Kluwer.

Neale, Stephen. 1990. *Descriptions*. Cambridge: MIT Press.

Partee, Barbara H. 1986. Noun phrase interpretation and type-shifting principles. In Jeroen Groenendijk, Dick de Jongh & Martin Stokhof (eds.), *Studies in discourse representation theory and the theory of generalized quantifiers*, 115–143. Dordrecht: Foris.

Poesio, Massimo. 1994. Weak definites. *Proceedings of SALT* 4. 282–299.

Prince, Ellen F. 1981. Toward a taxonomy of given/new information. In Peter Cole (ed.), *Radical pragmatics*, 223–255. New York: Academic Press.

Puig Waldmüller, Estela Sophie. 2008. *Contracted preposition-determiner forms in German: Semantics and pragmatics*. Barcelona: Universitat Pompeu Fabra (Doctoral dissertation).

Recanati, François. 1996. Domains of discourse. *Linguistic and Philosophy* 19(5). 445–475.

Recanati, François. 2004. *Literal meaning*. Cambridge: Cambridge University Press.

Recanati, François. 2007. *Perspectival thought: A plea for moderate relativism*. Oxford: Oxford University Press.

Reuland, Eric J. & Alice G. B. ter Meulen. 1989. *The representation of (in)definiteness* (Current Studies in Linguistics 14). Cambridge: MIT Press.

Roberts, Craige. 2002. Demonstratives as definites. In Deemter van Kees & Rodger Kibble (eds.), *Information sharing: Reference and presupposition in language generation and interpretation* (CSLI Lecture Notes 143), 89–196. Stanford: CSLI.

Roberts, Craige. 2003. Uniqueness in definite noun phrases. *Linguistics and Philosophy* 26(3). 287–350.

Roberts, Craige. 2004. Context in dynamic interpretation. In Laurence R. Horn & Gregory Ward (eds.), *The handbook of pragmatics* (Blackwell Handbooks in Linguistics 16), 197–220. Oxford: Blackwell.

Roberts, Craige. 2010. Retrievability and definite noun phrases. (Talk given at the Philosophy Department of The Ohio State University, February 5 2010.)

Russell, Bertrand. 1905. On denoting. *Mind* 14(56). 479–493.

Schürcks, Lilia, Anastasia Giannakidou & Urtzi Etxeberria. 2014. *The nominal structure in Slavic and beyond* (Studies in Generative Grammar 116). Berlin: De Gruyter Mouton.

Schwarz, Florian. 2009. *Two types of definites in natural language*. Amherst: University of Massachusetts. (Doctoral dissertation).

Stanley, Jason. 2002. Nominal restriction. In Gerhard Preyer & Georg Peter (eds.), *Logical form and language*, 365–388. Oxford: Oxford University Press.

Stanley, Jason & Zoltán Gendler Szabó. 2000. On quantifier domain restriction. *Mind and Language* 15(2–3). 219–261.

Stavrou, Melita. 1983. *Aspects of the structure of the noun phrase in Greek*. Cambridge: University of Cambridge. (Doctoral dissertation).

Stavrou, Melita & Geoffrey Horrock. 1989. Clitic and demonstrative pronouns in the NP. *Studies in Greek Linguistics* 10. 225–245.

Strawson, Peter F. 1952. *Introduction to logical theory*. London: Methuen.

Szabolcsi, Anna. 1987. Functional categories in the noun phrase. In Istvan Kenesei (ed.), *Approaches to Hungarian 2: Theories and analyses*, 161–191. Szeged: JATE.

Szabolcsi, Anna. 2010. *Quantification* (Research Surveys in Linguistics). Cambridge: Cambridge University Press.

von Fintel, Kai. 1994. *Restrictions on quantifier domains*. Amherst: University of Massachusetts. (Doctoral dissertation).

von Fintel, Kai. 1998. The semantics and pragmatics of quantifier domains. (Paper presented at the Vilem Mathesius Lectures, Prague, March 1998.)

Ward, Gregory & Betty Birner. 1995. Definiteness and the English existential. *Language* 71(4). 722–742.

Westerståhl, Dag. 1984. Determiners and context sets. In Johan van Benthem & Alice G. B. ter Meulen (eds.), *Generalized quantifiers in natural language*, 45–71. Dordrecht: Foris.

Westerståhl, Dag. 1985. Logical constants in quantifier languages. *Linguistics and Philosophy* 8(4). 387–413.

Zeijlstra, Hedde. 2004. *Sentential negation and negative concord* (LOT Dissertation Series 101). Utrecht: LOT.

Zwarts, Joost. 1986. *Categoriale Grammatica en Algebraische Semantiek: Een studie naar negatie en polariteit in het Nederlands.* Groningen: University of Groningen. (Doctoral dissertation).

3

On kinds and anaphoricity in languages without definite articles

Miloje Despić
Cornell University

This paper investigates the availability of anaphoric readings with bare nouns in languages without definite articles, with a special focus on kind-level interpretation. Various facts from Serbian, Turkish, Japanese, Mandarin, and Hindi shows that the anaphoric reading of bare nouns is constrained by two general factors: (i) number morphology; in particular, whether the language in question has number morphology to begin with, and if it does, whether the bare noun in question is mass or count, and (ii) kind interpretation. It seems that mass and plural nouns can have anaphoric readings only if they are not interpreted as kinds. Singular count bare nouns, on the other hand, do not seem to be restricted in this way: they can have anaphoric readings regardless of whether or not they are interpreted as kinds. I argue that this state of affairs naturally follows from the system developed in Dayal (2004), which is based on a limited set of type-shifting operations and a particular analysis of number morphology. Alternative approaches to interpretation of bare nouns, on the other hand, do not seem to directly predict this sort of variation and require additional assumptions to account for it.

1 Introduction

In this paper, I explore the anaphoric definite interpretation of bare nouns in languages without definite articles. Evidence presented here reveals an interesting generalization about the availability of anaphoric readings with bare nouns, which requires an adequate explanation. In particular, it seems that the anaphoric interpretation of a bare noun depends on (i) whether or not the noun in question is singular or mass/plural and (ii) whether or not it is interpreted as kind-denoting. I will present data from Serbian, Turkish, Japanese, Mandarin and Hindi to illustrate this phenomenon. Before introducing the main empirical puzzle, it is useful to go over two major types of approaches to the structure and interpretation of NPs in languages without definite articles.

A theoretical challenge for anyone dealing with bare nouns in languages with-out articles is how to formally treat the absence of the definite determiner.[1] On the one hand, there is what we may call the Universal DP Approach (UDP), on which DP is present in all languages, regardless of whether they have a definite article or not (e.g. Longobardi 1994; Cinque 1994; Scott 2002; Pereltsvaig 2007) etc.). The central claim of this line of research is that even article-less languages have a definite article (i.e. a D head) in syntax, but unlike in languages like En-glish, the article is unpronounced/covert. In some versions of it, a fixed layer of functional projections is present in the nominal domain of all languages:

(1)   Determiner > Ordinal Number > Cardinal Number > Subjective
       Comment > ?Evidential > Size > Length > Height > Speed > ?Depth >
       Width > Weight > Temperature > ?Wetness > Age > Shape > Color >
       Nationality/Origin > Material > Compound Element > NP (Scott 2002:
       114)

The idea here is that the structure of the nominal domain of all languages is underlyingly identical and involves a functional spine in (1), which is very similar to the adverbial functional spine proposed in Cinque (1999), for example. On the other hand, the DP/NP approach assumes that DP is present only in languages with articles. In this kind of approach, the lack of (overt) articles actually indicates a simpler syntactic structure, i.e. NP (Baker 2003; Bošković 2008; 2012; Despić 2011; 2013; 2015). The contrast between the two types of languages in the DP/NP approach is illustrated in (2).

---

[1]This is part of a more general question of how to treat a construction/language which lacks a particular morpheme that is otherwise present in other constructions/languages.

(2)   a.   Languages *with* definite articles

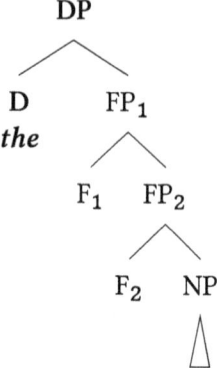

             (F_1 and F_2: potential functional projections)

     b.   Languages *without* definite articles

        (DP projection absent)

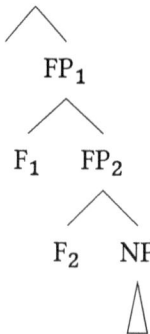

             (F_1 and F_2: potential functional projections)

There seems to be a number of cross-linguistic (and language-specific) syntactic patterns which are strongly correlated with whether or not definiteness marking is overtly present (e.g. Bošković 2008). Two such generalizations are given in (3) (see Bošković 2008 for more):

(3)   a.   Only languages without articles may allow Left Branch Extraction (Bošković 2008; 2012).

     b.   Reflexive possessives are available only in languages which lack definiteness marking, or which encode definiteness postnominally. Languages which have prenominal (article-like) definiteness marking, on the other hand, systematically lack reflexive possessives (Reuland 2011; Despić 2015).

Correlations like these are expected on the DP/NP approach, since the presence of the definite article in a language indicates a richer syntactic structure in the nominal domain. For example, to explain (3b), Despić (2015) proposes that DP is a binding domain, in contrast to NP, which is not (see Bošković 2012 and Despić 2015 for discussion of 3a).[2] Then in languages with prenominal definite articles, illustrated with English in (4), the reflexive possessive is not bound in its binding domain.

(4)   a.

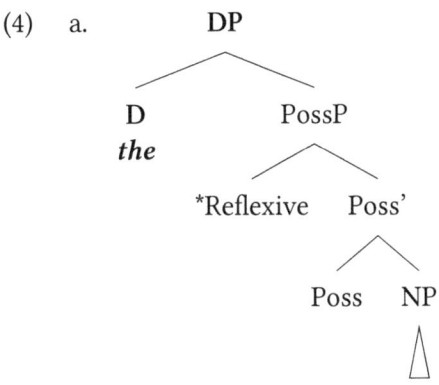

b. *John_i likes his_i/*himself_i's dog.*

In languages without definite articles, on the other hand, the nominal domain lacks DP and a binding domain by assumption and reflexive possessives are, therefore, in principle ruled in. Finally, for languages with postnominal definiteness marking, it can be assumed that PossP moves out of DP (as indicated by the

---

[2]LEFT BRANCH EXTRACTION (LBE) refers to situations in which a nominal modifier can be syntactically moved/fronted to the exclusion of the noun it modifies. Bošković (2008; 2012) observes that LBE is possible only in languages without articles. For example, while a construction like (i.a) is grammatical in Serbian, an article-less language, its English counterpart is ungrammatical (see i.b).

(i)   a. Serbian
          Lepe_i   je vidio [t_i kuće].
          beautiful is seen   houses
          'Beautiful houses, he saw.'

      b. English
          **Beautiful_i he saw [t_i houses].*

This strongly suggests that languages with and without definite articles have different nominal structures; e.g. while languages with articles project DP, which can block movement/LBE, languages without articles seem to lack this projection (i.e. their nominal structure is simpler; see 2b).

word order), which again rules in reflexive possessives. The general point is that, in the DP/NP approach, it is expected that at least some syntactic patterns would be directly sensitive to the overt presence/absence of the definite article.

In the UDP, such correlations appear *accidental*, since the presence of DP in the syntactic structure is independent of its morpho-phonologi-cal manifestation. To be clear, they are not strictly incompatible with the UDP, but additional assumptions are necessary to account for them. The question is, of course, whether these additional assumptions would simply re-describe the facts or actually provide true insight and be independently motivated. At the same time, one may wonder about the predictive power of the UDP; i.e. what kind of facts would ultimately be able to falsify it?

On the semantic side, it is clear that bare nouns in languages without articles can have definite, anaphoric readings, unlike in languages like English. The question is then what is responsible for the availability of this anaphoric reading, given that the anaphoric reading in languages like English requires the definite article. In the UDP, the presence of a phonologically null determiner creates this interpretation (e.g. Longobardi 1994). There is ultimately very little difference between English and an article-less language like Serbian: the definite, anaphoric reading in both of them is created by a definite D head. The only difference is that, in contrast to English, D is not overtly realized in Serbian. On the other hand, approaches that do not assume null D heads argue that a limited set of type-shifting operations is responsible for the general interpretation of bare nouns, including the anaphoric reading (e.g. Chierchia 1998; Dayal 2004).

In this paper, I focus on anaphoric, definite readings of bare nouns in languages without definite articles.[3] I show that their availability crucially depends on two factors (among other things): (i) number morphology and (ii) kind interpretation. I argue that the particular cross-linguistic variation discussed here is expected in the system developed in Dayal (2004), which employs type-shifting operations and a specific view of number morphology. As discussed in §3–5, the system based on type-shifting operations developed in Chierchia (1998) and Dayal (2004) is far from being unconstrained. That is, type-shifting operations do not apply arbitrarily. For example, the so-called BLOCKING PRINCIPLE regulates the availability of covert type-shifting operations by making sure that if a language has a lexical item whose meaning is a particular type-shifting operation, then that item must be used instead of the covert version. For this reason, for example, bare nouns in English (mass or plural) cannot have definite meaning – the covert type-shifting operation that would create this meaning is blocked by the existence of

---

[3]For an overview of different aspects of the meaning of definite descriptions see Schwarz (2009) and references therein.

the overt lexical item *the*. Also, covert type-shifting operations that are not excluded by the Blocking Principle are not equally available, but are rather ranked in terms of meaning preservation/simplicity; e.g. the operation responsible for kind reference $^\cap$ is more highly ranked than $\exists$, and the latter may apply only if $^\cap$ is undefined for some argument (see §3). Both of these principles are independently motivated; e.g. the Blocking Principle follows the general logic of the ELSEWHERE CONDITION (language particular choices win over universal tendencies).

At the same time, the data discussed in this paper raise certain questions for the UDP, which seems to require extra assumptions to explain them and it is not clear to which extent these assumptions could be independently motivated. In the remainder of the paper, I will therefore focus on demonstrating how th facts presented in the next section follow from Dayal's (2004) proposal.

The paper is organized as follows. In §2 I present the main empirical puzzle, while in §3 I show how it can be explained under Dayal's (2004) approach. In §4 I discuss some predictions and consequences of the data and analysis introduced in §2 and §3. Finally, a summary and concluding remarks are offered in §5. Here I also offer some thoughts on how the generalizations presented in this paper and Dayal (2004) can be connected to the distinction between weak and strong definiteness (e.g. Schwarz 2009).

2 The puzzle: Anaphoricity and kinds

In this section, I present the central empirical problem of the paper. Bare singular count nouns in languages without articles can be used anaphorically to refer to a previously introduced individual. Thus, the bare noun *book* in both Serbian (see 5) and Turkish (see 6) can refer to *Crime and Punishment* in the antecedent clause. English, on the other hand, must use the definite article (or demonstrative) in the same situation.

(5) Serbian
 Juče   sam pročitao "Zločin i Kaznu"   – knjiga   mi
 yesterday am read   Crime and Punishment   book-NOM me-DAT
 se   zaista svidela.
 REFL really liked
 'Yesterday I read *Crime and Punishment* – I really liked the book.'

(6) Turkish
 Dün   "Suç ve Ceza"   okudum – kitap harikaydı.
 yesteday   Crime and Punishment read-PST book terrific-PST
 'Yesterday I read *Crime and Punishment*. The book was terrific.'

As shown in (7–11), similar holds for Mandarin, Japanese and Hindi, also languages without definite articles (note that Mandarin and Japanese do not mark number, which will become relevant in §3 and §4). In Mandarin examples in (7), bare nouns *shu* 'book' and *ta* 'tower' are used to refer anaphorically to *Crime and Punishment* and *Oriental Pearl*, respectively. In (8), the bare noun *mao* 'cat' is referring to the NP in the antecedent clause. Japanese examples in (9) illustrate the same point: *hon* 'book' in (9a) refers to *Crime and Punishment*, while *roojin* 'old man' in (9b) refers to the proper name *Yahachi*. Examples from Hindi are given in (10) and (11). Now, although anaphoric readings with bare nouns are available in these languages, it should be noted that nouns with demonstratives or simple pronouns are preferred in many contexts, for a number of pragmatic and discourse reasons, which I will not discuss here. What is crucial is that such use of bare nouns in languages like English is disallowed regardless of discourse/context properties (that is, bare singular nouns are in general ungrammatical in English).

(7) Mandarin

    a. *Wo kan le   Zuiyufa   Shu zai zhuo zi-shang.*
       I   read ASP Crime and Punishment book be at   table-TOP
       'I read *Crime and Punishment*. The book is on the table.'

    b. *Wo canguan le   dongfangmingzhu. Ta   hen gao.*
       I   visit   PTCP Oriental Pearl   tower very tall
       'I visited the Oriental Pearl. The tower is high.'

(8) Mandarin
    Wo kanjian yi-zhi   mao. Mao zai huayuan-li.
    I   see   one-CLF cat   cat at garden-inside
    'I see a cat. The cat is in the garden.' (Dayal 2004: 403)

(9) Japanese

    a. *Kinou   "Tsumi to Batsu"-o   yonda.   Hon-wa*
       yesterday Crime and Punishment-ACC read-PST book-TOP
       subarashikatta.
       fantastic-PST

       'Yesterday I read *Crime and Punishment*. The book was fantastic.'

    b. *Yahachi-o   miru-to,   roojin-wa   damatte unazuita.*
       Yahachi-ACC see-when old man-TOP silently nodded

       'When I saw Yahachi, the old man silently nodded.' (Fujisawa 1992: 14)

(10) Hindi
      Kal   mei-ne Crime and Punishment pari aur kitaab bariya   hai.
      yesterday I-ERG   Crime and Punishment read and book   excellent is
      'Yesterday I read *Crime and Punishment* and the book is excellent.'

(11) Hindi
      Kuch bacce   andar aaye. Bacce   bahut khush the.
      some children inside came children very   happy were
      'Some children came in. The children were very happy.' (Dayal 2004: 403)

Consider now bare mass nouns. When they are used in a kind-denoting context they *cannot* be used anaphorically in these languages. For example, *meyve* 'fruit' in (12) cannot pick out *üzüm* 'grapes' in the antecedent clause, just like *voće* 'fruit' cannot refer to *grožđe* 'grapes' in (13). They only have the implausible general meaning – the second clause in these examples can be interpreted only as a statement about fruit in general, not about a particular kind of fruit (grape) introduced in the antecedent clause.

(12) Turkish
      Ömrüm boyunca   üzüm yetiştirdim. #(Bu) meyve herşeyim
      my life throughout grape produce   this fruit   my everything
      oldu.
      became
      'I have been producing grapes my whole life. (This) fruit is everything to me.'
      → * if *meyve* 'fruit' is anteceded by *üzüm* 'grapes'
      → OK if *bu meyve* 'that fruit' is anteceded by *üzüm* 'grapes'

(13) Serbian
      a. *Naše mesto već   generacijama proizvodi belo   grožđe. Sve*
         our town already generations   produces white grape   everything
         dugujemo #(tom) voću.
         owe   (that) fruit-DAT
         'Our town has been producing white grapes for generations. We owe everything to (that) fruit.'
         → * if *voću* 'fruit' is anteceded by *grožđe* 'grapes'
         → OK if *tom voću* 'that fruit' is anteceded by *grožđe* 'grapes'

b. ... #(*To*) *voće je jako ukusno.*
          that fruit is very tasty

'...(That) fruit is very tasty.'

→ * if *voće* 'fruit' is anteceded by *grožđe* 'grapes'

→ OK if *to voće* 'that fruit' is anteceded by *grožđe* 'grapes'

In order to get the anaphoric reading, a demonstrative must be used. These examples are minimally different from those in (5–6), which in contrast do allow anaphoric interpretation of the bare noun. Also note that whether *voće* 'fruit' in Serbian is in the subject or object position is irrelevant for anaphoricity.[4],[5]

We see a similar pattern in Mandarin, Japanese and Hindi, as illustrated with some examples below. All of my informants find a strong contrast in the availability of anaphoric reading between examples (7–11), on the one hand, and the ones in (12–16), on the other. Just like in (12–13), the second clause in (14–16) below can be interpreted only as a general statement about fruit, not as a statement about a particular kind of fruit mentioned in the antecedent clause; i.e. 'Fruit is our life' in (14) cannot be interpreted as 'Apples are our life'.

(14) Mandarin

Women shidai   zhong pingguo shuiguo jiu   shi women de   ming.
we   generation grow apple   fruit   PTCP is we   GEN life

'We have been growing apples for generations. Fruit is our life.'

---

[4]Turkish, however, has differential object marking and in accusative case makes a morphological distinction between specific and non-specific objects (e.g. Enç 1991).

[5]Other mass nouns behave in a similar way; e.g. *vino* 'wine' in (i.b) below cannot be anteceded by *Vranac* (a special type of wine) in (i.a) without the demonstrative. Both *voće* 'fruit' and *vino* 'wine' in Serbian in general require a classifier phrase (like truckload of or glass of) or a measure phrase (like lot of) for counting, which is typical of mass nouns. At the same time, they are very useful here because they have well-established subclasses/subtypes (in contrast to, say, *sand*), which could in principle serve as pragmatically plausible antecedents. The fact that the anaphoric relationship cannot be formed in these examples, thus, cannot be due to pragmatic factors.

(i) Serbian

a. *Naše mesto već   generacijama proizvodi "Vranac".*
    our town already generations sproduces Vranac

    'Our town has been producing Vranac for generations.'

b. *Sve   dugujemo #(tom) vinu.*
    everything owe   (that) wine

    'We owe everything to (that) wine.'

(15) Japanese

Watashitachi-wa daidai   budou-o   sodatetekita. #(*Kono*)
we-TOP   for-generations grapes-ACC have grown   this
Kudamono-wa subarashi.
fruit-TOP   fantastic

'We have been growing grape for generations. This fruit is fantastic.'

(16) Hindi

Mei-ne angur ki kheti   mei saari jeevan biaayi hai aur #(*ye*) *phal-ne*
I-ERG grapes of farming in all   life   spend is and this fruit-ERG
mujh-ko ameer bana   dija   hai.
me-ACC rich   make-PST give-PST is

'I have been growing grapes all my life and the fruit has made me rich.'

Now, a mass noun with a kind reading can be used anaphorically in English, if it is accompanied by the definite article. Consider, for instance, (17) in which 'the fruit' is anteceded by 'grapes'. Many speakers I have consulted find the anaphoric reading in (17) perfectly possible, although some of them would still prefer the demonstrative 'that' instead of 'the', presumably for the same type of reasons mentioned in the discussion of (5–11).[6,7]

(17) *We have been growing grapes for generations – and you know, we have made millions on the fruit.*

Why would this be the case? Why would the existence of kind-reference affect the anaphoric potential of a bare noun in article-less languages in such a way? This state of affairs seems to raise some non-trivial questions for the basic version

---

[6]What seems to be clear is that the bare noun *fruit* in (i) has no anaphoric potential; i.e. the second clause in (i) is interpreted as a general statement about fruit, which is exactly the kind of judgment speakers of languages without articles discussed here have for (12–16).

(i) *We have been growing grapes for generations – and you know, we have made millions on fruit.*

[7]Similar facts about anaphoricity of mass nouns interpreted as kinds have also been observed by Dayal (2004: ft. 43, 435–436), who points out that "...mass terms can occur with a definite if anaphorically linked to an antecedent, even if such anaphoricity leads to kind reference, as in (i)."

(i) *Patients need medicine and food. (The) medicine fights the disease and (the) food builds up strength.*

See §5 for a discussion of kinds in connection with the distinction between unique and familiar definites.

of the UDP approach. In particular, if the covert version of the definite article, which is overt in English, is responsible for the definite reading of the bare nouns in (5–11) (e.g. *knjiga* 'book'), why cannot it produce the same effect in (12–16) (with the bare noun *grožđe* 'fruit') given that 'the fruit' in English (17) has the definite article? In the UDP all languages have identical underlying structure in the nominal domain, and the phonologically null/covert D in Serbian or Turkish should in principle perform the same function as its overt version in languages like English; e.g. it assigns the definite/anaphoric interpretation to, say, *knjiga* or *kitap* 'book' in (5–6), just like the overt article *the* does in English. One could assume that, for some reason, covert versions of D are more limited in meaning, and cannot combine with, for instance, kind-denoting nouns, but this would have to be independently supported. That is, these additional assumptions would have to explain why the opposite situation does not arise.

Note that the real culprit here is the presence of kind-reference. In other words, bare mass nouns in languages without definite articles *can* have anaphoric readings in the absence of kind interpretation. This is shown in (18–22): in all of these examples the antecedent clause describes a particular object-level entity, and the bare mass nouns in the second clause ('fruit' or 'wine') can be anaphorically anteceded by it. This is true even though these examples are overall very similar to those in (12–16) – the only difference is that the latter force the kind-level interpretation. That is, bare mass nouns can have both kind-level and object-level interpretation, but the anaphoric reading is possible only in the latter case (see Chierchia 1998: §4 and references therein) for the kind vs. object level distinction). Compare (18a–b) with (13), for instance. As discussed in Chierchia (1998), from an intuitive, pretheoretical point of view, kinds are seen as regularities that occur in nature – although they are similar to individuals, "their spatiotemporal manifestations are typically "discontinuous"" (Chierchia 1998: 348). That is, a kind can be identified in any given world with the totality or sum of its instances. It may lack instances in a world/situation (e.g. *dodo*), but something that is necessarily instantiated by just one individual (e.g. *Noam Chomsky*), would not qualify as a kind (this contrast will in fact play one of the central roles in the explanation offered in the next section). So in (13), for example, we interpret the mass noun as an idealized sum of its instances with discontinuous spatiotemporal manifestations, which is highlighted by the use of the expression 'for generations' – we clearly do not interpret it as a particular object-level instantiation of the mass noun (e.g. *a bowl of fruit*). In (18b), on the other hand, we have exactly that – a specific, object-level interpretation of the mass noun, with a specific quantity, at a specific time/situation. And exactly in this case the anaphoric relationship can be established.

Also, as in the case of examples in (5–11), an NP with a demonstrative or a simple pronoun might be preferred in (18–22), but the bare noun is nevertheless quite possible. What is important is that there is a substantial contrast between this set of examples and those in (12–16), in which the anaphoric reading is not available without the demonstrative.

(18) Serbian

    a. *Juče   sam po prvi put   pojeo nekoliko braziliskih papaja. Voće je*
        yesterday am   at first time ate   a few   Brazilian   papaya fruit is
        zaista fantastično!
        truly   fantastic
        'Yesterday I ate a few Brazilian papayas for the first time. The fruit is fantastic!'

    b. *Danas sam kupio   malo grožđa, hleb i   mleko. Voće sam stavio un*
        today am   bought bit   grapes bread and milk   fruit am   put   in
        frižider a   sve ostalo na sto.
        fridge   and all else   on table
        'Today I bought some grapes, bread and milk. I put the fruit in the fridge and the rest on the table.'
        → OK if *voće* 'fruit' is anteceded by *grožđe* 'grapes'

    c. *Sa   prijateljima sam juče   popio tri   flaše Dom Perinjon-a.*
        with friends   am   yesterday drank three bottles Dom Perignon
        Vino je zaista fantastično.
        wine is truly   fantastic
        'I drank three bottles of Dom Pérignon yesterday. The wine is truly fantastic.'
        → OK if *vino* 'wine' is anteceded by *Dom Pérignon*

The examples below behave the same way:

(19) Turkish
    Dün   üzüm, peynir ve   süt   aldım.   Meyve pahalıydı   ama
    yesterday grape cheese and milk buy-1.PST fruit   expensive-PST but
    diğerleri hesaplıydı.
    rest   affordable-PST
    'I bought grapes, cheese and milk yesterday. The fruit was expensive but the rest was affordable.'

(20)   Mandarin

    a. *Wo ba na   dai   pinguo fang dao   zhuozi-shang, danshi shuiguo*
       I   ba that packet apple   put   towards table-TOP   but   fruit
      yixia zi   jiu   diao-chulai le.
      all-of-a-sudden PTCP fall-out   ASP

      'I put the packet with apples on the table, but the fruit immediately
      fell out of it.'

    b. *Wo mai   le   san   ge   pingguo niunai he   baozhi   shuiguo hen*
       I   bought ASP three CLF apple   milk   and newspaper fruit   very
      gui,   qita   dongxi dou hen pianyi.
      expensive other things all   very cheap

      'I bought three apples, milk and newspapers. The fruit was expensive;
      the other things were cheap.'[8]

(21)   Japanese

    a. *Tana-no   ue-no   ringo-o   miruto,   kudamono-wa sudeni kusatte*
      shelf-GEN top-GEN apple-ACC saw time fruit-TOP   already rotten
      ita.
      was

      'When I saw the apple on the shelf, the fruit was already rotten.'

    b. *Kinou   budou to   chiizu to   gyuunyuu-o katta. Kudamono-wa*
      yesterday grape and cheese and milk-ACC   bought fruit-TOP
      teeburu-ni oite,   hoka-wa reizouku-ni ireta.
      table-at   put-and rest-TOP fridge-in   insert-PST

      'Yesterday I bought grapes, cheese and milk. I put the fruit on the
      table and the rest in the fridge.'

---

[8]Contrastive particle *jiu* before 'fruit' in (20b) makes the anaphoric relation clearer, but it is
not necessary – (20b) is fine without it. Also, Jenks (to appear) observes that Mandarin seems
to make a principled distinction between unique and anaphoric definites (e.g. Schwarz 2009);
while unique definites are realized as bare nouns, anaphoric definites are realized with a demonstrative, except in subject positions, where bare nouns can also be interpreted anaphorically.
For this reason, in all Mandarin examples in this paper bare nouns are located in subject
positions.

(22) Hindi
   Aaj   mei-ne angur, dudh, aur paneer kharidi aur phal mehenga tha
   today I-ERG grapes milk and cheese bought and fruit expensive was
   par baki sab theek-thak tha.
   but rest all okay   was
   'I bought grapes, milk, and cheese today and the fruit was expensive but
   the rest was okay.'

   I argue in the next section that this contrast follows from Dayal's (2004) approach.

3 Solution: Dayal (2004)

Dayal's (2004) work is based on Chierchia (1998) and Carlson (1977), who take
English bare plurals to refer to kinds (as opposed to Wilkinson 1991; Diesing 1992;
Krifka & Gerstner-Link 1993; Kratzer 1995, who take bare plurals as ambiguous
between kind terms and indefinites). Chierchia (1998), in particular, attempts to
derive the typology and distribution of bare nominals across different types of
languages. Chierchia (1998) focuses on two parameters: (i) presence vs. absence of
determiners, and (ii) presence vs. absence of number morphology. Dayal (2004)
modifies Chierchia's (1998) theory, most importantly in the way languages with
number morphology but without determiners should be analyzed (see §4), but
many core assumptions are adopted from Chierchia (1998). I will provide a brief
overview of two assumptions of Chierchia's (1998) system that are most important for the purposes of this paper. The first assumption is that languages may
employ a number of type-shifting operations, a subset of which is given in (23):

(23) a. $\langle e, t \rangle = (^{\cap}, \iota, \exists) \Rightarrow \langle e \rangle / \langle \langle e, t \rangle t \rangle$
   b. ι: $\lambda P\ \iota x[Ps(x)]$
   c. $^{\cap}$: $\lambda P\lambda s\ \iota x[Ps(x)]$
   d. $\exists$: $\lambda P\lambda Q\exists x[Ps(x) \ni Qs(x)]$

   (Dayal 2004: 413)

   The main idea is that English bare plurals are derived via a nominalization
operation ('down') $^{\cap}$, defined as in (23c) (like other common nouns, they start
life as type $\langle s, \langle e, t \rangle \rangle$). $^{\cap}$ is a function from properties to functions from situations
to the maximal entity that satisfies that property in that situation. The function
is partial in that it requires the kind term to pick out distinct maximal individuals

across situations, thereby capturing the inherently intensional nature of the term. As shown in (24), this term can be a direct argument of a kind-level predicate:

(24)   *Dodos are extinct.*

In object-level contexts, however, further operations (see 25a) come into play to repair the sort mismatch. This repair (DERIVED KIND PREDICATION – DKP; see Chierchia 1998: 364, Dayal 2004: 399) involves the introduction of existential quantification over the instantiations of the kind in a given situation. It draws on the inverse of $^\cap$, the predicativizer or 'up', operation $^\cup$ (see 25b) to take kinds and return their instantiation sets in a given situation:

(25)   a.   DKP: If P applies to objects and k denotes a kind, then
             $P(k) = \exists x[^\cup k(x) \wedge P(x)]$
       b. $^\cup : \lambda k_{\langle s,e \rangle} \lambda x[x \leq k_s]$
       c.   Dogs didn't bark = $\neg\text{bark}(^\cap\text{dogs})$ = DKP $\Rightarrow \neg\exists x[^{\cup\cap}\text{dogs}(x) \wedge \text{bark}(x)]$

The source of existential quantification over instances of the kind in episodic sentences is an automatic, local adjustment triggered by a type mismatch. Bare plurals are in many ways different from indefinite singulars (e.g. Carlson 1977), for instance in scope:

(26)   a.   *John didn't read a book.* $\neg\exists$ and $\exists\neg$
       b.   *John didn't read books.*   only: $\neg\exists$

The indefinite denotes a generalized quantifier, and it can therefore take wide or narrow scope with respect to negation, as shown in (26a). The bare plural, on the other hand, is a kind term, which is a direct argument of the predicate (see 25c). Thus, whenever a kind (in an episodic frame) fills an object-level slot, the type of the element in question is automatically adjusted by introducing a local existential quantification over instances of the kind. The existential introduced by DKP therefore necessarily takes scope below negation. One prediction of this system is that non-kind denoting bare plurals should behave like regular existentially quantified NPs. For instance, they could take different scope with respect to negation: this prediction appears to be borne out (Carlson 1977; Chierchia 1998):

(27)   a.   * *Parts of this machine are widespread.*
       b.   *John didn't see parts of this machine.* $\neg\exists$ and $\exists\neg$
       (Dayal 2004: 419)

Parts of this machine in (27a) is not compatible with true kind predication, presumably because the definite inside the NP would force the extension of the noun phrase to be constant across worlds. But, as shown in (27b), this bare plural can now interact with negation, a diagnostic that separates indefinites from kind terms. Compare then (27) to (28):

(28)   a.   *Spots on the floor are a common sight.*
       b.   *John didn't see spots on the floor.*   *only:* ¬∃

In (28), possibility of kind reference results in the loss of scope interaction. The bare plural *spots on the floor* in (28a) is compatible with the kind-level predicate, which indicates that it has a kind reference. As a result, it can only have the low scope in (28b). Thus, this sort of system neatly explains this state of affairs. What needs to be assumed then is that $^\cap$ (see 23c) should apply whenever it can; i.e. it should take precedence over ∃ (see 23d). In (27b) $^\cap$ is unavailable, and therefore ∃ applies, as confirmed by the scope ambiguity. Chierchia (1998) thus ranks $^\cap$ above ∃ arguing that the former is simpler, since it does not introduce quantificational force (see 29).

(29)   **Meaning Preservation:** $^\cap > \{\iota, \exists\}$ (Dayal 2004: 419)

The immediate question that arises here concerns the availability of ι. In particular, if $^\cap$ is not available in (27) and ι (see 23b) is an available type-shifting operation, why cannot *parts of this machine* be interpreted as definite? This brings us to the second important component of the Chierchia (1998)/Dayal (2004) system called BLOCKING PRINCIPLE, which is given in (30):

(30)   **Blocking Principle (Type Shifting as Last Resort)**
       For any type-shifting operation ϕ and any X: $^*\phi(X)$ if there is a
       determiner D such that for any set X in its domain, $D(X) = \phi(X)$. (Dayal
       2004: 216)

The intuition behind this principle is that for considerations of economy lexical items must be exploited to the fullest before covert type-shifting operations can be used. So, since English has *the*, which is the lexical version of ι, it will always block ι. Thus, in English, bare plurals can avail of $^\cap$ (or ∃ when $^\cap$ is blocked for independent reasons, as in 27b), but not ι, because of the presence of the lexical determiner *the*. This in turn also explains the following contrast between Hindi (a determiner-less language) and English (Dayal 2004: 417):

(31)   a. English
            *Some children came in. *(The) children were happy.*
        b. Hindi
            Kuch bacce$_i$ aaye. Bacce$_i$ bahut khush lage.
            some children came children very   happy seemed
            'Some children came. The children seemed very happy.'

While bare nouns in Hindi can be used anaphorically, as shown in (31b), this is not possible in English (see 31a). This is because there is no lexical definite determiner in Hindi, which makes ι as well as $\cap$ available options for bare nominals. For this reason, *bacce* 'children' in (31b) can be interpreted as definite. In English, on the other hand, bare plurals can avail of $\cap$ but not ι. $\cap$ is a function whose extension varies from situation to situation, while ι is a constant function to a contextually anchored entity. Thus, the bare noun *children* in (31a) cannot be interpreted as definite/anaphorically. In other words, the underlying assumption of Chierchia (1998) and Dayal (2004) about $\cap$ is that it manufactures a kind out of a property (i.e. an intensional entity) by taking the largest member of its extension at any given world; it creates a saturated object with concrete, but possibly spatiotemporally discontinuous manifestations. But $\cap$ cannot establish an anaphoric relationship with a contextually anchored entity. Only ι, which selects the greatest element from the *extension* of the predicate, can do this. That is, even though $\cap$ (*nom*) is simply an intensional counterpart of ι, "...*nom* cannot be used referentially" (Dayal 2011: 1103). In §5 I offer some remarks on how Dayal's (2004) typological observations about the relationship between $\cap$ and ι relate to Schwarz's (2009; 2013) typology of definiteness marking (i.e. *strong* vs. *weak* definite articles).

Now, since in Dayal (2004) mass kinds are treated on a par with plural kinds, we have the solution to the puzzle introduced in §2. Recall first that a bare singular noun in an article-less language like Serbian can be interpreted as definite. This is expected: ι is allowed, since there is no lexical article to block it. This is illustrated by (5), repeated below as (32):

(32)   Serbian
        Juče   sam pročitao Zločin i Kaznu   – knjiga   mi se
        yesterday am   read   Crime and Punishment book-NOM me REFL
        zaista svidela.
        really liked
        'Yesterday I read *Crime and Punishment* – I really liked the book.'

However, a bare mass noun in a kind-denoting context cannot be interpreted as definite in language like Serbian, as shown in (33) (=13a) below.

(33) Serbian
      Naše mesto već   generacijama proizvodi belo   grožđe. Sve
      our town already generations   produces white grape   everything
      dugujemo #(tom) voću.
      owe   (that) fruit
      'Our town has been producing white grapes for generations. We owe everything to (that) fruit.'
      → * if *voću* 'fruit' is anteceded by *grožđe* 'grapes'
      → OK if *tom voću* 'that fruit' is anteceded by *grožđe* 'grapes'

This is exactly expected on this approach since kind-denoting terms must be derived via $\cap$; thus, the bare noun *voće* 'fruit' in (33) behaves similarly to the bare noun *children* in (31a) with respect to anaphoricity/definiteness. But bare mass nouns which do not denote kinds can avail of ι in languages like Serbian, because there is no lexical determiner to block it. Therefore they can be interpreted as definite, as illustrated in (34) (=18b):

(34) Serbian
      Danas sam kupio   malo grožđa, hleb   i   mleko. Voće sam stavio un
      today am bought bit   grapes bread and milk   fruit am put   in
      frižider a   sve ostalo na sto.
      fridge   and all else   on table
      'Today I bought some grapes, bread and milk. I put the fruit in the fridge and the rest on the table.'
      → OK if *voće* 'fruit' is anteceded by *grožđe* 'grapes'

Dayal's (2004) approach also makes some interesting predictions about the availability of definite interpretations for bare singular and plural (i.e. non-mass) kinds in languages without determiners. I discuss these predictions in §4 and show that they are borne out.

4 Predictions and consequences

An important observation about languages with number marking but no determiners, which is central to Dayal's (2004) modification of Chierchia's (1998) system, is that bare plurals in such languages behave more or less like English bare plurals, but bare singulars are substantially different. Although bare singulars and bare plurals in such languages allow for kind as well as anaphoric readings, their existential reading, however, is distinct from that of regular indefinites in two respects: (i) they cannot take wide scope over negation or other operators, and (ii) they cannot refer non-maximally. Thus, bare NPs cannot be used in translating (35b) or (35c) to refer to a subset of the children mentioned in (35a) (Dayal 2011: 1100):

(35)   a. *There were several children in the park.*
        b. *A child was sitting on the bench and another was standing near him.*
        c. *Some children were sitting on the bench, and others were standing nearby.*

So, even though there are no definite or indefinite determiners in these languages, only readings associated with definites are available to bare NPs. Dayal argues that this shows that the availability of covert type shifts is constrained, as proposed by Chierchia (1998), but that the correct ranking is as in (36) not (29) (note that both $\cap$ and ι are simpler than $\exists$):

(36)   **Revised Meaning Preservation:** $\{\cap, \iota\} > \exists$ (Dayal 2004: 219)

This is also motivated by the fact that the Hindi version of 27b (i.e. 37b) does not allow a wide scope reading of *parts of this machine*, even though this bare plural is not compatible with true kind predication, as shown in (37a).

(37)   Hindi

       a. * *Is   mashin   ke TukRe aam   haiN.*
            this machine of parts   common are

            'Parts of this machine are common.'

       b. *Anu-ne is   mashiin ke TukRe nahiiN dekhe.*
            Anu-ERG this machine of parts   not   see

            'Anu didn't see any/the parts of this machine.'
            (Dayal 2004: 420)

Thus, given the revised ranking in (36), in the absence of $\cap$, the availability of ι blocks $\exists$. What one might take to be the frozen existential reading in (37b) is, in fact, the (non-familiar) definite reading of a sentence with negation.[9] Dayal (2004) also observes that bare singulars are not trivial variants of bare plurals in languages like Hindi, and that these languages raise important questions about the connection between singular number and kind reference. For example, the Hindi example in (38a) has only the implausible reading whereby the same child is assumed to be playing everywhere. Its plural counterpart in (38b), however, readily allows for a plausible reading:

(38)   Hindi

    a.   # *CaaroN taraf bacca khel rahaa thaa.*
          four   ways child was playing

        'The (same) child was playing everywhere.'

    b.   *CaroN taraf bacce   khel rahe the.*
          four   ways children were playing

        'Children (different ones) were playing everywhere.' (Dayal 2004: 406)

In order to explain this contrast, Dayal argues that singular and plural kind terms differ in the way they relate to their instantiations, as illustrated by the following quote:

> An analogy can be drawn with ordinary sum individuals *the players* whose atomic parts are available for predication, and collective nouns or groups like *the team* which are closed in this respect: *The players live in different cities* vs. **The team lives in different cities* (Barker 1992; Schwarzschild 1996).

---

[9]It seems rather clear that bare NPs in languages like Hindi are not true indefinites, but there are cases for which the most natural translation into English uses an indefinite (Dayal 2011: 1101):

(i)   Hindi
    Lagtaa hai kamre meN cuhaa hai.
    seems be room in   mouse be
    'There seems to be a mouse in the room.'

Dayal argues that covert and overt type shifts agree on semantic operations but not on presuppositions. So, English article *the* encodes the operation ι, which Hindi bare NPs use to shift to type $\langle e \rangle$ covertly. Both of these variants entail maximality/uniqueness. In addition, the lexical definite article *the* has a familiarity requirement that Hindi bare NPs do not. The assumption is that familiarity presuppositions are attached to lexical items, and that a language that does not have a lexical definite determiner will not enforce familiarity presuppositions. This non-familiar maximal reading can then be confused with a true existential reading (see also Heim 2011).

$\cap$ applies only to plural nouns and yields a kind term that allows semantic access to its instantiations, analogously to sums. A singular kind term restricts such access and is analogous to collective nouns. (Dayal 2011: 1100)

Thus, $\cap$ is taken to be undefined for singular terms, which makes a prediction and raises a question. The prediction is that in article-less languages without singular-plural distinction (e.g. Mandarin) a sentence like (38a) should be fine. This is because a language that does not mark number on kind terms should not impose any constraints on the size accessibility of their instantiation sets, effectively aligning it with bare plurals. The prediction is borne out:

(39)   Mandarin
       Gou zai meigeren-de   houyuan-li   jiao.
       dog at everyone-PTCP backyard-inside bark

       'Dogs (different ones) are barking in everyone's backyard.' (Dayal 2004: 413)

The question is how to characterize singular kind formation. Dayal argues that in these cases, the common noun has a taxonomic reading and denotes a set of taxonomic kinds. It can then combine with any determiner and yield the relevant reading.

(40)   a. *Every dinosaur is extinct.*
       b. *The dinosaur is extinct.*

In (40a), the presupposition that *every* ranges over a plural domain is satisfied if the quantificational domain is the set of sub-kinds of dinosaurs. The uniqueness requirement of *the* with a singular noun in (40b) is satisfied if the quantificational domain is the set of sub-kinds of animals. There is, therefore, nothing special about the definite article in definite singular kinds like (41), according to Dayal. The definite singular generic is derived compositionally from the regular definite determiner plus a common noun under its taxonomic guise:

(41)   *The lion comes in several varietis, the African lion, the Asian lion ...*

Specifically, in the case of kind formation out of singular nouns, there is a clash between singular morphology and plurality associated with kinds, which is repaired as in (42), where X ranges over entities in the taxonomic domain. (42) then forces the application of ι, which in English comes out/is lexicalized as *the*.

(42)   PredK($\cap$lion $=^{*\cap}$(SING) $\Rightarrow$ PredK (ιX[LION(X)]) (Dayal 2004: 435)

At the same time, mass kinds must be bare in English (43), which is expected given that $\cap$ is defined for them. Mass kinds thus behave like plural kinds.

(43)   (*The) wine comes in several varieties, (*the) red wine, (*the) white wine and (*the) rosé.

We expect then that plural kinds and singular kinds in English should differ in their ability to be interpreted as definite, i.e. only the latter could be interpreted anaphorically. This is because in the case of singular kinds $\cap$ cannot apply (it clashes with the singular number morphology), and the (lexical realization of ι in English) is introduced via (38). This appears to be true, as the contrast between (44) and (45) illustrates. The definite singular the bird can be anteceded by the dodo in (45), while establishing the anaphoric relationship between bare plurals birds and dodos in (44) does not seem to be possible.

(44)   Only dodos and gorillas survived on the continent.
       After the humans arrived birds were wiped out.
       → ?* if birds is anteceded by dodos

(45)   Only the dodo and the gorilla survived on the continent.
       After the humans arrived the bird was wiped out.
       → OK if the bird is anteceded by the dodo

Crucially, the same kind of contrast should in principle appear in article-less languages with number morphology. $\cap$ should not be defined for singular terms, and ι should be available for them via (42) – thus, the definite/anaphoric interpre-tation should be available for singular kinds in languages without articles. How-ever, since $\cap$ is defined for plural kinds, they should pattern with mass kinds in terms of the availability of definite interpretation; i.e. they should lack the anaphoric interpretation. I believe that the following contrasts from Serbian and Turkish are clear enough to confirm this prediction. For example, Serbian exam-ples in (46) and (47) differ only in terms of number. However, there is a noticeable contrast between them in the availability of anaphoric interpretation, similar to

(44–45). Turkish examples in (48–51) illustrate the same point.[10,11]

---

[10]As indicated in the translation of (47), the object here can be modified with the expression 'as a kind', which shows that what we are dealing with here is not an object-level but a kind-level expression. This is true for previous examples involving kind reference as well. Also, the object in (46) can be replaced with 'the kind of bird known as 'bald eagle" (e.g. *My whole life, I have been studying the kind of bird known as bald eagle*). Similar can be done to other relevant examples. Moreover, one can dedicate one's entire career to studying the work of Abraham Lincoln, and use (i.a) to express that, but 'as a kind' cannot modify the object in this particular case; e.g. (i.b) is clearly more marked than (i.c). This follows from the fact that something that is necessarily instantiated by just one individual (Abraham Lincoln) does not qualify as a kind. All of this shows that these examples truly involve kind reference.

(i) a. *I have been studying Abraham Lincoln my whole life.*

  b. # *I have been studying Abraham Lincoln, as a kind, my whole life.*

  c. *I have been studying the bald eagle, as a kind, my whole life.*

[11]Recall that due to the Blocking Principle, ɩ is never available for bare nouns in English, singular or plural (the existence of the definite article blocks it); for this reason, bare nouns can never be interpreted anaphorically in English. On the other hand, ɩ is in principle available to both singular and plural bare nouns in languages like Serbian and Turkish. In the case of bare plurals, both ∩ and ɩ are available depending on whether the noun in question has a kind or object-level interpretation, respectively. In such languages, the context and the type of predicate could play a crucial role: a kind-selecting predicate (*rare, widespread, extinct...*) could, for instance, make the contrast clearer for some speakers; compare (i–ii) with (46–47) respectively. In general, it is not unexpected that this contrast would be somewhat subtler in languages like Serbian or Turkish than in English.

(i) Serbian

  Ceo   život proučavam beloglavog   orla   — na žalost,   pre   deset godina ptica
  whole life   study-1.PRS white-headed eagle   unfortunately before ten   years   bird
  je istrebljena.
  is exterminated

  'I have been studying the bald eagle my whole life. Unfortunately, ten years ago the bird was exterminated.'
  → OK if *ptica* 'bird' is anteceded by *beloglavog orla* 'bald eagle'

(ii) Serbian

  Ceo   život proučavam beloglave   orlove — na žalost,   pre   deset godina ptice
  whole life   study-1.PRS white-headed eagles   unfortunately before ten   years   birds
  su   istrebljene.
  are exterminated

  'I have been studying bald eagles my whole life. Unfortunately, ten years ago birds were exterminated.'
  → ?* if *ptice* 'birds' is anteceded by *beloglave orlove* 'bald eagles'

(46) Serbian (singular)
Ceo   *život proučavam beloglavog   orla   – ptica je fantastična.*
Whole life   study-PRS   white-headed eagle   bird   is fantastic
'I have been studying the bald eagle (as a kind) my whole life. The bird is fantastic.'
→ OK if *ptica* 'bird' is anteceded by *beloglavog orla* 'bald eagle'

(47) Serbian (plural)
Ceo   *život proučavam beloglave   orlove – ptice su   fantastične.*
Whole life   study-PRS   white-headed eagles   birds are fantastic
'I have been studying bald eagles (as a kind) my whole life. Birds are fantastic.'
→ ?* if *ptice* 'birds' is anteceded by *beloglave orlove* 'bald eagles'

(48) Turkish (singular)
Kel   kartal, Kuzey Amerika'da   bulunur. Güç   ve   hız-ın
bald eagle   North America-LOC is found   strength and speed-GEN
sembolü olarak tanınır.   Ancak,   küresel ısınma   nedeniyle, kuş
symbol as   recognized however global warming because   bird
yakında tamamen   yok olabilir.
soon   completely may disappear
'The bald eagle is found in North America. It is the symbol of strength and speed. However, because of the global warming, the bird may soon completely disappear.'
→ OK$^?$ if *kuş* 'bird' is anteceded by *kel kartal* 'bald eagle'

(49) Turkish (plural)
Kel   kartallar, Kuzey Amerika'da   bulunurlar. Güç   ve   hız-ın
bald eagles   North America-LOC are found   strength and speed-GEN
sembolü olarak tanınırlar. Ancak,   küresel ısınma   nedeniyle, kuşlar
symbol as   recognized however global warming because   birds
yakında tamamen   yok olabilir.
soon   completely may disappear
'Bald eagles are found in North America. They are the symbol of strength and speed. However, because of the global warming, birds may soon completely disappear.'
→ * if *kuşlar* 'birds' is anteceded by *kel kartallar* 'bald eagles'

(50)   Turkish (singular)

Kel kartal, Kuzey Amerika'da bulunur. Güç   ve hız-ın sembolü
bald eagle North America-LOC is found strength and speed-GEN
olarak tanınır. Ayerica,   kuşun gözleri   oldukça keskindir.
symbol as   recognized also bird-GEN eyes   quite   sharp

'The bald eagle is found in North America. It is the symbol of strength and speed. Also, the bird's eyes are quite sharp.'

→ OK if *kuş* 'bird' is anteceded by *kel kartal* 'bald eagle'

(51)   Turkish (plural)

Kel kartallar, Kuzey Amerika'da bulunurlar. Güç   ve hız-ın
bald eagles   North America-LOC are found strength and speed-GEN
sembolü olarak tanınırlar. Ayerica, kuşların   gözleri oldukça keskindir.
symbol as   recognized Also   birds-GEN eyes   quite   sharp

'Bald eagles are found in North America. They are the symbol of strength and speed. Also, birds' eyes are quite sharp.'

→ * if *kuşlar* 'birds' is anteceded by *kel kartallar* 'bald eagles'

Finally, bare non-mass kinds in article-less languages without number morphology (e.g. Mandarin, Japanese) are expected *not to* have definite/anaphoric interpretations. $^\cap$ is defined for such nouns, since these languages do not have singular morphology that would clash with plurality associated with kind formation (recall also 39; see Dayal 2004: 411–413). In terms of anaphoricity/definiteness, bare non-mass kinds in these languages should pattern with plural kinds (and mass kinds) in languages like Serbian and Turkish. This also appears to be borne out, as shown in (52) and (53). The non-mass noun *tori* 'bird' in (52) cannot be anteceded by *hagetaka* 'bald eagle', in contrast to (46–48). As already mentioned in footnote 8, Jenks (to appear) shows that Mandarin makes a systematic distinction between unique and anaphoric definites (e.g. Schwarz 2009); while unique definites are realized as bare nouns, anaphoric definites are realized with a demonstrative, except in subject positions, where bare nouns can also be interpreted anaphorically. Examples in (20) which involve object-level interpretation are consistent with Jenks' observations in that bare nouns in subject positions can be used anaphorically. Bare nouns in (14) and (53), on the other hand, lack anaphoric readings precisely because they are derived by $^\cap$, which is responsible for the kind-level interpretation.

(52) Japanese
Watashi-wa nagai aida hagetaka-o   kenkyu shitekita. Tori-wa
I-TOP   long time bald eagle-ACC studied   bird-TOP
subarashi.
fantastic
'I have been studying the bald eagle for a long time. The bird is fantastic.'
→ * if *tori* 'bird' is anteceded by *hagetaka* 'bald eagle'

(53) Mandarin
Zhiyou gezi   he daxingxing xingcun zai zhe pian dalu   shang.
only   pigeon and gorilla   survive LOC this CLF continent on
Danshi hen kuai   niao jiu   miejue le.
but   very quickly bird PTCP exinct ASP
'Only the pigeon and the gorilla survived on the continent. But very quickly the bird went extinct.'
→ * if *niao* 'bird' is anteceded by *gezi* 'pigeon'

5 Summary and further questions

The initial contrast in interpretation between mass kinds in English and languages without definite articles led us to an analysis from which some rather systematic patterns appear to emerge.

Table 1: Languages without definite articles: Bare nouns

	+Number						−Number			
	Kind-level			Object-level			Kind-level		Object-level	
	Mass	Count		Mass	Count		Mass	Count	Mass	Count
		SG	PL		SG	PL					
Anaphoric	*	✓	*	✓	✓	✓	*	*	✓	✓
Type-shift	∩	ι	∩	ι	ι	ι	∩	∩	ι	ι

↑ ∩ undefined for singular nouns; ι applies to the taxonomic domain

As Table 1 above shows, the availability of anaphoric/definite readings of bare nominals in languages without definite articles correlates with the availability of ∩ and ι. More specifically, whenever ∩ applies, the anaphoric/definite reading is missing. We see that object-level and kind-level readings are available both in languages with number marking (e.g. Serbian) and in languages without number-marking (e.g. Japanese). ι is responsible for anaphoric interpretation of object-level bare nouns in both types of languages. Where the two language types differ is how they manufacture kinds. In languages without number marking, all kinds are created via $\cap$, which means that bare kind-level nouns in these languages cannot be interpreted anaphorically. In other words, since count nouns in these languages do not mark number (and are used with classifiers etc.), they pattern with mass nouns and are accessible to $\cap$. But in languages with number marking, kind-level singular count bare nouns cannot be formed via $\cap$, due to a clash with singular number morphology. This is repaired by (42), which introduces ι. As a result, only this type of bare kind-level noun will have anaphoric potential. For bare mass and plural nouns, both ι and $\cap$ are available, given the modified ranking of operations in (36), according to which they are both more highly ranked than $\exists$. Which one of them applies will depend on the context (among other things). In contexts like (31b), ι applies and creates the anaphoric reading. But if a kind-level interpretation of the antecedent noun is forced by the context (as in 33), the anaphoric relation will be missing; ι maps property extension to individuals, and a kind is identified with the totality of its instances in any given world (or situation). If, on the other hand, $\cap$ applies, the anaphoric relation will still be absent, since $\cap$ is a function whose extension varies from world/situation to world/situation (while ι is a constant function to a contextually anchored individual).

Now, as already noted, $\cap$ is the intensional counterpart of ι, and Dayal (2004) takes the latter to be the canonical meaning of the definite determiner. One of significant cross-linguistic patterns discussed in Dayal (2004) is the absence of dedicated kind determiners in natural language. That is, plural kind terms are either bare (e.g. English, Hindi), or definite (e.g. Italian, Spanish). A simple explanation for this robust generalization is that $\cap$ is the intensional counterpart of ι and that languages do not lexically mark extensional/intensional distinctions. There are additional systematic restrictions: for example, if a language uses bare nominals for anaphoric readings, then it also uses them as plural kind terms. Also, if a language uses definites as plural kind terms, it also uses them for anaphoric readings. Thus, correlations are not completely arbitrary; e.g. there are no attested languages in which bare plurals could be used anaphorically and at the same time definite plurals could refer to kinds. To account for these facts, Dayal proposes a universal principle of lexicalization in which ι (which is canonically used for anaphoric reference) and $\cap$ (which is canonically used for generic reference) are mapped along a scale of diminishing identifiability: $\iota > \cap$. Languages can then lexicalize at distinct points on this scale, proceeding from ι to $\cap$. Languages without determiners like Serbian use the extreme left as the cut-off for lexicalization – in such languages both ι and $\cap$ are covert type shifts. The cut-off point for mixed languages like English is in the middle – here ι is lexicalized (*the*) and $\cap$ is a covert type-shift. ι and $\cap$ are both encoded lexically in obligatory determiner languages like Italian, where the cut-off point is at the extreme right. So if a language has a lexical determiner for plural kind formation, this automatically means that its cut-off point is at the extreme right. The principle of lexicalization above therefore entails that such a language could not have a covert ι. The unattested language type mentioned above would then not conform to the proposed direction of lexicalization.[12]

We can also view the relationship between ι and $\cap$ from the perspective of Schwarz's (2009) account of strong/weak definites. Schwarz discusses a distinction between *strong* and *weak* definite articles in German: strong articles are used in familiar definite environments and are anaphoric to a previously introduced referent, while weak articles occur in unique definite contexts. Schwarz proposes that strong (anaphoric) definites take an index as an argument, while unique definites do not (see also Jenks to appear). That is, anaphoric articles are more complex than their unique counterparts since they take one extra argument. At the same time, both types of articles presuppose the existence of a unique individual. Jenks (to appear) shows that different languages lexicalize/mark these two types of definites differently. Languages like German and Lakhota (see Schwarz 2013) have two separate lexical items/markers to encode unique definites (i.e. ι) or anaphoric definites (i.e. ι^x). There are also languages like Fante Akan and Mandarin (see footnote 8) which have a lexical definite marker for definite anaphoric environments (i.e. ι^x), but no marker for unique definite contexts (covert type shift is used). And finally there are languages like English that use a single lexical item for both types of definites. We could add to this list languages like Serbian which can use covert type shifts for both environments. But if Schwarz and Jenks are right in making a distinction between the unique ι and the anaphoric ι^x (which I believe they are), then the facts discussed here strongly suggest that $\cap$ is the intensional counterpart of the unique ι and not the anaphoric ι^x. This is further supported by the fact that in German it is the weak (unique definite)

---

[12]Languages like Brazilian Portuguese and German are particularly interesting because they allow a certain degree of optionality. Brazilian Portugese admits bare singulars while some dialects of German allow both bare and definite plurals/mass terms for kind reference, but the variation in available meanings is still quite limited. For detailed discussion of these languages see Dayal (2004; 2011), Krifka (1995), Müller (2002), Munn & Schmitt (2005), Cyrino & Espinal (2015) and references therein.

article that is used for kind reference (e.g. Schwarz 2009: 65-66). That is, if languages do not lexically mark extensional/intensional distinctions and if $^\cap$ is the intensional counterpart of the unique ι, then it follows that in languages which use two separate markers for unique and anaphoric definites, the unique definite marker will also be used for kind reference.

I have to leave some questions for future work, since they are outside of the scope of this study. For example, I showed that if a demonstrative is added to the constructions with kind-level context, the anaphoric reading becomes possible. The question is, of course, how this should be formalized. At this point I have to assume that this is due to some specific property of this lexical element.[13] For instance, Chierchia (1998: 353) proposes (for independent reasons) that determiners may semantically come in two variants: those that apply to predicates and those that apply to kinds. One possibility is that a demonstrative like Serbian *to* 'that' has both types of interpretations and can therefore combine with kinds.[14,15] Another question which should be more directly investigated is what kind of discourse factors facilitate or inhibit the anaphoric reading of bare nouns and how they can be distinguished from those discussed in this paper. It is clear that, in terms of anaphoricity, ι (i.e. a bare noun) is less potent than demonstratives and pronouns (see Footnote 13). The question is then whether this

---

[13]Similar questions can be raised with respect to kind-referring pronouns that can be anteceded by non-kind NPs. In (i) below, for example, the antecedent *Martians* refers to some Martians, while *themselves* refers to the kind (see Rooth 1985 and Krifka 2003 for details). So the next step would be to check whether constructions like (i) are allowed in languages discussed here (in particular, whether both coreference and anaphoric binding are possible) and then what kind of implications would such facts have for the analysis presented here. I have to leave this for future work.

    (i)   *At the meeting,* **Martians** *presented* **themselves** *as almost extinct.*

[14]This line of reasoning would be supported by a language which makes some kind of morphological distinction between the two determiner variants. This seems to be true for Serbian (and some other Slavic languages), at least to a first approximation: in addition to *taj* 'that', which seems to be ambiguous as noted above, there are also determiners like *takav* which are best translated as 'that kind' (also *kakav* 'what kind', *onakav* 'that kind', etc.). This, however, requires a more careful examination, which I leave for future work.

[15]It needs to be clarified that the presence of demonstratives does not necessarily indicate the presence of DP (or some other functional projection) in languages without articles. For example, as discussed in Bošković (2005), Despić (2011; 2013), Zlatić (1997), etc., it is much more plausible to analyze demonstratives (and possessives) in Serbian as NP-adjuncts. A number of morpho-syntactic arguments support this claim: the availability of LBE, the appearance of Serbian possessives and demonstratives in adjectival positions (and adjective-like agreement), stacking up, impossibility of modification, specificity effects, etc. This is based on syntactic evidence, and as long as the demonstrative is assigned appropriate meaning, semantic composition is not affected.

contrast can ultimately be reduced to some version of blocking (elsewhere) condition that governs the distribution of covert and overt elements (e.g. use overt demonstratives/pronouns wherever you can and avoid the covert ι), or whether the anaphoric potential of ι is truly impoverished compared to that of demonstratives/pronouns.

Overall I hope to have shown that the general pattern of cross-linguistic variation given in Table 1 follows from Dayal's (2004) approach, which is based on a limited set of type-shifting operations constrained by the Blocking Principle, and which incorporates an appropriate analysis of number morphology.

Acknowledgements

For helpful discussion of the material presented here (and related ideas), I would like to thank Greg Carlson, Gennaro Chierchia, Amy Rose Deal, Jeff Runner, Neda Todorović, John Whitman, the participants of the Definiteness across Languages conference (Mexico City, June 2016) and the Dimensions of D workshop (Rochester, September 2016). For their generous help with data, I am very grateful to Shohini Bhattasali, Sachiko Komuro, Yanyu Long, Hasan Sezer, Deniz Özyıldız, Hao Yi and Lingzi Zhuang. Finally, I also want to thank anonymous reviewers and the editors for their careful and helpful suggestions. All errors are my own responsibility.

Abbreviations

1	first person	PTCP	particle
ACC	accusative	PST	past
CLF	classifier	PRS	present
DKP	Derived Kind Predication	REFL	reflexive
ERG	ergative	TOP	topic
GEN	genitive	UDP	Universal DP (Approach)
LBE	Left Branch Extraction		
LOC	locative		

References

Baker, Mark. 2003. *Lexical categories: Verbs, nouns and adjectives* (Cambridge Studies in Linguistics 102). Cambridge: Cambridge University Press.

Barker, Chris. 1992. Group terms in English: Representing groups as atoms. *Journal of Semantics* 9(1). 69–93.

Bošković, Željko. 2005. On the locality of left branch extraction and the structure of NP. *Studia Linguistica* 59(1). 1–45.

Bošković, Željko. 2008. What will you have, DP or NP? *Proceedings of NELS* 37(1). 101–114.

Bošković, Željko. 2012. On NPs and clauses. In Günther Grewendorf & Thomas Ede Zimmermann (eds.), *Discourse and grammar: From sentence types to lexical categories* (Studies in Generative Grammar 112), 179–242. Berlin: De Gruyter Mouton.

Carlson, Greg N. 1977. *Reference to kinds in English*. Amherst: University of Massachusetts. (Doctoral dissertation).

Chierchia, Gennaro. 1998. Reference to kinds across languages. *Natural Language Semantics* 6(4). 339–405.

Cinque, Guglielmo. 1994. On the evidence for partial N-movement in the Romance DP. In Guglielmo Cinque, Jan Koster, Jean-Yves Pollock, Luigi Rizzi & Raffaella Zanuttini (eds.), *Paths towards universal grammar: Studies in honor of Richard S. Kayne* (Georgetown Studies in Romance Linguistics), 85–110. Washington, D. C.: Georgetown University Press.

Cinque, Guglielmo. 1999. *Adverbs and functional heads: A cross-linguistic perspective* (Oxford Studies in Comparative Syntax). Oxford: Oxford University Press.

Cyrino, Sonia & M.-Teresa Espinal. 2015. Bare nominals in Brazilian Portuguese: More on the DP/NP. *Natural Language and Linguistic Theory* 33(2). 471–521.

Dayal, Veneeta. 2004. Number marking and (in)definiteness in kind terms. *Linguistics and Philosophy* 27(4). 393–450.

Dayal, Veneeta. 2011. Bare noun phrases. In Paul Portner, Claudia Maienborn & Klaus von Heusinger (eds.), *Semantics: An international handbook of natural language meaning*, vol. 2, 1088–1108. Berlin: De Gruyter Mouton.

Despić, Miloje. 2011. *Syntax in the absence of determiner phrase*. Storrs: University of Connecticut. (Doctoral dissertation).

Despić, Miloje. 2013. Binding and the structure of NP in Serbo-Croatian. *Linguistic Inquiry* 44(2). 239–270.

Despić, Miloje. 2015. Phases, reflexives, and definiteness. *Syntax* 18(3). 201–234.

Diesing, Molly. 1992. *Indefinites* (Linguistic Iinquiry Monographs 20). Cambridge: MIT Press.

Enç, Mürvet. 1991. The semantics of specificity. *Linguistic Inquiry* 22(1). 1–25.

Fujisawa, Shuhei. 1992. *Zenshū*. Vol. 11, heisei 5. Tōkyō: Bungei Shunjū.

Heim, Irene. 2011. Definiteness and indefiniteness. In Paul Portner, Claudia Maienborn & Klaus von Heusinger (eds.), *Semantics: An international handbook of natural language meaning*, vol. 2, 996–1024. Berlin: De Gruyter Mouton.

Jenks, Peter. to appear. Articulated definiteness without articles. *Linguistic Inquiry*.

Kratzer, Angelika. 1995. Stage-level and individual-level predicates. In Greg N. Carlson & Francis Jeffry Pelletier (eds.), *The generic book*, 125–175. Chicago: University of Chicago Press.

Krifka, Manfred. 1995. Common nouns: A contrastive analysis of English and Chinese. In Greg N. Carlson & Francis Jeffry Pelletier (eds.), *The generic book*, 398–411. Chicago: University of Chicago Press.

Krifka, Manfred. 2003. Bare NPs: Kind-referring, indefinites, both, or neither? *Proceedings of SALT* 13. 180–203.

Krifka, Manfred & Claudia Gerstner-Link. 1993. Genericity. In Joachim Jacobs, Arnim von Stechow, Wolfgang Sternefeld & Theo Venneman (eds.), *Syntax: Ein internationales Handbuch zeitgenössischer Forschung / An international handbook of contemporary research*, 966–978. Berlin: De Gruyter.

Longobardi, Giuseppe. 1994. Reference and proper names: A theory of N-movement in syntax and logical form. *Linguistic Inquiry* 25(4). 609–665.

Müller, Ana. 2002. The semantics of generic quantification in Brazilian Portuguese. *Probus* 14(2). 279–298.

Munn, Alan & Cristina Schmitt. 2005. Number and indefinites. *Lingua* 115(6). 821–855.

Pereltsvaig, Asya. 2007. The universality of DP: A view from Russian. *Studia Linguistica* 61(1). 59–94.

Reuland, Eric J. 2011. *Anaphora and language design* (Linguistic Inquiry Monographs 62). Cambridge: MIT Press.

Rooth, Mats. 1985. *Association with focus*. Amherst: University of Massachusetts. (Doctoral dissertation).

Schwarz, Florian. 2009. *Two types of definites in natural language*. Amherst: University of Massachusetts. (Doctoral dissertation).

Schwarz, Florian. 2013. Two kinds of definites cross-linguistically. *Language and Linguistics Compass* 7(10). 534–559.

Schwarzschild, Roger. 1996. *Pluralities* (Studies in Linguistics and Philosophy 59). Dordrecht: Kluwer.

Scott, Gary-John. 2002. Stacked adjectival modification and the structure of nominal phrases. In Guglielmo Cinque (ed.), *Functional structure in DP and IP: The cartography of syntactic structures*, vol. 1 (Oxford Studies in Comparative Syntax), 91–122. Oxford: Oxford University Press.

Wilkinson, Karina Jo. 1991. *Studies in the semantics of generic noun phrases.* Amherst: University of Massachusetts. (Doctoral dissertation).

Zlatić, Larisa. 1997. *The structure of the Serbian noun phrase.* Austin: University of Texas. (Doctoral dissertation).

4

Most vs. *the most* in languages where *the more* means *most*

Elizabeth Coppock

Boston University
University of Gothenburg

Linnea Strand

University of Gothenburg

This paper focuses on languages in which a superlative interpretation is typically indicated merely by a combination of a definiteness marker with a comparative marker, including French, Spanish, Italian, Romanian, and Greek (DEF+CMP LANGUAGES). Despite ostensibly using definiteness markers to form the superlative, superlatives are not always definite-marked in these languages, and the distribution of definiteness-marking varies across languages. Constituency structure appears to vary across languages as well. To account for these patterns of variation, we identify conflicting pressures that all of the languages in consideration may be subject to, and suggest that different languages prioritize differently in the resolution of these conflicts. What these languages have in common, we suggest, is a mechanism of Definite Null Instantiation for the degree-type standard argument of the comparative. Among the parameters along which languages are proposed to differ is the relative importance of marking uniqueness vs. avoiding determiners with predicates of entities that are not individuals.

1 Introduction

In French, placing a definite article before a comparative adjective, as in (1), suffices to produce a superlative interpretation:

(1)   *Elle est la plus grande.*   (French)
      she is   the CMP tall
      'She is **the tallest**.'

French is not alone; other Romance languages, as well as Modern Greek, Maltese and others, make do with the same limited resources. Some examples are
given in Table 1.[1] This paper considers such languages, which we call DEF+CMP
LANGUAGES, against the background of a growing literature on cross-linguistic
variation with respect to the relationship between definiteness-marking and the
interpretation of superlatives.

Table 1: Comparative and superlative degree of 'tall' in selected
DEF+CMP languages

LANGUAGE	POS	CMP	SPRL
English	*tall*	*taller*	*tallest*
French	*grande*	*plus grande*	*la plus grande*
Spanish	*alto*	*más alto*	*el más alto*
Romanian	*inalt*	*mai inalt*	*cea mai inalt*
Italian	*alto*	*più alto*	*il più alto*
Greek	*psilós*	*pio psilós*	*o pio psilós*
Greek (alt 2)	*psilós*	*psilóteros*	*o psilóteros*

When it comes to the superlatives of ordinary gradable adjectives like *tall*,
the interpretive contrast of interest is the distinction between so-called *absolute*
and *relative* readings of superlatives in the domain of quality superlatives. In
Swedish, unlike English, this interpretive distinction is signalled morphologically
with definiteness:

---

[1]Besides Romance languages, languages reported to use this strategy include Modern Standard
Arabic, Assyrian Neo-Aramaic, Middle Armenian, Modern Greek, Biblical Hebrew, Livonian,
Maltese, Chalcatongo Mixtec, Papiamentu, Vlach Romani, Russian, and Tamashek (Bobaljik
2012; Gorshenin 2012). Note however that Gorshenin has rather liberal criteria for a given
construction being of this type; for Russian, the example given is *Etot žurnal **sam-yj** interesn-
yj* 'This magazine is the most interesting (one)'. Gorshenin (2012: 129) describes *sam-yj* as
an "emphatic pronoun" and reasons that "this pronoun indicates uniqueness, particularity of
the referent in some respect, and therefore it can be regarded as a functional equivalent of a
determiner in the corresponding superlative construction".

(2) a. *Gloria sålde **god-ast**   **glass.***   (Swedish)
         Gloria sold delicious-SPRL ice cream
         'Gloria sold **the most delicious ice cream.**' (relative only)

     b. *Gloria sålde **den god-ast-e**   **glass-en.***
         Gloria sold the delicious-SPRL-WK ice cream-DEF
         'Gloria sold **the most delicious ice cream.**' (relative or absolute)

As Teleman et al. (1999) discuss, (2a) means that Gloria sold more delicious ice cream than anyone else. It would not suffice for (2a) to be true for there to be a salient set of ice creams of which Gloria sold the most delicious. If someone else sold that ice cream as well, then (2a) would be false. In contrast, the English gloss and the definite-marked example (2b) could be true if both Gloria and someone else sold the ice cream that was more delicious than all other ice creams that are salient in the context. All that is required for that sentence to be true is that Gloria stands in the 'sold' relation to the ice cream satisfying that description.

In Heim's (1999) terms, (2a) has a *relative reading* (originally called a *comparative reading* by Szabolcsi 1986), and (2b), along with the English gloss, is ambiguous between a relative reading and an *absolute reading*. Relative readings are typically focus-sensitive, implying a comparison between the focus (e.g. Gloria) and the focus-alternatives, and on such readings the superlative noun phrase behaves like an indefinite despite the frequent presence of a definite determiner (Szabolcsi 1986; Coppock & Beaver 2014). On an absolute reading, comparisons are made only among elements satisfying the descriptive content of the modified noun, and the definite behaves as a definite. The contrast between absolute and relative readings was discussed early on by Szabolcsi (1986) with reference to Hungarian, and has been taken up in a fair amount of recent cross-linguistic research, mainly focused on English (Gawron 1995; Heim 1999; Hackl 2000; Sharvit & Stateva 2002; Hackl 2009; Teodorescu 2009; Krasikova 2012; Szabolcsi 2012; Bumford 2016; Wilson 2016), but also with reference to German (Hackl 2009), Swedish (Coppock & Josefson 2015), other Germanic languages (Coppock 2019), Hungarian (Farkas & Kiss 2000), Romanian (Teodorescu 2007), Spanish (Rohena-Madrazo 2007), Arabic (Hallman 2016), and Slavic languages including Macedonian, Czech, Serbian/Croatian and Slovenian (Pancheva & Tomaszewicz 2012). This paper extends this line of research insofar as it considers the morphosyntactic realization of both types of readings in DEF+CMP languages.

The landscape of possible interpretations is slightly different when it comes to the superlatives of quantity words, like English *much, many, little* and *few*. In English, *the most* has a relative reading ('more than everybody else'), while bare *most* has what is called a *proportional* reading ('more than half', roughly). In this domain, there is an especially great deal of cross-linguistic variability. As Hackl (2009) shows, German *die meisten*, lit. 'the most', can be translated into English either as *most* or *the most*. Even more dramatically, English and Swedish are near-opposites with respect to the impact of definiteness-marking on interpretation (Coppock & Josefson 2015); the definite quantity superlative definite *de flesta* has a proportional reading, corresponding to English *most*, while the bare *flest* has a relative reading, corresponding to English *the most*. Coppock (2019) shows that every possible correlation between definiteness and interpretation is attested among the Germanic languages. So the quantity domain is one that appears to be particularly volatile.

We might expect the landscape of variation with respect to the definiteness-marking of superlatives to be rather dull and flat within the realm of DEF+CMP languages. If superlatives are formed with definiteness-markers, then definiteness-markers should always appear, regardless of what reading is involved. But this is not what we find.

We find in fact several departures from the dull and flat picture one might expect. First, as Dobrovie-Sorin & Giurgea (2015) discuss, French is one of the many languages of the world where quantity superlatives do not have a proportional interpretation.

(3)   *De tout les enfants de mon école, je suis celui   qui joue **le   plus***
       of all   the kids   of my   school, I am the.one who plays DEF CMP
       d'instruments.   (French)
       of.instruments

       'Of all the kids in my school, I'm the one who plays the most instruments.'

(4)   * ***Le plus de cygnes*** *sont blancs.*   (French)
       the more of swans   are white

       Intended: 'Most swans are white.'

Example (3) shows that the quantity superlative *le plus* can be used with a relative interpretation (comparing the speaker to other kids in the school); (4) shows that it does not have a proportional interpretation; this example does not mean 'most swans are white'. Such languages are surprising from the perspective of Hackl (2000; 2009), according to which the proportional readings of quantity superlatives are parallel to absolute readings of quality superlatives. Romanian and Greek are more well-behaved from that perspective; there, the superlative of 'many' (literally 'the more many') can have a proportional interpretation. For example, the Greek sentence in (5) is ambiguous as indicated:

(5) *Éfaga ta perissotera biskóta.*   (Greek)
     ate.1SG the much.CMP   cookies

     'I ate **the most cookies**' or 'I ate **most of the cookies**.'

This is one point of variation.

Another point of variation is which types of superlatives are accompanied by definiteness-marking. We can distinguish between the following types:

- Quality superlatives

    - Adjectival quality superlatives

        * Predicative, as in *She is (**the**) **tallest**.*

        * Adnominal; absolute reading, as in ***The tallest girl** left.*

        * Adnominal; relative reading, e.g. *I'm not the one with **the thinnest waist**.*

    - Adverbial quality superlatives, as in *She runs **the fastest**.*

- Quantity superlatives

    - Adnominal quantity superlatives

        * Relative reading, as in *I ate **the most cookies**.*

        * Proportional reading, as in *I ate **most of the cookies**.*

    - Adverbial quantity superlatives, as in *She talks **the most**.*

In French and Romanian, definiteness-marking appears on superlatives of all of these types. The same is not the case for Italian, Spanish and Portuguese. Despite forming quality superlatives through the combination of a definiteness-marker with a comparative form, these languages do not use definiteness-marking for adverbial superlatives or quantity superlatives on relative readings (and they generally do not allow proportional readings for quantity superlatives at all). Sentence (6) is an example from Italian (cf. de Boer 1986, Dobrovie-Sorin & Giurgea 2015, i.a.):

(6) *Probabilmente è Hans che ha bevuto **più caffè**.*   (Italian)
     probably   it.is Hans who has drunk CMP coffee
     'It is probably Hans who has drunk **the most coffee**.'

(A comparative interpretation, 'It is probably Hans who has drunk more cof-fee', is also available here, although the cleft construction strongly biases toward a superlative interpretation.) The same happens in Spanish and Portuguese.

In Greek, as illustrated below, there is a split between quantity and quantity adverbials ('talk the most' vs. 'talk the fastest'): quantity adverbials are obligatorily definite-marked and quantity adverbials obligatorily lack definiteness-marking. All other superlatives have a definiteness marker, relative and proportional readings of quantity superlatives included.

So, in all of these languages, superlatives are generally formed by combining a definiteness-marker with a comparative, yet in some of these languages, superlatives may lack a definiteness-marker. This is certainly surprising if the superlative interpretation is supposed to rest fully in the hands of the definite determiner.

Generally, there are several analytical options we could consider for DEF+CMP superlatives. The one we have just ruled out (at least for some of these languages) is that the definite article itself is the marker of the superlative. Another is that the comparative is lexically ambiguous between a comparative and a superlative. Another would build on the stance argued for by Bobaljik (2012), where superlatives are composed of comparatives and a bit that means 'of all'. This latter piece could be taken to be silent in DEF+CMP languages; see Szabolcsi (2012) for a formal analysis of *the more* in English along these lines. A fourth possibility is that a superlative interpretation arises more or less directly from the composition of a comparative meaning and the meaning of the definite article, just as the surface form suggests.

We show that a moderate instantiation of the last-mentioned strategy is viable, both for DEF+CMP languages and for certain cases in English like *the more qualified candidate* (*of the two*). In a nutshell, the standard argument of the comparative is saturated by a degree-type pronoun. So *the more qualified candidate*, for example, denotes the candidate in the contextually-given comparison class C that is more qualified than contextually-given **d**, for appropriately chosen value of **d**. This is hypothesized to be possible in all of the languages under considera-tion (and even English, manifest in expressions like *the taller one of the two*).

This is the common core. But there are conflicting pressures that lead to varia-tion with respect to whether definiteness-marking occurs. On the one hand, there is pressure to mark uniqueness on phrases where uniqueness can be marked, and on the other hand, there is pressure to avoid definiteness-marking on descriptions of entities other than individuals. Different languages prioritize differently when it comes to resolving these conflicts. We suggest furthermore that proportional readings arise through grammaticalization, but via different routes for different languages.

The following sections will present data from Greek, Romanian, French, and Ibero-Romance, in that order. These sections will lay out the basic facts concerning the morphosyntax of superlatives in these languages. After a summary in §5, compositional treatments of the various varieties will be sketched in §6.

2 Greek

We begin with Greek, where a definite article may combine with either a synthetic or periphrastic comparative to form the superlative. The synthetic and periphrastic variants are in free variation. For example, the comparative form of *psilós* 'tall' has two varieties, *psilóteros* and *pio psilós*, and these can both combine with a definite determiner to form a superlative. These two variants appear to be freely interchangeable, although the synthetic one may be slightly more commonplace. For all of the types of examples we elicited, many of which are presented below, both variants were judged to be acceptable.

Table 2: Declension of the definite article in Greek

SINGULAR			
	MASC.	NEUT.	FEM.
NOM	*o*	*to*	*i*
GEN	*tou*	*tou*	*tis*
ACC	*to(n)*	*to*	*ti(n)*
PLURAL			
	MASC.	NEUT.	FEM.
NOM	*oi*	*ta*	*oi*
GEN	*ton*	*ton*	*ton*
ACC	*tous*	*ta*	*tis*

2.1 Quality superlatives

In adnominal superlatives, there is always a definite article, which agrees in gender and number with the modified noun.[2] The definite article is present regardless of whether an absolute or relative interpretation is intended. Hence, example (7) is ambiguous:[3]

(7) *O Stellios odigei **to pio grigoro aftokinito**.*
     the Stellios drives DEF CMP fast   car
     'Stellios drives **the fastest car**.'

Example (8) strongly favors a relative interpretation; definiteness-marking is obligatory here as well.

(8) *Den eimai ego afti me **ti leptoteri mesi** stin oikogeneia.*
     not I   self she with DEF thin.CMP middle in family
     'I'm not the one with **the thinnest waist** in the family.'

Note that the periphrastic variety *ti pio lepti mesi* 'the thinnest waist', lit. 'the more thin waist', is equally acceptable here according to our consultants.

Absolute and relative readings of adnominal superlatives are similar to each other and to ordinary adjectives with respect to syntactic behavior as well. Greek has a much-discussed construction in which the order of the adjective and the noun can be reversed called "determiner spreading"; see Alexiadou (2014: 19) for an extensive list of references. The interpretive effect of determiner spreading is similar to that of placing an adjective postnominally in Romance: generally, it is restricted to restrictive modifiers (Alexiadou & Wilder 1998). But unlike in Romance, this construction involves an extra definite determiner, as can be seen in (9):

(9) a. *to kokino to podilato*
         DEF red   DEF bicycle
         'the red bicycle'
     b. *to podilato to kokino*
         DEF bicycle DEF red
         'the red bicycle'

---

[2]For reference, the inflectional paradigm for the definite article is as in Table 2. We suppress the agreement features in our glosses for the sake of readability.

[3]Thanks to Haris Themistocleous and Stergios Chatzikyriakidis for judgments and discussion.

Determiner spreading can involve superlatives; Alexiadou (2014) discusses the example in (10), which has an absolute reading, referring to a particular cat:

(10) *Spania haidevo **tin mikroteri ti gata.***
      seldom pet   DEF smallest   the cat
      'I seldom pet **the smallest cat**.'

Intuitions appear to be somewhat murky when it comes to determiner spreading with relative readings, but example (11), a variant of (8), was judged as acceptable by our consultants:

(11) *Den eimai ego afti me **ti leptoteri ti   mesi** stin oikogeneia.*
      not be.1SG I   she with the thin.CMP DEF waist in   family
      'I'm not the one with **the thinnest waist** in the family.'

This evidence suggests that the comparative adjective in an adnominal superlative may be structurally analogous to an ordinary adjective in a determiner-adjective-noun sequences, and that the article is in its ordinary position.

Adverbial quality superlatives are different, however; they do not involve a definite article, as can be seen in (12) and (13):

(12) *I   aderfi mou trechei **pio grigora.***
      DEF sister my runs   CMP fast
      'My sister runs **the fastest**.'

(13) *Pios tragoudái **pio   kalá?***
      who sings   more good
      'Who sings the best?' (Dobrovie-Sorin & Giurgea 2015: 16, ex. 71)

Inserting a definite article before *pio* is not possible in this sentence, e.g. **I aderfi mou trechei **to** pio grigora.* As Dobrovie-Sorin & Giurgea (2015) point out, this shows that the definite article is not an integral part of superlative-marking in Greek.

2.2 Quantity superlatives

Like quality superlatives, quantity superlatives are formed though the combination of a definite article with a comparative form, which may be either periphrastic, as in (14), or synthetic, as in (15). These two examples have relative readings.

(14) *Apó óla ta   paidiá sto scholeío, egó paízo **ta   pio pollá órgana**.*
      of all DEF kids   at school, I   play DEF CMP many instruments
      'Of all the kids in my school, I'm the one who plays **the most
      instruments**.'

(15) *Eimai aftos pou pinei   **ton ligotero kafe**.*
      I   he   who drinks DEF little.CMP coffee
      'I am the one who drinks **the least coffee**.'

Definiteness-marking is not optional here. Note that the word for 'many' is
transparently contained within the superlative phrase in (14).

Definite-marked quantity superlatives are also regularly used for expressing a
proportional interpretation. Sentences (16–18) are some examples from our data:

(16) ***S-ta   perissótera paidiá** sto scholeío mou arései na paízoun mousikí.*
      DAT-DEF many.CMP   kids   at school mine like to play   music
      'Most of the kids in my school like to play music.'

(17) *I   mamá éftiaxe biskóta chthes   kai éfaga **ta   perissótera**.*
      the mom made cookies yesterday and ate   DEF many.CMP
      'Mom baked cookies yesterday and I ate **most of them**.'

(18) *Ípia   epísis **to   perissótero gála**.*
      drank also DEF much.CMP milk
      'I drank **most of the milk**, too.'

Definiteness-marking is not optional here either.

Interestingly, there is a contrast between quality and quantity in the adverbial
domain. Adverbial quantity superlatives appear to require a definite article, as in
(19):[4]

(19) *O   Pavlos milaei **to   ligotero**.*
      DEF Paul talks DEF little.CMP
      'Paul talks the least'

---

[4]Thanks to a reviewer for pointing this out, and to Stavroula Alexandropoulou for discussion.

Removing the definite article in (19) yields a comparative interpretation, 'Paul talks less'. Notice that *talk* is intransitive, so it is unlikely that *to ligotero* is serving as the object of the verb. Further evidence that the construction in question is really adverbial comes from the fact that definite-marked quantity superlatives can be coordinated with non-definite-marked adverbial quality superlatives, as is the case in (20):

(20)   O   *Pavlos milaei* [*pio grigora apo olus   ke **to   perisotero**].
       DEF Paul   talks   [CMP fast   of all.ACC and DEF much.CMP]
       'Paul talks the fastest of all and the most'

Thus adverbial quantity superlatives pattern with adnominal quantity superlatives and quality superlatives, and differently from adverbial quality superlatives.

Although quantity superlatives look morphologically very much like quality superlatives, there is a slight difference in their syntactic behavior. Definiteness spreading appears to be somewhat less acceptable with quantity superlatives than with quality superlatives. None of our consultants were entirely comfortable with examples (21-22) (although they were characterized as "syntactically perfect"), and some rejected them:

(21)   a. ?? *Éfaga **ta perissotera ta biskóta**.*
          ate.1SG DEF much.CMP   the cookies
          Intended: 'I ate **the most cookies**' or 'I ate **most of the cookies**.'

       b. ?? *Éfaga **ta biskóta ta perissotera**.*
          ate.1SG DEF cookies DEF much.CMP
          Intended: 'I ate **the most cookies**' or 'I ate **most of the cookies**.'

(22)   a. ?? *Eimai aftos pou pinei   **ton ligotero ton kafe**.*
          be.1SG him who drinks DEF little.CMP DEF coffee
          'I'm the one who drinks **the least coffee**.'

       b. ?? *Eimai aftos pou pinei   **ton kafe   ton ligotero**.*
          be.1SG him who drinks DEF coffee DEF little.CMP
          'I'm the one who drinks **the least coffee**.'

So definiteness-spreading appears to be somewhat more restricted in the quantity domain.

However, Giannakidou (2004) gives examples such as the following:

(23)   *I   perissoteri i   fitites*   *efygan noris.*
       DEF most   DEF students left   early
       'Most of the students left early.'

It is unclear to us whether this should be seen as an instance of determiner spreading or a construction in which *i perissoteri* behaves as a quantifier for which *i fitites* serves as the restrictor. According to one native Greek speaker we have consulted, the variant in (23) is much better than a version in which the noun precedes the quantifier:

(24)   ? *I   fitites   i   perissoteri* *efygan noris.*
       DEF students DEF most   left   early

Example (24) is fully acceptable only with comma intonation separating *the students* from *the most*, and serves as an answer to the question *What happened with the students?*, rather than *Who left early?* We see an even stronger contrast with *ligotero* 'less', which doesn't give rise to proportional readings.

(25)   *Ton ligotero ton kafe*   *ton ipia*   *egho.*
       DEF less   DEF coffee it   drink.1SG I
       'I drink the least coffee.'

(26)   * *Ton kafe   ton ligotero* *ton ipia*   *egho.*
       DEF coffee DEF less   it   drink.1SG I

Note that (25) is ungrammatical without the subject pronoun *egho*, even though Greek is normally a pro-drop language; this is presumably because of the requirement of focus for relative readings.

This evidence suggests that the structure in (23) is not actually a definiteness-spreading structure but actually one in which *i fitites* behaves like a partitive argument of *i perissoteri*. More generally, we take these facts to show that definiteness-spreading is not possible with quantity superlatives in Greek.

To summarize the situation for Greek: definiteness-marking appears with every type of superlative *except* adverbial quality superlatives. This list includes adnominal quality superlatives on both relative and proportional readings, and both adnominal and adverbial quantity superlatives. Relative and proportional readings are available for adnominal quantity superlatives modifying both mass nouns and count nouns. There is also full agreement with the noun in all cases where there is a noun to agree with. So quantity superlatives are morphologically very similar to quality superlatives overall. However, quantity superlatives differ from quality superlatives with respect to definiteness-spreading, suggesting that the two types are not syntactically parallel.

3 Romanian

We turn now to Romanian, which is like Greek is some respects, but not in others. It uses DEF+CMP for both relative and proportional readings, but there is evidence that the definite article is more tightly knit with the comparative here than it is in Greek.

3.1 Quality superlatives

Example (27) shows a predicative use of a superlative in Romanian, (28) an attributive use, and (29) an adverbial use.

(27) *Pentru că* *eram* **cea mai entuziasmată.**
for   that I.was DEF CMP enthustiastic

'Because I (fem.) was **the most enthusiastic**.'

(28) *A   scris*   **cea mai frumoasă compunere.**
has written DEF CMP beautiful   composition.ACC

'She wrote **the most beautiful composition**.'

(29) *Sora   mea poate alerga* **cel mai repede.**
sister my can   run   DEF CMP fast

'My sister can run **the fastest**.'

In (27) and (28), *cea* is a feminine singular form of *cel*. In (29), we have the invariant, default form.[5] We will not gloss the agreement features, but simply refer the reader to the inflectional paradigm for the demonstrative in Table 3, taken from Cojocaru (2003: 53). Note also that the adjective *frumosă* 'beautiful' shows feminine singular agreement with the noun *compunere* 'composition'.

We gloss *cel* here as DEF, in order to bring out the parallels with other DEF+CMP languages, but it should be kept in mind that this element is not the most direct correlate of English *the* in the language. *Cel* is not found in ordinary, simple definites; instead a suffix is used. For example, in (30a), we have a feminine singular definite ending *-a*, modified from the stem-inherent *-ă* illustrated in (30b). We gloss this ending here as DEF as well.

---

[5]Pană Dindelgan (2013: 315) points out that adverbial *cel* can receive dative case marking, so it is not entirely invariable.

(30)   a. *Carte-a   e   pe   mas-a   mare.*
           map-DEF is on table-DEF big
           'The map is on the big table.'

       b. *Carte-a   e   pe   o masă mare.*
           map-DEF is on a table big
           'The map is on a big table.'

Note also that in traditional grammar (e.g. Cojocaru 2003), *cel* is classified as a demonstrative, though it has additional functions as well. For instance, it can double a definite suffix (Alexiadou 2014):

(31)   *Legile   (cele) importante n'au fost   votate.*
       laws-DEF (DEF) important have not_been voted
       'The laws which were important have not been passed.'

See Alexiadou (2014: 53–62) for a recent discussion of this phenomenon and its relation to Greek determiner spreading.

As (31) implies, Romanian has two word order options for adjectives, including superlatives. This choice bears on the presence or absence of a definite suffix on the noun. If the adjective precedes the modified noun as in (28), repeated in (32a), this noun remains uninflected. If the noun precedes the adjective, as in (31) and (32b), the noun receives definiteness marking (Cojocaru 2003: 53).

Table 3: Inflectional paradigm for *cel* in Romanian

SINGULAR		
	MASC., NEUT.	FEM.
N., A.	*cel*	*cea*
G, D.	*celui*	*celei*
PLURAL		
	MASC.	FEM., NEUT.
N., A.	*cei*	*cele*
G., D.	*celor*	*celor*

(32)   a. *A scris   cea mai frumoasă compunere.*
          has written DEF CMP beautiful   composition.ACC
          'She wrote **the most beautiful composition**.'

       b. *A scris   compunere-a   cea mai frumoasă.*
          has written composition-DEF DEF CMP beautiful
          'She wrote **the most beautiful composition**.'

According to Teodorescu (2007), the prenominal variant (32a) and the postnominal variant (32b) have the same interpretive options. The following is an example favoring a relative interpretation; both orders, shown in (33a) and (33b), are reportedly fine, although all four of the Romanian speakers we consulted spontaneously translated the sentence indicated in the English gloss using the prenominal variant (33a).[6]

(33)   a. *Eu nu sunt cea din   familie   cu   cel mai subțire talie.*
          I   not be.1SG DEF from family.ACC with DEF CMP thin   waist
          'I am not the one in my family with **the thinnest waist**.'

       b. *Eu nu sunt cea din   familie   cu   tali-a   cea mai subtire.*
          I   not be.1SG DEF from family.ACC with waist-DEF DEF CMP thin
          'I am not the one in my family with **the thinnest waist**.'

Note that postnominal adjectives typically receive an intersective interpretation (Cornilescu 1992; Marchis & Alexiadou 2009; Teodorescu 2007):

(34)   a. *o poveste advărată*
          a story   true
          'a story that is true' (not 'quite a story')

       b. *o advărată poveste*
          a true   story
          'a story that is true' or 'quite a story'

       c. *Această poveste este advărată.*
          this   story   is   true
          'This story is true.'

The postnominal adjective in (34a) has only the interpretation that the adjective in (34c) has, while the prenominal adjective in (34b) can also have a nonintersective interpretation. If this applies to superlatives, then the fact that both

---

[6]Thanks to Gianina Iordachioaia for help and discussion.

relative and absolute readings of superlatives are possible in post-nominal position suggests that both relative and absolute readings are, or can be, restrictive readings.

Dobrovie-Sorin & Giurgea (2015) give a number of arguments that *cel mai +* AP form a constituent that sits in the specifier of DP. One is the striking fact that *cel* can be preceded by an indefinite article as in (35) (Dobrovie-Sorin & Giurgea 2015: 15, ex. 64):

(35)   *Există întotdeauna **un cel mai mic   divizor comun** a două elemente.*
       exists always   a   DEF CMP small divisor common of two elements
       'There always exists **a smallest common factor** of two elements.'

Their second argument is that *cel* is always present in superlatives, both when the superlative is post-nominal as in (32b), and when it is adverbial as in (36).

(36)   *Vi fi premiat   cel care   va   scrie #(**cel**) **mai clar**.*
       will be awarded-prize DEF which will write DEF more clearly
       'The one who writes **the most clearly** will be awarded a prize.'
       (Dobrovie-Sorin & Giurgea 2015: 15, ex. 66)

Their third argument is that definite comparatives involve the suffix (which appears on the adjective preceding the head noun) rather than *cel*, as in (37):

(37)   *... dar cu   **mult mai difficil-ul   obiectiv** al ...*
       ... but with much more difficult-the goal   of ...
       '... but with **the much more difficult goal** of ...'

So *cel* must have some meaning or function distinct from the suffix. They also observe that the unmarked position of comparatives is postnominal, whereas the unmarked position for superlatives is prenominal, and note that *cel* cannot be separated from a prenominal comparative by numerals (though numerals can normally follow *cel*), which can be seen in the contrast between (38a) and (38b):

(38)   a. * *cei doi mai înalţi munţi*
            DEF two more high mountains

       b. *cei mai înalţi doi munţi*
            DEF more high two mountains
            'the two highest mountains'

These arguments have us convinced that *cel* in superlatives is not a direct dependent of the modified noun, but rather forms a phrase with the comparative marker and the adjective to the exclusion of the noun. So the structure of *cea mai frumoasă compunere* 'the most beautiful composition' appears to be:

(39)

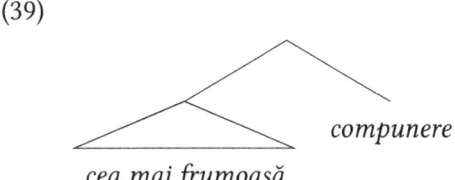

compunere

cea mai frumoasă

3.2 Quantity superlatives

Now let us turn to quantity superlatives in Romanian. As with quality superlatives, definiteness-marking is ubiquitous, even with adverbials, as in (40):

(40) *Personajele de care   se   râdea   **cel mai mult** erau Leana și   nea*
      characters of which they laughed DEF CMP much were Leana and uncle
      Nicu.
      Nicu
      'The characters they laughed at the most were Leana and uncle Nicu.'

And the DEF+CMP construction can have both proportional and relative readings in Romanian. Examples (41) and (42) have relative readings (the latter from Teodorescu 2007: 11).

(41) *Eu sunt cel care   canta la **cele mai multe instrumente**.*
      I   am   the which plays to DEF CMP much   instruments
      'I am the one who plays **the most instruments**.'

(42) *Dan a   băut   **cea mai multă bere**.*
      Dan has drunk DEF CMP much   beer
      'Dan drank **the most beer**.'

Example (43) is a case with a proportional reading, using the partitive preposition *dintre*:[7]

---

[7]The preposition *dintre* (*din* with singular complements) is used in Romanian to introduce an

(43) **Cele mai multe dintre copiii**   care merge la scoala mea place să se
     DEF CMP much of   kids.DEF who go   at school mine like to REFL
     joace muzica.
     play music
     '**Most of the kids** who go to my school like to play music.'

We also find non-partitive uses as in (44) and (45):

(44) **Cei mai mulţi elevi**   din   clasa   mea au   plecat devreme.
     DEF CMP many students from class.the my have left   early
     '**Most of the students** in my class have left early.'

(45) **Cele mai multe lebede** sunt albe.
     DEF CMP many swans are white
     '**Most swans** are white.'

But the syntactic position of the superlative phrase may not be the same as with quality superlatives: in contrast to quality superlatives, quantity superlatives are normally only permitted prenominally (Teodorescu 2007: 11), as example (46) shows.

(46) * Dan a   băut   bere-a   **cea mai multă.**
     Dan has drunk beer-DEF DEF CMP much
     Intended: 'Dan drank **the most beer.**'

Dobrovie-Sorin (2015) does give the example of a postnominal *cel mai mult*-construction in (47a) and (47b), but says that it does not give rise to a relative *or* proportional reading, but "comparison between predefined groups", where the noun phrase refers to one of these groups.

(47)   a.   **Cele mai multe lebede** sunt albe.
         DEF CMP many swans are white
         '**Most swans** are white.'

---

explicit comparison class in superlative constructions, e.g. *El scrie cel mai bine dintre toţi*, 'He writes the best of all', lit. 'He writes the more good among all' (Cojocaru 2003: 169). *Dintre* is also used in quantificational partitive constructions, e.g. *Unul dintre ei prezintă proiectul* 'One of them is presenting the project'.

b. ? *Lebedele   cele mai multe sunt albe.*

   swans.DEF DEF CMP many are   white

   'The more/most numerous (group of) swans are white.'

This reading is referential, and distinct from the proportional reading that arises in prenominal position, rather than quantificational.

Interestingly, (42) above does not have a proportional interpretation. According to Dobrovie-Sorin (2015), this is tied to the fact that a mass noun is involved. Indeed, in our data, a proportional interpretation, in the case of mass quantification (shown in 48 and 49), typically involves a 'majority' or 'part' noun instead, just as in other Romance languages:

(48)   *Am   baut   majoritatea laptelui.*

       have drunk majority   milk

       'I drank **most of the milk.'**

(49)   *Am   baut   mai mare parte a   laptelui.*

       have drunk CMP big   part   GEN milk

       'I drank **most of the milk.'**

Dobrovie-Sorin argues that *cel mai mult* functions as a complex proportional quantifier, one that expects a count down denotation as an argument. Providing further evidence for this view, she claims that a proportional reading is not *always* available for count nouns, either, pointing to a contrast in acceptability between (50) and (51):

(50)   *Cei mai mulți elevi   din clasa   mea au   plecat devreme.*

       DEF CMP many students.DEF of class.DEF my have left   early.

       '**Most students** in my class left early.' (Dobrovie-Sorin 2015: 395)

(51)   * *Cei mai mulți băieți s-au   adunat în sala   asta.*

       DEF CMP many boys   REFL-have gathered in room.DEF this.

       '**Most of the boys** have gathered in this room.' (Dobrovie-Sorin 2015: 395)

She ascribes these differences to whether or not the nuclear scope is filled with a distributive predicate. The unacceptability of (51) is explained under the assumption that the subject noun phrase is quantificational rather than referential. This adds to the evidence in favor of Dobrovie-Sorin's (2015) idea that *cel mai mult* has grammaticalized as a proportional determiner.

To summarize: superlatives are always definite in Romanian. Evidence involving quality superlatives suggests that the definite element is integrated more closely with the comparative element than with the modified noun, i.e. lower down in the structure, not signalling definiteness at the level of the full nominal. Both relative and proportional readings are available for adnominal quantity superlatives, although the proportional readings are limited to count nouns. The existence of proportional readings only with count nouns as well as the unacceptability of collective predicates suggests that *cel mai mult* has grammaticalized into a proportional determiner (Dobrovie-Sorin 2015).

4 Ibero-Romance

4.1 Quality superlatives

Predicative adjectival superlatives in Italian, as in (52), and Spanish, as in (53), normally involve a definite article:

(52) *Carla è **la più intelligente** di tutte queste studentesse.*   (Italian)
      Carla is DEF CMP intelligent   of all   these students

      'Carla is **the most intelligent** of all these students.' (de Boer 1986: 53)

(53) *Ese carro es **el mejor**.*   (Spanish)
      that car is DEF better

      'That car is **the best**.' (Rohena-Madrazo 2007: 1)

One exception, as illustrated in (54), is noted by de Boer (1986: 53), who gives the following predicative example without definiteness-marking.

(54) *il giorno in cui   il nostro lavoro era **più faticoso***   (Italian)
      DEF day in which DEF our   work was CMP tiresome

      'the day on which our work was **most tiresome**'

Here, even though the example is grammatically predicative, it has the flavor of a relative reading, comparing days rather than alternatives to the subject of the sentence *il nostro lavoro* 'our work'. The same example in French, shown in (55), involves a definite article (Alexandre Cremers, p.c.):

(55) *le   jour où   notre travail était le   plus fatiguant*   (French)
      DEF day when our   work   was DEF CMP tiresome
      'the day on which our work was **most tiresome**'

Matushansky (2008a: 75) reports a similar phenomenon in Spanish presented in examples (56) and (57):

(56) *la   que es más alta*   (Spanish)
      DEF who is CMP tall
      'the one who is **tallest**'

(57) *la   que está más enojada*   (Spanish)
      DEF who is   CMP annoyed
      'the one who is **most annoyed**'

In both these examples and in the Italian example (54), uniqueness is indicated with the help of a relative clause. These patterns suggest that superlatives require marking of uniqueness in some fashion, not necessarily with an accompanying definite article.

As in French, adnominal superlatives can appear both pre- and post-nominally in Italian, as the reader can see in (58a) and (58b):

(58) a. *La mamma fa   i   biscotti più buoni del   mondo.*   (Italian)
         DEF mom   makes DEF cookies CMP tasty of.DEF world
         'Mom bakes **the yummiest cookies** in the whole world.'
      b. *La mamma fa   i   più buoni biscotti del   mondo.*
         DEF mom   makes DEF CMP tasty cookies of.DEF world

Normally, there is no definite article on a postnominal superlative in Italian, although Plank (2003) reports that both variants in (59a) and (59b) are acceptable, the latter "putting greater emphasis on the adjective":

(59) a. *l'uomo   più forte*   (Italian)
         DEF'man more strong
         'the **stronger** / **strongest** man'
      b. *l'uomo   il più forte*
         DEF'man the more strong
         'the **strongest** man'

Example (60) displays a postnominal superlative in Italian with a relative reading; here again there is no definite article:[8]

(60)   a.   *Non sono quello con **il** **girovita più sottile** in famiglia.*   (Italian)
        not am the.one with DEF waist   CMP thin   in family

        'I'm not the one with **the thinnest waist** in the family.'

     b.   # *Non sono quello con **il** **più sottile girovita** in famiglia.*
        not am the.one with DEF CMP thin   waist   in family

Adverbial quality superlatives systematically lack definiteness-marking in Italian, as shown in example (61) from de Boer (1986: 53):

(61)   *Di tutte queste ragazze, Marisa lavora **più diligentemente**.*   (Italian)
     of all   these kids   Marisa works CMP diligently

     'Of all these kids, Marisa works **the most diligently**.'

The same holds in Spanish:

(62)   *Juan es el   que corre **más rápido**.*   (Spanish)
     Juan is DEF who runs CMP fast

     'Joan is the one who runs **the fastest**.' (Rohena-Madrazo 2007: 1–2)

As Rohena-Madrazo (2007) notes, the relative clause in (62) is necessary in order for a superlative interpretation to arise. Example (63) has only a comparative interpretation:

(63)   *Juan corre **más rápido**.*   (Spanish)
     Juan runs CMP fast

     'Joan runs **faster**.'

Thus a superlative interpretation does not freely arise on its own here; uniqueness must somehow be signaled in the absence of a determiner.

---

[8] According to Cinque (2010: 11–12), only the postnominal syntax is possible on relative readings. Here is a speculation as to how one might explain this in semantic/pragmatic terms: the prenominal position is normally hostile to non-restrictive modifiers in Italian (e.g. *la presenza mera* vs. *la mera presenza* 'the mere presence'). Matushansky (2008b) proposes that the modified noun saturates the comparison class argument of a superlative, so that a superlative modifier combines with the noun via Functional Application rather than Predicate Modification. This kind of analysis would yield an absolute reading; suppose this is how absolute readings arise. Then absolute readings would be non-restrictive and relative readings would be restrictive. Placing a superlative postnominally could then serve as an indication that an absolute reading is not intended.

4.2 Quantity superlatives

Naturally, we expect the definite article to mark the superlative degree with quantity superlatives as it does with quality superlatives. However, the definite article is sometimes absent even in superlative constructions. De Boer (1986: 53) gives the example in (64); our informants consistently gave us translations like that in (65) and (66) for sentences involving relative readings:

(64) *Dei   nostri amici Luigi è quello che ha **più soldi**.*   (Italian)
      of.DEF our   friends Luigi is the.one who has CMP money
      'Of our friends, Luigi is the one who has **the most money**.'

(65) *Ma probabilmente è   Hans che   ha   bevuto **più caffè**.*   (Italian)
      But probably   it.is Hans who has drunk CMP coffee
      'But it is probably Hans who has drunk the most coffee.'

(66) *Di tutti i   ragazzi della   mia scuola io sono quello   che suona **più***
      of all   DEF kids   in.DEF my school I   am   the.one that plays CMP
      ***strumenti**.*   (Italian)
      instruments
      'Of all the kids in my school, I'm the one who plays the most instruments.'

Hence there is no overt morphological distinction between 'more coffee' and 'most coffee'.

Following Bosque & Brucart (1991), Rohena-Madrazo (2007) uses comparative and superlative "codas" to distinguish between comparative and superlative interpretations in Spanish, as in (67) and (68) respectively:

(67) ***el   niño más rápido** (que   todos nosotros)*   (Spanish)
      DEF boy CMP fast   (than all   we)
      '**the boy faster** (than all of us)'

(68) ***el   niño más rápido** (de todos nosotros)*   (Spanish)
      DEF boy CMP fast   (of all   we)
      '**the fastest boy** (of all of us)'

In (67), the boy is among 'us', but not in (68). Using this technique, he shows that so-called "free" superlatives in Spanish, as shown in (69), can be fronted before the verb, but comparatives cannot:[9]

(69)   *Juan es el   niño que **más libros** leyó (de/*que todos ellos).*   (Spanish)
      John is DEF boy that CMP books read (of/*than all   them)
      'Juan is the boy that read **the most books** (of/*than all of them).'

This evidence suggests that the comparative and the superlative interpretations are really distinct.

Similarly, *the most instruments* in 'I'm the one who plays the most instruments' and *the most coffee* in 'Hans has drunk the most coffee' are translated without definiteness-marking in other Ibero-Romance languages, as we can see in the sets of examples in (70) and (71):

(70)   a.   *Yo soy el que toca **más instrumentos**.*   (Spanish)
      b.   *Eu sou o que toca **mais instrumentos**.*   (Portuguese)
      c.   *Jo sóc qui toca **més instruments**.*   (Catalan)
         'I am the one who play **the most instruments**.'

(71)   a.   *Hans es el que ha bebido **más café**.*   (Spanish)
      b.   *Hans quem bebeu **mais café**.*   (Portuguese)
      c.   *Hans és probablement qui ha begut **més cafè**.*   (Catalan)
         'Hans is the one who has drunk **the most coffee**.'

Adverbial quantity superlatives also lack definiteness-marking, as (72) and (73) show:

(72)   *... uno che lavora **più** di tutti e   parla **meno**   di tutti.*   (Italian)
      ... one who works CMP of all   and speaks little.CMP of all
      '... one who works **most** of all and speaks **least** of all'

---

[9]"Free superlatives" include adverbial superlatives like *más rápido* 'the fastest' and quantity superlatives like *más libros* 'the most book'. In contrast, "incorporated superlatives" such as *el niño más rápido* 'the fastest boy' are defined as being contained within an NP. The free/incorporated distinction in Spanish happens to draw a line between adnominal quality superlatives on the one hand and quantity and adverbial superlatives on the other.

(73) *Alberto es el   que trabaja **más**.*   (Spanish)
      Alberto is DEF that works CMP
      'Alberto is the one who works **the most**.'

Unlike in French and Romanian, a definite article would be ungrammatical preceding the comparative word here. Rather, adverbial quantity superlatives the pattern of adnominal quantity superlatives here (as in all of the languages under consideration, in fact).

The DEF+CMP construction is generally not used to express proportional readings. Proportional *most* is generally translated using other types of constructions, such as 'the greater part' in (74):

(74) **Alla   maggior parte dei**   **bambini** *nella mia scuola piace suonare.*
      of.DEF big.CMP part of.DEF kids   in   my school like play
      '**Most of the kids** in my school like to play (music).'   (Italian)

The same holds for the entire Ibero-Romance subfamily, as far as we can see, including Spanish, Portuguese, and Catalan. For example, *most of the kids* in *Most of the kids in my school like to play music* is translated using a majority noun in these languages, as can be seen in (75):

(75) a. *La mayoría de los niños...*   (Spanish)
      b. *A maioria das crianças...*   (Portuguese)
      c. *La majoria dels nens...*   (Catalan)
      '**Most of the kids...**'

However, according to Dobrovie-Sorin & Giurgea (2015: 20), "Italian allows the article and a proportional meaning in the *partitive* construction":

(76) **Il più degli uomini** *predicano ciascuno la sua benignità.*   (Italian)
      the more of.DEF men   preach   each   the his kindness
      'Most men preach their own kindness.'

Dobrovie-Sorin & Giurgea (2015: 21) also write that this is possible with no overt partitive complement.

(77) *Gli ospiti sono partiti. I **più** erano già   stanchi.*   (Italian)
      DEF guests have left   DEF CMP were already tired
      'The guests left. **Most (of them)** were already tired.'

This shows that to the extent that proportional readings for quantity superlatives are allowed in Italian, they are signalled with the definite article. In this respect, Italian is like Swedish: definite for proportional and non-definite for relative. But this construction appears more restricted than Swedish *de flesta* 'most', given that it can only occur with partitive complements. Our Spanish and French informants do not accept the DEF+CMP construction in the same environment, so this appears to be specific to Italian among the Ibero-Romance languages.

To summarize: Italian and other Ibero-Romance languages use definiteness-marking for adnominal quality superlatives, and ordinary predicative quality superlatives, but not quantity superlatives, adverbial superlatives, or predicative quality superlatives embedded in phrases uniquely characterizing a given discoursediscourse referent. Proportional readings are generally not available for quantity superlatives, with the exception of *il più* in Italian accompanied by a partitive complement.

5 Summary

Table 4 gives a summary of the definiteness-marking patterns we have observed. For a set of languages in which superlatives are formed with the help of a definite article, there is a remarkable diversity of definiteness-marking patterns on superlatives.

Table 4: Definiteness-marking in superlatives in DEF+CMP languages

	Greek	Romanian	French	Italian	Spanish
Qual./pred.	+	+	+	+	+
Qual./pred. (rel. clause)	+	+	+	−	−
Qual./prenom.	+	+	+	+	+
Qual./postnom.	+	+	+	−	−
Qual./adv.	−	+	+	−	−
Quant./prop.	+	+	NA	+	NA
Quant./rel.	+	+	+	−	−
Quant./adv.	+	+	+	−	−

The contrasts raise a number of questions, including:

- Why do quantity superlatives in Ibero-Romance lack definiteness-marking, in contrast to Greek, Romanian, and French?

- Why are adverbial superlatives marked definite in French and Romanian, but not Italian, and why is there a split among adverbial superlatives in Greek?

- Why is definiteness-marking absent on predicative superlatives in relative clauses in Italian, but not in French?

- Why do Greek and Romanian allow proportional readings for DEF+CMP but not Spanish or French, and why is it limited to partitive environments in Italian?

We cannot address all of these issues adequately here. However, we will suggest a certain perspective that may bring some of this apparent chaos to order.

The perspective is as follows. The variety of different definiteness-marking patterns we see suggests that the grammars of these languages may be pulled by a number of competing pressures. One pressure is to mark uniqueness of a description overtly. Another pressure, we suggest, is to avoid combining a definite determiner with a predicate of entities other than individuals, such as events or degrees. In conjunction with certain additional assumptions regarding the semantics of various types of superlatives, these pressures result in a dispreference for certain patterns. These assumptions are made explicit in the following section.

6 Formal analyses

6.1 Quality superlatives

6.1.1 Prenominal quality superlatives

To derive a superlative meaning for DEF+CMP constructions, let us start with the assumption that the basic meaning for a comparative like Greek *pio* is a function from measure functions to degrees to individuals to truth values, roughly following Kennedy (2009), Alrenga et al. (2012), and Dunbar & Wellwood (2016), among others.[10]

---

[10]This presentation glosses over the fact that not all comparatives are alike. An illustration of this point of particular relevance to the case at hand are the detailed studies of comparison in Greek by Merchant (2009; 2012), where there are three morphosyntactic strategies for marking the standard: (i) the preposition *apo* 'from' introducing a phrasal standard; (ii) a genitive case marker, also introducing a phrasal standard; and (iii) a complex standard marker *ap-oti* 'from-wh' which introduces both reduced and unreduced clausal standards. Merchant (2012) concludes that if all of the work is to be done by the comparative, then three different lexical entries for the comparative are needed. But there is hope for a unified analysis; the two phrasal

(78) $pio \rightsquigarrow \lambda g \lambda d \lambda x . g(x) > d$

In (78), g denotes a measure function, a function that maps individuals to degrees. A gradable adjective like *long* is assumed to denote such a function.[11] Modulo lambda-conversion, this yields the translation in (79) for *pio grigoro* 'faster':

(79)   *pio grigoro* $\rightsquigarrow \lambda d \lambda x . \text{FAST}(x) > d$

The next ingredient is a meaning shift that we refer to as Definite Null Instantiation, in homage to Fillmore (1986), as defined in (80). It takes any function and saturates its argument with an unbound variable.[12]

(80)   **Definite Null Instantiation (Meaning Shift)**
       If $\alpha \rightsquigarrow \alpha'$, and α' is an expression of type $\langle \sigma, \tau \rangle$, then $\alpha \rightsquigarrow \alpha'(v)$ as well, where v is an otherwise unused variable of type σ.

Applying this gives (81), where $\mathbf{d}$ is an unbound degree-type variable:

(81)   *pio grigoro* (after DNI) $\rightsquigarrow \lambda x . \text{FAST}(x) > \mathbf{d}$

We have written $\mathbf{d}$ in bold-face in order to draw attention to the fact that it is unbound. (We could of course have chosen a variable other than $\mathbf{d}$; all we needed was a degree variable that is not otherwise used.) This description can combine with a noun like *aftokinito* 'car' using Predicate Modification to produce (82):

---

comparatives differ only in the order in which they take their arguments, and Kennedy (2009) shows that one of the phrasal meanings can be derived from the clausal meaning. Moreover, Alrenga et al. (2012) offer a new perspective on the division of labor between the comparative and the standard marker, allowing for a unified view on the comparative morpheme across these constructions, with differences attributed to the standard markers. They use a lexical entry like (78) for the comparative, and clausal and phrasal standard markers each combine with it appropriately in their own way. In light of this work, we may continue to operate under the assumption that (78) constitutes a viable candidate for a unified treatment of the comparative morpheme across different types of constructions and across the languages under consideration.

[11]The arrow $\rightsquigarrow$ signifies a translation relation from a natural language expression (part of an LF representation) to an expression of a typed extensional language; we thus adopt an "indirect interpretation" framework, in which expressions of natural language are translated to a formal representation language. Within this framework we assume the standard rule of Functional Application:

   (i)   **Functional Application (Composition Rule)**
         If $\alpha \rightsquigarrow \alpha'$ and $\beta \rightsquigarrow \beta'$, and α' is of type $\langle \sigma, \tau \rangle$ and β' is of type σ, and γ is a phrase whose only constituents are α and β, then $\gamma \rightsquigarrow \alpha'(\beta')$.

[12]Note that this meaning shift depends on the assumption that the $\rightsquigarrow$ relation is not a function; a given natural language expression can have multiple translations into the formal language and they need not be equivalent. See Partee & Rooth (1983) for precedent for this assumption.

(82)   [*pio grigoro*] *aftokinito* ⤳ $\lambda x . \text{FAST}(x) > \mathbf{d} \wedge \text{CAR}(x)$

If there is a unique fastest car, then there will be a way of choosing a value for **d** in such a way that this description picks it out. Hence, given an appropriate choice of value **d**, the definite article should be able to combine with this description to pick out the most qualified candidate. Normally, the range of potential referents will be limited to a class **C**, which we may suppose is referenced by the definite determiner, as displayed in (83).

(83)   *to* ⤳ $\lambda P_{\langle \tau, t\rangle} . \iota x_\tau . P(x) \wedge C(x)$

Where τ is a variable over types, constrained in specific ways by different languages. Applied to *pio grigoro aftokinito*, this denotes the unique car in **C** that is faster than **d**. The structure of the derivation is the one in (84).

(84)

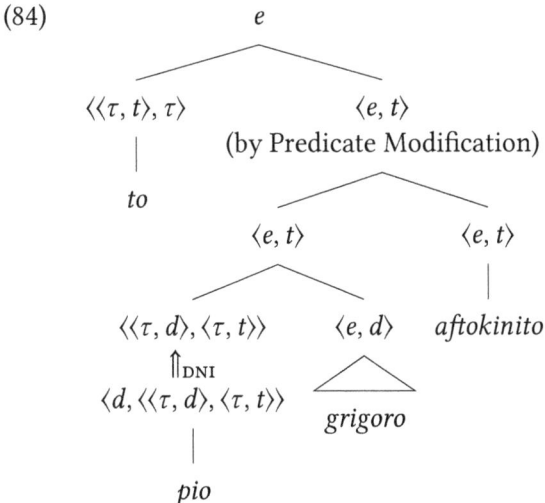

This clearly gives an absolute superlative reading. What about relative readings such as (8), with *ti leptoteri mesi* 'the thinnest waist'? The analytical landscape is quite different under the assumption that there is no superlative morpheme. One influential analysis of the absolute vs. relative distinction, due to Szabolcsi (1986) and developed in Heim (1999), holds that relative readings arise through movement of -*est* at LF to a position adjacent to the constituent of the sentence corresponding to one of the elements being compared, typically the focus. With no -*est* to undergo movement, this analytical route is not available to us.

A prominent class of alternatives to the movement view is that *-est* remains *in situ*, the absolute vs. relative contrast resulting from different settings of the comparison class (Gawron 1995; Farkas & Kiss 2000; Sharvit & Stateva 2002; Gutiérrez-Rexach 2006; Teodorescu 2009; Pancheva & Tomaszewicz 2012; Coppock & Beaver 2014; Coppock & Josefson 2015). This type of approach is more amenable to the assumptions that we have made here. Although we have no superlative morpheme to provide a comparison class, the definite article is restricted to a contextually-determined domain C, and the contrast could concern the value of that contextually-set variable. On an relative reading of *the fastest car*, for example, C might consist of cars standing in a salient correspondence relation to the focus alternatives.

Heim (1999) notes that so-called "upstairs *de dicto*" readings pose a challenge for the *in situ* approach. The problem is that *John wants to climb the highest mountain* can be true in a context where there is no specific mountain that John wants to climb, nor does John's desire pertain to the relative heights of mountains climbed by various competitors; it just so happens that he wants to climb a 5000 mountain (any such mountain), and the ambitions of the others in the context with respect to the heights of mountains they want to climb are not so great. This reading can be obtained by scoping just *-est* over the intensional verb *want*. Such a reading is apparently available in at least Greek and French, according to our informants.

Various responses to that challenge have been offered. Sharvit & Stateva (2002) offer an *in situ* theory designed to handle these readings, but it relies on a non-standard definite determiner, so that solution is not directly compatible with our analysis. Solomon (2011) points out that upstairs *de dicto* readings can be handled if the comparison class is thought to be a set of degrees rather than individuals. This is more amenable to the assumptions we have made, and would only require us to allow for the possibility that the definite article combine directly with a d-saturated version of CMP that compares degrees rather than individuals and serve to pick out a specific degree.

Other routes may be compatible with the analysis as it stands. Coppock & Beaver (2014) argue that the "upstairs *de dicto*" phenomenon is part of a more general phenomenon that requires an explanation anyway, namely cases like *Adrian wants to buy a jacket like Malte's*, discussed by Fodor (1970) and in much subsequent literature under the heading of "Fodor's puzzle". If indeed upstairs *de dicto* readings can be seen as an instance of Fodor's puzzle, then the problem can be explained away. Another alternative is offered by Bumford (2016), who posits a sort of definiteness that is subordinated to the modal element. Although

Bumford's theory of the definite article is different from the simple one we have sketched here, his suggested approach for dealing with intensional contexts may be viable even in the context of a more standard analysis. In any case, we believe it is an open question whether upstairs *de dicto* readings can indeed be managed in the context of an *in situ* approach using the sort of approach to the definite article that we have taken here, and the success of our analysis in dealing with them depends on a general solution to this problem.

Another fact to be accounted for is the fact that, as Szabolcsi (1986) pointed out, superlatives on relative readings behave like indefinites, suggesting that they are, in Coppock & Beaver's (2015) terms, *indeterminate*. We refer to Coppock & Beaver (2014) for ideas on how to capture the indeterminacy of relative readings in the context of an *in situ* analysis.

Another question that this proposal raises is how to rule out overt standard phrases with comparatives that combine with definite articles. These are entirely ungrammatical:

(85)   * *Elle est la   plus belle   que {Marie, j'ai imaginé}.*   (French)
        she is   the CMP beautiful than {Marie, I've imagined}

The same is true for definite comparatives in English, as Lerner & Pinkal (1995) observe:

(86)   *George owns the faster car (*than Bill).*

Lerner & Pinkal (1995) also observe that this is part of a larger pattern, where weak determiners allow overt standard arguments and strong determiners disallow them:

(87)   *George owns a/some/a few faster car(s) than Bill.*

(88)   * *George owns every/most faster car(s) than Bill.*

Beil (1997) offers an explanation of this contrast on the basis of the fact that strong determiners have a domain that has to be presupposed in previous context. Xiang (2005) offers an alternative explanation, on which strong quantifiers induce an LF intervention effect blocking the movement that the *than* phrase needs to undergo. This idea is quite compatible with the present analysis. In a case where Definite Null Instantiation has applied, the target of comparison does not need to undergo movement, so no intervention effect is predicted to arise.

6.1.2 Postnominal quality superlatives

In all of the languages we have seen, there are constructions in which the superlative occurs post-nominally; (89–92) are some examples repeated from the discussions above.

(89)   *Spania haidevo **tin mikroteri ti gata.***   (Greek)
       seldom pet   DEF smallest   DEF cat
       'I seldom pet **the smallest cat.**'

(90)   *A scris   compunere-a   cea mai frumoasă.*   (Romanian)
       has written composition-DEF DEF CMP beautiful
       'She wrote **the most beautiful composition.**'

(91)   *celui   de la famille avec **la taille la plus fine***   (French)
       the.one of the family with the waist DEF CMP fine
       'the one in the family with the thinnest waist.'

(92)   *La mamma fa   i   **biscotti più buoni** del   mondo.*   (Italian)
       DEF mom   makes DEF cookies CMP tasty of.DEF world
       'Mom bakes **the yummiest cookies** in the whole world.'

In Greek, Romanian and French, the postnominal superlative is accompanied by a second definiteness-marker (this is specific to superlatives only in Romanian and French). For such cases, it is convenient to adopt Coppock & Beaver's (2015) predicative treatment of the definite article, whereby it denotes a function from predicates to predicates, presupposing uniqueness but not existence. It is also important for our purposes to restrict the domain of a definite determiner to a salient comparison class **C**. Thus we adopt the lexical entry shown in (93) for Romanian *cel*, for example.

(93) $cel_C \rightsquigarrow \lambda P \lambda x . \partial(|P \cap C| \leq 1) \wedge P(x) \wedge C(x)$

(Here ∂ is the 'partial' operator, whose scope is presupposed material. It evaluates to the 'undefined' truth value unless its scope is true.) With this, we derive the interpretation in (94) for the superlative phrase in (90):

(94) cel_C *mai frumoasă*
       $\rightsquigarrow \lambda x . \partial(|\lambda x' . \textsc{beautiful}(x') > \mathbf{d} \wedge C(x)| \leq 1) \wedge \textsc{beautiful}(x) > \mathbf{d} \wedge C(x)$

This description characterizes a composition x in C that is the only one whose beauty exceeds **d**. Combining this phrase with the definite article on the noun yields a derivation of the following form for the the full noun phrase (we assume that the suffix *-a* in *compunere-a* 'the composition' is interpreted in D, and we represent it in 95 as an iota operator for simplicity, although it can also be given a treatment along the lines of 93):

(95)

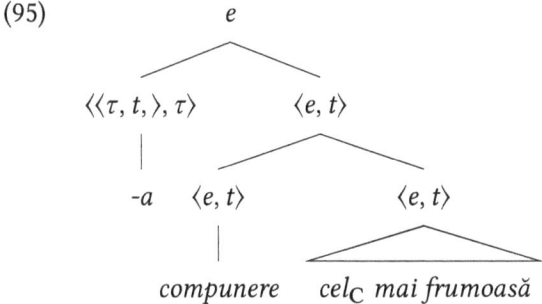

6.2 Quantity superlatives

The picture is much richer when it comes to quantity superlatives. In all of the languages we have considered, quantity superlatives differ at least to some extent from quality superlatives, if not with respect definiteness-marking (as in Italian) then with respect to definiteness-spreading in object position (Greek), use of a pseudopartitive construction (French), or pre- vs. postnominal word order (Romanian). We therefore posit that quantity superlatives are of a different semantic type from quality superlatives (across the board), namely: predicates of degrees, rather than individuals. We have adopted a measure function approach to the semantics of gradable predicates, so that an adjective like *tall* for example is translated as an expression of type $\langle e, d \rangle$, mapping an individual to a degree. The parallel treatment for a quantity word like *much* or *many* would then be $\langle d, d \rangle$; just as *tall* maps an individual to its height, *much* maps a quantity to its magnitude. The magnitude of a quantity might as well be seen as the quantity itself, so we will simply treat quantity words as identity functions on degrees. Thus for Greek, we have (96) and (97):

(96)   *pollá* $\rightsquigarrow \lambda d \, . \, d$

(97)   *pio pollá* (after DNI) $\rightsquigarrow \lambda d' \, . \, d' > \mathbf{d}$

Now, we cannot use Predicate Modification to combine with the noun (and this predicts that definiteness spreading should be problematic.) Let us assume that what happens instead is that the degree predicate is linked to the nominal predicate by the same glue that holds a pseudopartitive together. We implement this with the composition rule called Measure Identification in (98). he result is a predicate that holds of some individual x if the nominal predicate holds of x and x has an extensive measure satisfying the degree predicate.

(98) **Measure Identification (Composition Rule)**

If γ is a subtree whose only two immediate subtrees are α and β, and $\alpha \rightsquigarrow D$, where D is of type $\langle d, t \rangle$, and $\beta \rightsquigarrow P$, where P is of type $\langle \tau, t \rangle$, where τ is any type, then

$$\gamma \rightsquigarrow \lambda v \,.\, D(\mu_i(v)) \wedge P(v)$$

where v is a variable of type τ and μ_i is a free variable over measure functions (type $\langle \tau, d \rangle$).

We use μ_i to denote a contextually-salient measure function along the lines of Wellwood (2014), with i as a free variable index presumed to be constrained by context. So given a predicate of degrees D and a predicate of individuals P, this operation yields $\lambda x \,.\, D(\mu_i(x)) \wedge P(x)$. (99) is an example (assuming the plural is translated using the cumulativity operator *; cf. Link 1983):

(99) *pio pollá órgana* $\rightsquigarrow \lambda x \,.\, \mu_i(x) > \mathbf{d} \wedge {}^*\textsc{instrument}(x)$

This is the right sort of thing to combine with a definite article as long as $\mathbf{d}$ is chosen appropriately. The definite article introduces a comparison class $\mathbf{C}$. So *ta pio pollá órgana* will be predicted to denote the plurality of instruments in $\mathbf{C}$ whose contextually-relevant extensive measure is $\mathbf{d}$. The structure of the derivation is thus as in (100):

(100)

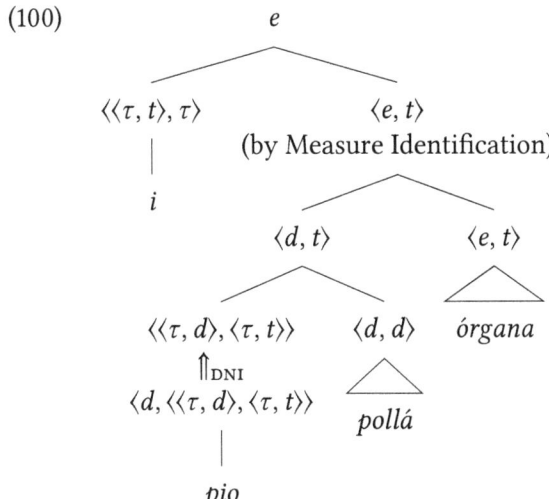

In Romanian, the definite element *cel* forms a constituent with the comparative element and the quantity word to the exclusion of the noun. We therefore posit the structure in (101) for the semantic derivation:

(101)

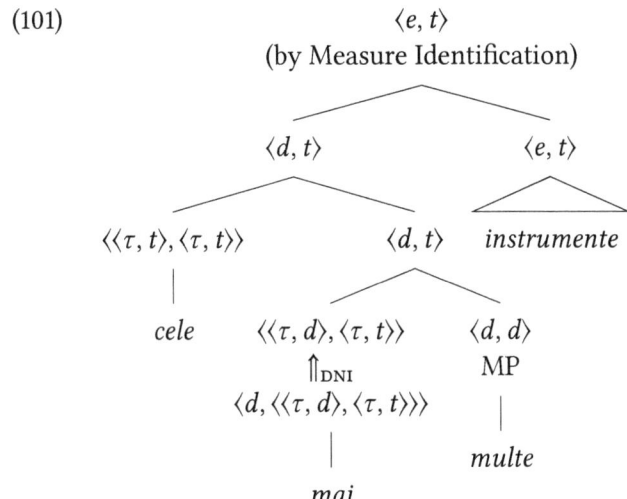

The meaning for this expression as a whole characterizes a plurality of instruments whose measure is greatest among any of the degrees in the context. In the case of a relative reading, the set of degrees that are salient in the context are aligned in a one-to-one relationship with some salient set of individuals, typically those individuals that are alternatives to the focused constituent.

French has yet a different structure, involving a pseudopartitive, as illustrated in (102).

(102) *Je suis celui   qui joue **le plus d'instruments.***   (French)
       I am the-one who plays DEF CMP of-instruments

       'I am the one who plays **the most instruments.**'

Since French does not use a word for *many* parallel to Greek *pollá* or Romanian *mult*, we might posit either a silent underlying form with the same meaning, or we might imagine that French simply makes do without such an element. In the latter case, it is convenient to treat *plus* using the simplest imaginable lexical entry for comparison (Heim 2006; Beck 2010), namely (103):

(103) *plus* ⤳ $\lambda d . \lambda d' . d' > d$

Given this, we have the derivation in (104):

(104)

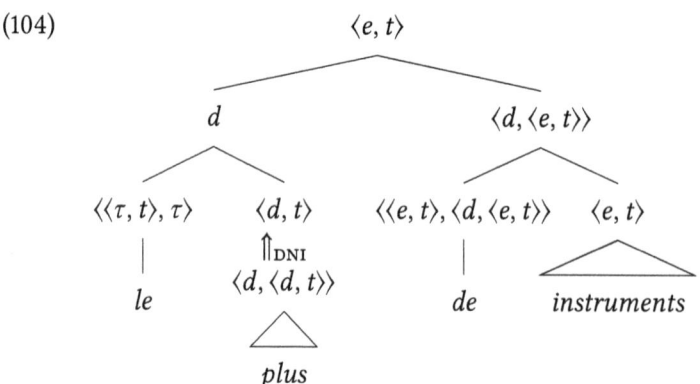

We assume that the Meas head acts as glue, linking the degree denoted by *le plus* with the denotation of the noun phrase such that the noun phrase is constrained to have an extensive measure of that degree. The resulting denotation is just the same as that posited for Romanian.

Finally, we come to Italian, which has the simplest overt form, as shown in (66) above, repeated here as (105):

(105) *... che suona **più strumenti.***   (Italian)
       ... that plays CMP instruments

       '... who plays the most instruments.'

One possible analysis is the one in (106), using a lexical entry for *più* like the one given for French *plus* above.

(106)

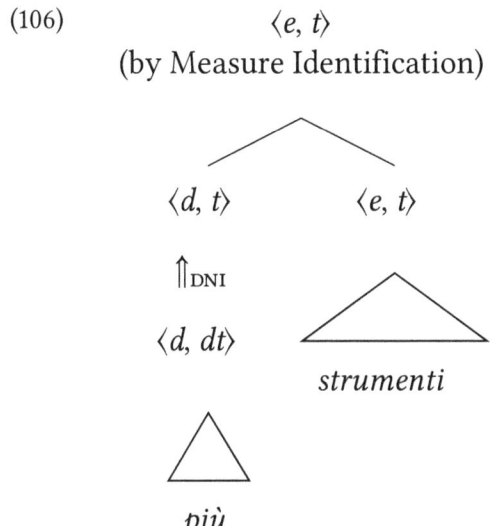

The predicate that this derives holds of any plurality of instruments *x* whose quantity exceeds **d**. his of course does not necessitate that there be no larger plurality of instruments in the context, so we have not captured a superlative interpretation. Assuming the same analysis carries over to Spanish, it remains an open question why superlatives undergo fronting and comparatives do not.

6.3 Adverbial superlatives

For adverbial quantity superlatives, we start with the assumption that a verb phrase denotes a property of events, translating to an expression of type $\langle v, t \rangle$, and that the DEF+CMP construction combines with it via Measure Identification. For example, in Greek we have (107):

(107) $\langle v, t \rangle$
          (by Measure Identification)

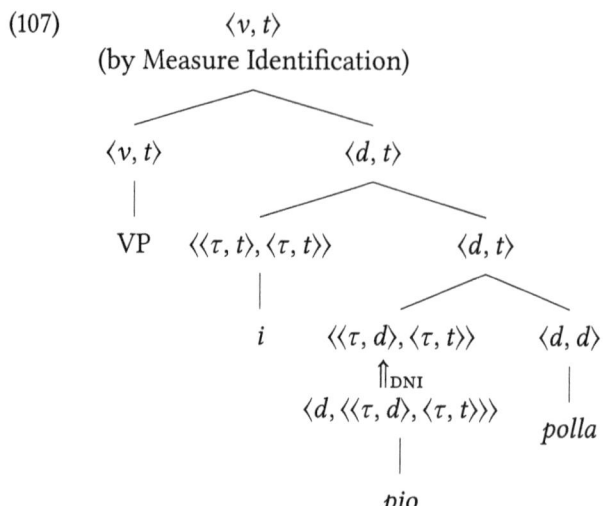

Adverbial quality superlatives, on the other hand, involve gradable predicates that measure events as in (108):

(108) $\langle v, t \rangle$
          (by Predicate Modification)

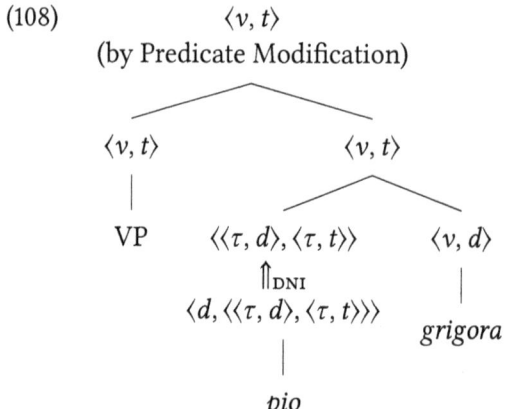

We suggest that this difference in type underlies the contrast between quantity and quality adverbial superlatives in Greek: the Greek definite determiner applies to predicates of type $\langle d, t \rangle$ but not ones of type $\langle v, t \rangle$. In Italian, neither type of adverbial superlative is marked definite; this can be understood as an aversion to definiteness-marking on predicates of both types. In French and Romanian, on the other hand, both types are definite, and this can be understood under the lens of a maximally polymorphic definite determiner.

6.4 Proportional readings

Proportional readings for quantity superlatives are not fully available in French, Spanish, or Italian, but they are available in Greek and Romanian. From a larger typological perspective, Greek and Romanian are the odd ones out; most languages lack proportional readings for the superlative of 'many' (Coppock et al. 2017). In line with Coppock et al. (in prep), we suggest that this is related to our proposal that quantity words typically denote predicates of degrees rather than individuals, and their comparatives likewise compare degrees rather than individuals. A definite determiner that combines directly with the comparative of a quantity word after Definite Null Instantiation produces a phrase denoting a degree or amount that is greatest among some contextually-salient set of degrees. Thus for example *le plus* in *le plus d'instruments* would a denotation like 'the greatest number' or 'the greatest amount'. Notice that the phrase *the greatest number* only has a relative reading. Consider (109):

(109)   *Maria has visited the greatest number of continents.*

This cannot mean that Maria has visited more than half of the continents. If *le plus* means the same thing as *the greatest number*, then it, too, should only have relative readings. According to Coppock et al. (in prep), the reason that such cases have only relative readings is related to a general constraint on the interpretation of superlatives. This view makes a distinction in principle between the entities that are actually measured by the gradable predicate to which superlative morphology attaches, the *measured entities*, and what they call the *contrast set*, following Coppock & Beaver (2014). On relative readings, the contrast set and the measured entities are distinct and related by a salient association relation given by the sentence. On absolute readings, they are conflated. Coppock et al. (in prep) posit a constraint on the contrast set, according to which it must consist of individuals. When the gradable predicate measures degrees rather than individuals, the contrast set must be distinct from the set of measured entities; hence a relative reading is forced.

How, then, do proportional readings arise? Dobrovie-Sorin & Giurgea (2015) suggest that they arise through grammaticalization, which requires full grammatical agreement (present in both Greek and Romanian), and is preempted by the pseudopartitive construction that French uses with relative readings. On this perspective, it is a matter of historical accident whether a given language has developed a proportional determiner from a quantity superlative. We are sympathetic to this view. We would only note that if indeed Greek and Romanian involve different constituency relations when it comes to relative readings, as suggested above, then the putative grammaticalization process must be of a different nature for the two languages. We would like to suggest that in Greek, proportional readings arise through a process similar to the one envisioned by Hoeksema (1983), where the quantity word comes to denote a gradable predicate of (plural) individuals, and the comparison class for the superlative is constituted by two non-overlapping pluralities, one consisting of atoms that satisfy the predicate in question and one consisting of atoms that do not. Such an analysis is consonant with the idea that the definite determiner is in its ordinary position in Greek, rather than more tightly integrated with the comparative marker. In Romanian, on the other hand, there is a constituent containing the definite article, the comparative marker, and the quantity word; this phrase could potentially be reanalyzed as a complex determiner.

7 Conclusion and outlook

We have suggested that superlative interpretations arise in DEF+CMP languages with the help of an interpretive process called Definite Null Instantiation for the target argument of a comparative. It is reasonable to ask whether this process is restricted to DEF+CMP languages or available more broadly. We suggest that it is available at least somewhat more broadly, and that English is one of the languages that avails itself of it, in constructions like *the taller of the two* (discussed from a formal semantic perspective by Szabolcsi 2012). Why English doesn't generally form superlatives using this strategy could be explained in terms of markedness; since there is a dedicated superlative morpheme in English, it should be used whenever the comparison class contains more than two members.

The pattern of variation suggests that a number of competing pressures are at play. One pressure is to mark uniqueness of a description overtly. Another pressure is to avoid combining a definite determiner with a predicate of entities other than individuals, such as events or degrees. We have assumed that quality adverbs denote gradable predicates of events, and that quantity words denote predicates of degrees. The pressure to avoid combining definite determiners with predicates of events rules out definiteness-marking on adverbial quality superlatives, and similarly for predicates of degrees and quantity superlatives.

In Optimality Theoretic terms, we might conceive of these forces as constraints that we could label *DEF/d ("do not use a definite determiner with a predicate of degrees"), *DEF/v ("do not use a definite determiner with a predicate of events") and MARK-UNIQUENESS. Italian ranks the former two over the latter:

$$^*\text{DEF}/d, {}^*\text{DEF}/v > \text{MARK-UNIQUENESS}$$

while French ranks the latter over the former two:

$$\text{MARK-UNIQUENESS} > {}^*\text{DEF}/d, {}^*\text{DEF}/v$$

An adverbial superlative like *le moins fort* (French, lit. 'the less fast') violates $^*\text{DEF}/v$ but not MARK-UNIQUENESS, while one like *más rápido* (Spanish, lit. 'more fast') violates MARK-UNIQUENESS but not $^*\text{DEF}/v$. Greek draws the line at adverbial quality superlatives, which suggests that it ranks MARK-UNIQUENESS over $^*\text{DEF}/v$, but not over $^*\text{DEF}/d$:

$$^*\text{DEF}/d > \text{MARK-UNIQUENESS} > {}^*\text{DEF}/v$$

Intuitively, MARK-UNIQUENESS should require that any descriptive phrase which is presupposed to apply to at most one individual is marked with a lexical item that conventionally signals this presupposition. But there may be slightly different shades of this constraint for different languages. Recall that in Italian (and Spanish), the definite article is normally used in predicative superlatives, presumably to distinguish between the comparative and the superlative interpretations. But the relative clause construction serves to mark uniqueness in some sense, rendering the definite article unnecessary. This sort of explanation could be made more precise by imagining a version of the MARK-UNIQUENESS constraint in Ibero-Romance that imposes slightly different requirements. Suppose that in Ibero-Romance, the operative MARK-UNIQUENESS constraint may be satisfied in some cases where a candidate phrase with unique descriptive content is not actually marked as unique, as long as it is embedded in a larger phrase with unique descriptive content which *is*. So Ibero-Romance might have a "once per discourse referent" rule, while French might have a "once per phrase" rule. Syntactic restrictions would presumably also come into play.

This hypothesized difference could also apply to bare postnominal superlatives, which are found in Italian but not French. This idea would have to be evaluated in light of previous ideas regarding this contrast. According to Kayne (2008), the reason has to do with the licensing of bare nouns in general. Alexiadou (2014: 74–75) suggests an approach appealing to the richness of agreement features. Matushansky (2008a) argues that superlatives are always attributive modifiers of nouns, so a nominal structure is projected around a superlative in the postnominal case; perhaps Italian does not do that. We leave it to future research to compare among these possible explanations for the difference.

Future research on this topic should also bring into the discussion a wider range of languages that use this strategy. For example, Plank (2003) briefly discusses the very interesting case of Maltese, which makes use of fronting to distinguish the superlative degree (110c) from the comparative (110b).

(110)   a. *il-belt   il-qawwi*   (Maltese)
            DEF-city DEF-powerful
            'the powerful city'

        b. *il-belt   l-aqwa*
            DEF-city DEF-powerful.CMP
            'the more powerful city'

        c. *l-aqwa   belt*
            DEF-powerful.CMP city
            'the most powerful city'.

As Plank (2003: 361–362) points out, "Paradoxically, as a result of this fronting, NPs with superlatives thus end up less articulated than NPs with other adjectives in normal postnominal position." Plank posits that "Just like *le plus jeune homme* [...] in French, [superlatives in Maltese] are in fact under-articulated: there ought to be two definiteness markers on the initial superlative, one by virtue of it being a superlative, another by virtue of it being NP-initial." Further issues for future work include whether and how the approach we have taken here, in terms of competing pressures, can be fruitfully applied to Maltese and other DEF+CMP languages.

Acknowledgements

We are very grateful to our consultants who have been so generous with their time, and to the organizers and participants of the Definiteness Across Languages conference in Mexico City, July 2016. Extra special thanks are due to Stavroula Alexandropoulou for help with the Greek judgments. This research was carried out under the auspices of the Swedish Research Council project 2015-01404 entitled *Most and more: Quantity superlatives across languages* awarded to PI Elizabeth Coppock at the University of Gothenburg.

Abbreviations

CMP comparative   DEF definite
SPRL superlative   WK weak ending

References

Alexiadou, Artemis. 2014. *Multiple determiners and the structure of DPs* (Linguis-tik Aktuell/Linguistics Today 211). Amsterdam: John Benjamins.

Alexiadou, Artemis & Chris Wilder. 1998. Adjectival modification and multiple determiners. In Artemis Alexiadou & Chris Wilder (eds.), *Possessors, predicates and movement in the determiner phrase* (Linguistik Aktuell/Linguistics Today 22), 305–332. Amsterdam: John Benjamins.

Alrenga, Peter, Chris Kennedy & Jason Merchant. 2012. A new standard of com-parison. In Nathan Arnett & Ryan Bennett (eds.), *Proceedings of the 30th West Coast Conference on Formal Linguistics*, 32–42. Somerville: Cascadilla Proceed-ings Project.

Beck, Sigrid. 2010. Quantifiers in *than*-clauses. *Semantics and Pragmatics* 3. 1–72.

Beil, Franz. 1997. The definiteness effect in attributive comparatives. *Proceedings of SALT* 7. 37–54.

Bobaljik, Jonathan David. 2012. *Universals in comparative morphology: Suppletion, superlatives, and the structure of words* (Current Studies in Linguistics). Cam-bridge: MIT Press.

Bosque, Ignacio & José María Brucart. 1991. QP Raising in Spanish superlatives. (Madrid: Universidad Complutense de Madrid. Manuscript).

Bumford, Dylan. 2016. Split-scope definites: Relative superlatives and Haddock descriptions. (New York: New York University. Manuscript).

Cinque, Guglielmo. 2010. *The syntax of adjectives: A comparative study* (Linguistic Inquiry Monographs 57). Cambridge: MIT Press.

Cojocaru, Dana. 2003. *Romanian grammar*. Durham, NC: Slavic & East European Language Research Center (SEELRC), Duke University.

Coppock, Elizabeth. 2019. Quantity superlatives in Germanic, or, "Life on the fault line between adjective and determiner". *Journal of Germanic Linguistics* 31(2). 109–200. DOI:10.1017/S1470542718000089

Coppock, Elizabeth & David Beaver. 2014. A superlative argument for a minimal theory of definiteness. *Proceedings of SALT* 24. 177–196.

Coppock, Elizabeth & David Beaver. 2015. Definiteness and determinacy. *Linguis-tics and Philosophy* 38(5). 377–435.

Coppock, Elizabeth, Elizabeth Bogal-Allbritten & Golsa Nouri-Hosseini. in prep. Proportional MOST is more than MANY plus -EST: Evidence from typological universals and variation. (Boston University and University of Gothenburg. Manuscript.)

Coppock, Elizabeth & Christian Josefson. 2015. Completely bare Swedish superlatives. In Eva Csipak & Hedde Zeijlstra (eds.), *Proceedings of Sinn und Bedeutung 19*, 179–196. Götingen: University of Göttingen.

Coppock, Elizabeth, Golsa Nouri-Hosseini, Elizabeth Bogal-Allbritten & Saskia Stiefeling. 2017. Proportional implies relative: A typological universal. *Proceedings of the Linguistics Society of America* 2(12). 1–15.

Cornilescu, Alexandra. 1992. Remarks on the determiner system of Rumanian: The demonstratives *al* and *cel*. *Probus* 4(2). 189–260.

de Boer, Minne Gerben. 1986. Il superlativo italiano. *Revue Romane* 21(1). 53–64.

Dobrovie-Sorin, Carmen. 2015. Two types of *most*. *Proceedings of SALT* 25. 394–412.

Dobrovie-Sorin, Carmen & Ion Giurgea. 2015. Quantity superlatives vs. proportional quantifiers: A comparative perspective. (Abstract for the 25th Colloquium on Generative Grammar, Bayonne).

Dunbar, Ewan & Alexis Wellwood. 2016. Addressing the 'two interface' problem: Comparatives and superlatives. *Glossa: A journal of general linguistics* 1(1). 5.

Farkas, Donka F. & Katalin É. Kiss. 2000. On the comparative and absolute readings of superlatives. *Natural Language and Linguistic Theory* 18(3). 417–455.

Fillmore, Charles J. 1986. Pragmatically controlled zero anaphora. In Vassiliki Nikiforidou (ed.), *Proceedings of the 12th Annual Meeting of the Berkeley Linguistics Society*, 95–107. Berkeley, CA: Berkeley Linguistics Society.

Fodor, Janet Dean. 1970. *The linguistic description of opaque contexts*. Cambridge: Massachusetts Institute of Technology. (Doctoral dissertation).

Gawron, Jean Mark. 1995. Comparatives, superlatives, and resolution. *Linguistics and Philosophy* 18(3). 333–380.

Giannakidou, Anastasia. 2004. Domain restriction and the arguments of quantificational determiners. *Proceedings of SALT* 14. 110–126.

Gorshenin, Maksym. 2012. The crosslinguistics of the superlative. In Cornelia Stroh (ed.), *Neues aus der Bremer Linguistikwerkstatt – Aktuelle Themen und Projekte*, 55–159. Bremen: Brockmeyer.

Gutiérrez-Rexach, Javier. 2006. Superlative quantifiers and the dynamics of context-dependence. In Klaus von Heusinger & Ken Turner (eds.), *Where semantics meets pragmatics* (Current Research In The Semantics/Pragmatics Interface 16), 237–266. Amsterdam: Elsevier.

Hackl, Martin. 2000. *Comparative quantifiers*. Cambridge: Massachusetts Institute of Technology. (Doctoral dissertation).

Hackl, Martin. 2009. On the grammar and processing of proportional quantifiers: *Most* vs. *more than half*. *Natural Language Semantics* 17(1). 63–98.

Hallman, Peter. 2016. Superlatives in Syrian Arabic. *Natural Language and Linguistic Theory* 34(4). 1281–1328.

Heim, Irene. 1999. Notes on superlatives. (Cambridge: Massachusetts Institute of Technology. Manuscript.)

Heim, Irene. 2006. Notes on comparative clauses as generalized quantifiers. (Cambridge: Massachusetts Institute of Technology. Manuscript.)

Hoeksema, Jack. 1983. Plurality and conjunction. In Alice G. B. ter Meulen (ed.), *Studies in modeltheoretic semantics*, 63–84. Dordrecht: Foris.

Kayne, Richard S. 2008. Some preliminary comparative remarks on French and Italian definite articles. In Freidin Robert, Carlos Peregrín Otero & María Luisa Zubizarreta (eds.), *Foundational issues in linguistic theory: Essays in honor of Jean-Roger Vergnaud*, 291–321. Cambridge: MIT Press.

Kennedy, Christopher. 2009. Modes of comparison. In Malcolm Elliott, James Kirby, Osamu Sawada, Eleni Staraki & Suwon Yoon (eds.), *CLS 43-1: The Main Session. Papers from the 43rd Annual Meeting of the Chicago Linguistic Society*, 139–163. Chicago, IL: Chicago Linguistic Society.

Krasikova, Sveta. 2012. Definiteness in superlatives. In Maria Aloni, Vadim Kimmelman, Floris Roelofsen, Galit W. Sassoon, Katrin Schulz & Matthijs Westera (eds.), *Logic, language and meaning: 18th Amsterdam Colloquium, Amsterdam, The Netherlands, December 19-21, 2011. Revised selected papers* (Lecture Notes in Computer Science 7218), 411–420. Berlin: Springer.

Lerner, Jan & Manfred Pinkal. 1995. Comparative ellipsis and variable binding. *Proceedings of SALT* 5. 222–236.

Link, Godehard. 1983. The logical analysis of plurals and mass terms: A lattice-theoretical approach. In Rainer Bäuerle, Christoph Schwartze & Arnim von Stechow (eds.), *Meaning, use, and interpretation of language* (Grundlagen der Kommunikation und Kognition / Foundations of Communication and Cognition), 302–323. Berlin: de Gruyter.

Marchis, Michaela & Artemis Alexiadou. 2009. On the distribution of adjectives in Romanian: The *cel* construction. In Enoch Aboh, Elisabeth van der Linden, Josep Quer & Petra Sleeman (eds.), *Romance languages and linguistic theory: Selected papers from 'Going Romance' Amsterdam 2007* (Romance Languages and Linguistic Theory 1), 161–178. Amsterdam: John Benjamins.

Matushansky, Ora. 2008a. On the attributive nature of superlatives. *Syntax* 11. 26–90.

Matushansky, Ora. 2008b. On the linguistic complexity of proper names. *Linguistics and Philosophy* 31(5). 573–627.

Merchant, Jason. 2009. Phrasal and clausal comparatives in Greek and the abstractness of syntax. *Journal of Greek Linguistics* 9. 134–164.

Merchant, Jason. 2012. The two phrasal comparatives of Greek. (Chicago: University of Chicago. Manuscript).

Pană Dindelgan, Gabrielă (ed.). 2013. *The grammar of Romanian.* Oxford: Oxford University Press.

Pancheva, Roumyana & Barbara Tomaszewicz. 2012. Cross-linguistic differences in superlative movement out of nominal phrases. In Nathan Arnett & Ryan Bennett (eds.), *Proceedings of the 30th West Coast Conference on Formal Linguistics*, 292–302. Somerville: Cascadilla Proceedings Project.

Partee, Barbara H. & Mats Rooth. 1983. Generalized conjunction and type ambiguity. In Rainer Bäuerle, Christoph Schwarze & Arnim von Stechow (eds.), *Meaning, use and interpretation of language* (Grundlagen der Kommunikation und Kognition / Foundations of Communication and Cognition), 361–383. Berlin: De Gruyter.

Plank, Frans. 2003. Double articulation. In Frans Plank (ed.), *Noun phrase structure in the languages of Europe* (Empirical Approaches to Language Typology 20-7), 337–395. Mouton de Gruyter.

Rohena-Madrazo, Marcos. 2007. Superlative movement in Puerto Rican Spanish and General Spanish. *NYU Working Papers in Linguistics* 1. 1–32.

Sharvit, Yael & Penka Stateva. 2002. Superlative expressions, context, and focus. *Linguistics and Philosophy* 25(4). 453–505.

Solomon, Mike. 2011. Thoughts on Heim on superlatives. (New York: New York University. Manuscript).

Szabolcsi, Anna. 1986. Comparative superlatives. *MIT Working Papers in Linguistics* 8. 245–265.

Szabolcsi, Anna. 2012. Compositionality without word boundaries: *(the) more* and *(the) most. Proceedings of SALT* 22. 1–25.

Teleman, Ulf, Staffan Hellberg & Erik Andersson. 1999. *Svenska Akademiens Grammatik [The Swedish Academy Grammar]*. Stockholm: Svenska Akademien/Norstedts.

Teodorescu, Alexandra. 2007. Attributive superlatives in Romanian. In Gabriela Alboiu, Andrei Avram, Larissa Avram & Daniela Isac (eds.), *Pitar Mos: A building with a view. Papers in honor of Alexandra Cornilescu.* Bucharest: Editura Universitatii din Bucuresti.

Teodorescu, Alexandra. 2009. *Modification in the noun phrase: The syntax, semantics, and pragmatics of adjectives and superlatives.* Austin: University of Texas. (Doctoral dissertation).

Wellwood, Alexis. 2014. *Measuring predicates.* College Park: University of Maryland. (Doctoral dissertation).

Wilson, E. Cameron. 2016. Deriving the most internal reading. In Nadine Bade, Polina Berezovskaya & Anthea Schöler (eds.), *Proceedings of Sinn und Bedeutung 20*, 779–797. Semantics Archive. https://semanticsarchive.net/sub2015/BOOKLET_SuB_20.pdf.

Xiang, Ming. 2005. The degree argument and the definiteness effect. *Proceedings of NELS* 35. 647–662.

5

Is the weak definite a generic?
An experimental investigation

Thaís Maíra Machado de Sá
Universidade Federal de Minas Gerais

Greg N. Carlson
University of Rochester

Maria Luiza Cunha Lima
Universidade Federal de Minas Gerais

Michael K. Tanenhaus
University of Rochester
Nanjing Normal University

We discuss the properties of WEAK DEFINITE noun phrases, definite noun phrases (henceforth DP) which do not uniquely refer to an individual referent. Since one of the properties of generic noun phrases is that they do not uniquely refer, we asked whether weak definites might in fact be a form of generic noun phrase. We adopted a quantitative and experimental approach conducting a corpus analysis and four experiments that were designed to assess whether weak definites differ from DPs that are generic, weak and regular definites. A corpus analysis by de Sá et al. (2016) showed that generic DPs and weak definites are not in complementary distribution. A follow-up analysis on verb *aktionsart* showed that most weak definites appear in telic or activity DPs. The experiments also compared matched sentences with weak, regular and generic reading DPs. These studies do not find similarities between weak definites and generics. We conclude that weak definite noun phrases are not generics.

1 Introduction

Definite reference has played a central role in linguistics, the philosophy of language and in psycholinguistics (Russell 1905; Strawson 1950; Donnellan 1966; Clark & Marshall 1981; Heim 1982; Aguilar-Guevara & Zwarts 2013). Modulo some nuanced differences in the treatment of definite reference, there is general agreement that definite noun phrases carry a "familiarity", "uniqueness" or "identifiability" condition; the referent of a definite referring expression should be uniquely identifiable within a referential domain. In Example (1), *the hospital* denotes only one hospital in the world, being *unique*, and it is known by the interlocutors, being *familiar*.

(1)　*Workers picketed **the hospital** to protest layoffs.*

However, so-called *weak definite*[1] noun phrases (Carlson & Sussman 2005) such as *the hospital* in (2) violate uniqueness: the speaker does not need to have any specific hospital in mind when she utters *the hospital*. Moreover, John and Bill could even be going to different hospitals.

(2)　*John went to **the hospital** and so did Bill.*

It is also known that reference in definite noun phrases can be generic. In those cases, the definite noun has uniqueness of a kind, i.e. it denotes a kind, not an individual referent. *The hospital* in (3) is an example, because it does not have an unique individual referent, but a kind referent, *the hospital* is a kind of place.

(3)　*In the XVIII century, hygiene rules were introduced into **the hospital** in the Western world.*

For Aguilar-Guevara & Zwarts (2011: 193) weak and generic definites would be "different faces of a same phenomenon", because both of them would have the uniqueness of a kind property, denoting a kind. Indeed, if the lack of individual reference in weak definites can be reduced to the fact they are generic definites, it would be the most straightforward means of accounting for this lack of individual reference.

---

[1]Poesio (1994) was the first to use the name *weak definites*, questioning the Russellian uniqueness (1905) and Heim's familiarity (1982). He noted that in sentences like *John got these data from the student of a linguist* there is no need to have familiarity or characterize a single individual to *the student* in order to understand the sentence. He named this class of definites *weak definites*. Carlson & Sussman (2005) adopted the *weak definites* term, observing that weak definites lack uniqueness.

The current work does not directly address the specific analysis proposed by Aguilar-Guevara & Zwarts (2011). Instead we address the basic question of to what extent weak definites share the properties of generic noun phrases and regular noun phrases.

In this chapter, we employ empirical means to evaluate the hypothesis that definite generics and weak definites are the same phenomenon. We will examine corpus data form Brazilian Portuguese, and experimental data from English to evaluate this question.

We begin with a brief summary of the properties of weak definites.

2 Weak definites

The term *weak definite noun phrase* is used here to describe a certain kind of construction that Carlson and collaborators (Carlson & Sussman 2005; Carlson et al. 2006; 2013 and Klein et al. 2013) have been working on for some time under this designation. The contrasting class of definite noun phrases is called *regular definites* (sometimes "strong definites"), meaning that they trigger the familiarity/uniqueness presuppositions commonly focused in the literature on definite descriptions. The term *weak definite noun phrase(s)* is often elided to simply *weak definite(s)*, but we wish to be clear that we do not use this term in the present context to refer to just any noun phrase which, in a language differentiating "strong" vs. "weak" definite article forms, has the definite article in the "weak" form. When we wish to refer to the morphological forms of definite articles, we will do so explicitly.

Besides failing to trigger uniqueness presuppositions, these noun phrases, among other properties, must occur in construction with a specific verb or preposition, may only occur in the singular form or the plural form but not both, and are not subject to restrictive modification.[2] They appear to have the semantic truth-conditions of narrow-scope indefinites, and normally trigger semantically "enriching" implications – i.e. there is a non-compositional aspect to their meaning. Finally, the constructions appear to have a more "eventive" meaning than the corresponding compositional constructions, a matter we try to pin down a bit more precisely below.[3]

Our work was motivated in part by the incorporation hypotheses proposed by Carlson and colleagues. Weak definite noun phrases are treated as an incorpo-

---

[2] See Aguilar-Guevara (2014) for insight into the allowable modifiers.
[3] The constructions under consideration have a number of characteristics that are summarized in Carlson et al. (2006).

rated structure by Carlson et al. (2013) and Klein et al. (2013), in which the noun phrase and the verb have the semantics of an incorporated event in which the article, definite or indefinite, takes scope over the incorporated structure. This analysis unifies the observation that weak definites need not uniquely refer and the observation that they evoke habitual events associated with the noun. It also provides an explanation for the role of the definite article and makes the novel prediction that the same noun phrases that can have a weak definite interpretation can also appear in "weak indefinite" structures, which are incorporated structures that have properties more characteristic of an indefinite than a definite. Crucially this approach assumes that weak definites do not have the same properties as generic DP.

In an attempt to better understand the role of the definite article in the determined phrase and in the incorporated construction, we conducted a corpus analysis and a set of experiments that examined whether weak definites exhibit properties of generics (§3). Then, we report the results of four experiments (§4).

3 Corpus analysis

In order to observe if weak definites would pattern with generic definites, de Sá et al. (2016) analyzed data on a Brazilian Portuguese (BP) corpus. Four-hundred occurrences of 31 words, which may present the weak reading in BP (e.g. *the hospital*), were analyzed. They analyzed whether the word was determined by a definite article, and if so, whether the DP reading was weak (Carlson & Sussman 2005), strong – or regular – (Russell 1905), or generic (Carlson 2006). They then looked at the distribution of those three kinds of definites. As expected, the regular reading is significantly more frequent than the others, 45.6%, but surprisingly, according to the categorization criteria, the weak DPs occur significantly more often than the generic ones, 33.7% versus 27.5%.

The authors also described the DP's syntactic function – subject, object, adjunct – for occurrences of weak, regular and generic definites in the corpus analysis. The goal was to compare the distributional properties of weak definites, generic DPs and regular definites. They evaluated two hypotheses:

1. If weak definites are in fact generics, then generic DPs and weak definites should either occur in the same environments or be in complementary distribution with one another, indicating that they are variations of the same linguistic type.

2. The second hypothesis was motivated by an analysis that weak definites undergo semantic incorporation proposed by Carlson et al. (2013). The semantic incorporation hypothesis predicts that weak definites should occur primarily as the object of a verb or a preposition but rarely should occur in subject position.

They found that generics (Figure 1A) are more uniformly distributed between subject (25.1%) and object (20.3%), being adjuncts most frequently (54.6%). Regular definites showed the same overall pattern (Figure 1B), presenting a significant majority of adjuncts (43.7%), followed by objects (31.3%), and subjects (25%). Weak definites presented a different distribution in which they appear as adjuncts (45.7%) as often as objects (46.6%). Weak definites, however, seldom appear as subjects. Only 7.2% of the occurrences were as subjects, significantly less than the other categories (Figure 1C).

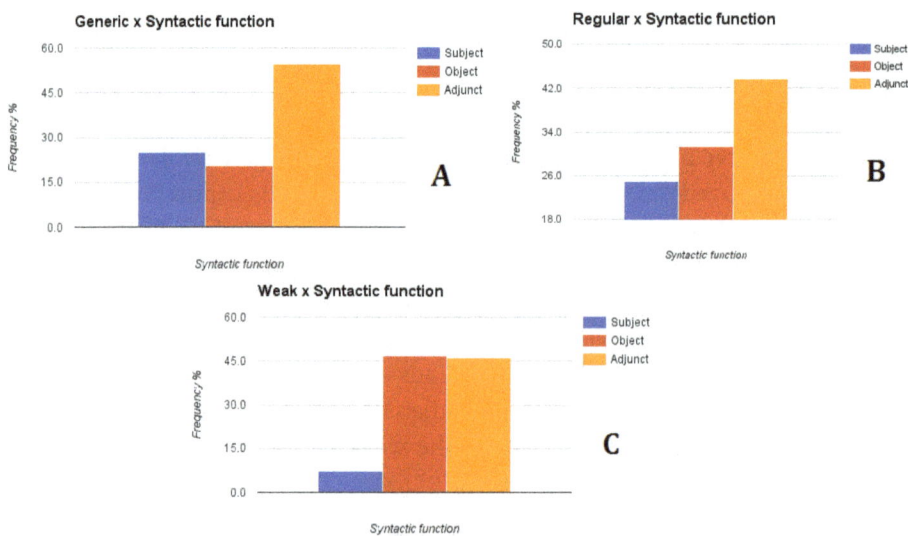

Figure 1: Definite types and syntatic function – Generic definites (A), Regular definites (B) and Weak definites (C) (de Sá et al. 2016: 114, 115)

The authors argued that the weak definites' high occurrence in adjunct and in object position could be interpreted as a reflex of an incorporation process, as proposed by Carlson et al. (2013) and Klein et al. (2013). But the fact that this kind of definite could also be found in subject position is a problem for the incorporation analysis. The data also did not point to a complementary distribution between weak and generic definites, which could be argued to provide support for the claim that they are the same phenomena.

3.1 Aktionsarten analysis

As a following analysis to the syntactic function analysis made by de Sá et al. (2016), we, with the same tagged corpus, used the verb to analyze the semantics of the clause in which the definite noun occurred. The verb aktionsarten[4] was the semantic property we focused on motivated by the incorporation analysis, which claims that weak definites are incorporated in event or activity verbs (Carlson et al. 2013).

Our hypothesis was that in aktionsart analyses, the semantic incorporation hypothesis predicts that weak definites (but not generic DPs) should primarily occur with activity and telic verbs, but not with state verbs. We also compared weak definites with generics, which are usually found in clauses with state verbs (Carlson 2006), to see if there is a complementary distribution between those categories.

For the same 2196 occurrences (of 31 words which could have generic, weak and regular readings)[5] from de Sá et al. (2016) we analyzed the lexical aspect of the verb for the clauses containing the definite expression.

The verbs were classified as *state*, *activity*, or *telic* (achievement and accomplishment), based on Vendler (1957). We classified as *state* verbs those that do not denote an action, for example the verb *ter* in BP, in the Example (4):[6] *tem* does not have a process which unfolds during time, it does not denote action and if we consider its thematic role, then the subject, *the school* is not an agent.

(4) Brazilian Portuguese
Além   do   atendimento pedagógico, a   escola **tem** responsabilidades
Beyond of+the service   pedagogical the school **has** responsibilities
sociais.
social

'The school has social responsibilities, which goes beyond the pedagogical service.'

---

[4]We analyzed Vendler (1957) aktionsarten's categories: state, activity and telic (achievement and accomplishment).

[5]Extracted from the *ptTenTen* corpus, in the platform *Sketch Engine*. See more information in de Sá et al. (2016).

[6]From here until the end of this section all the examples are from our data.

The *activity* verbs are actions which do not need a conclusion point, as the verb *nadar* in Example (5): *nadavam* is an action that unfolds during time, but it does not have a finishing point.

(5) Brazilian Portuguese
     *Os alunos **nadavam** todo dia na   escola.*
     The students **swam**   every day in+the school
     'The students swam every day in the school.'

We classified as *telic* the action verbs that needed a finishing point, as *quebrar*, in Example (6): *quebraram* is an action that requires a conclusion point.

(6) Brazilian Portuguese
     *Os vândalos **quebraram** a   escola durante a   festa.*
     The vandals **broke**   the school during the party
     'Vandals broke the school during the party.'

In addition to the notion of aktionsart proposed by Vendler (1957), we used the aspectual tests in Dowty (1979) to distinguish one category from another in our analysis. As the Dowty tests are proposed for English, we used a version proposed by Wachowicz & Foltran (2006) for Brazilian Portuguese.

3.1.1 Results

The results are summarized in Table 1 and Figure 2.

Table 1: Weak and generic definites and aktionsarten corpus occurrence (%)

Conditions	Aktionsarten	Corpus occurrence (%)
Generic	State	48.9
	Activity	37
	Telic	14.1
Weak	State	16.6
	Activity	55
	Telic	28.4

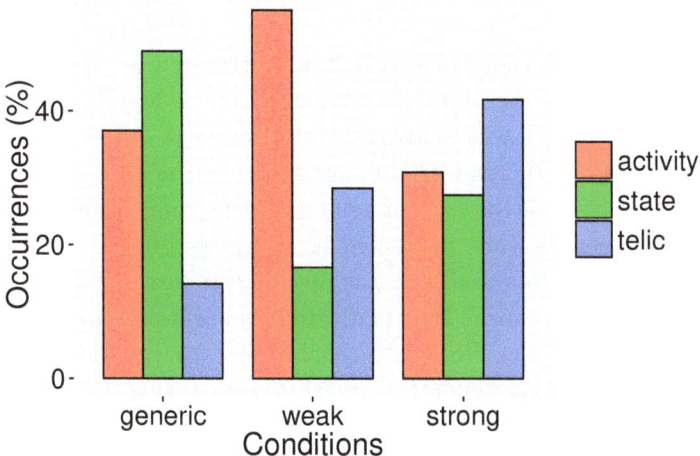

Figure 2: Aktionsarten occurrence percentage in Generic, Weak and Strong conditions

Weak definites showed a significant difference (χ^2 = 171.6676, df = 2, p < 0.001) among state, 16.6%, activity, 55%, and telics, 28.4%, with activity being the most frequent category. Generic definites also significantly differ (χ^2 = 85.2335, df = 2, p < 0.001) in occurrences of state, 48.9%, telic, 14.1%, and activity, 37%.

The aktionsarten analysis is consistent with the incorporation hypothesis, in that weak definites are more frequent as activity and telic verbs. Also, as expected, generics are more frequent as state verbs. One interesting finding is that weak and generic definites are not in a complementary distribution.

3.2 Corpus summary

The quantitative data presented in this corpus analysis introduces some interesting evidence about weak definites. Weak definites are more frequent than generic definites. Weak definites occur in subject position and they do so less frequently than in object or adjunct position. Another interesting fact about syntactic position is that there is no complementary distribution between weak and generic definites, which would have provided support for the generic hypothesis.

The analysis of lexical aspect again found no complementary distribution between weak and generic definites. Also, as expected by the incorporation hypothesis, the majority of weak definites occur in activity and telic clauses.

4 Experiments

We conducted four experiments in which we compared participant's production and comprehension for stimuli that were chosen to bias weak, regular and
generic readings. Our goal was to examine whether weak definites and generics
exhibited similar properties as would be predicted by the simple version of the
generic hypothesis. All of the experiments used the same materials, described
in §4.1. The experiments were conducted in American English, they were pro-
grammed in *JavaScript*, and used *Amazon Mechanical Turk*[7] by the software *Psi-
turk*.[8] We used the Mechanical Turk platform because it provides easy and fast
access to participants, data collection is reliable, and results are similar to those
obtained in laboratory-based experiments (cf. Mason & Suri 2012; Paolacci et al.
2010).

4.1 Materials

The experimental materials were 54 sentences divided in three groups containing
a noun phrase with a definite article which had: a clear generic reading (Example 7), a clear regular reading (Example 8) and a weak reading (Example 9):

(7)   *Henry Ford created **the bus** in his early years.*

(8)   *James crashed **the bus** during the night.*

(9)   *Linda took **the bus** to go to college.*

For all sentences, the target noun was presented in a definite noun phrase
which was an object of a telic verb or an activity verb. In our examples, *bus* is the
target word, it is preceded by *the*, a definite determiner *the bus*, in object position
of a telic verb, as *created, crashed, took*.

In Example (7) the sentence in the target DP has a prototypical generic reading,
in which *the bus* has a kind uniqueness (cf. Carlson & Pelletier 1995; Carlson
2006). In Example (8), the *the bus* has a unique referent in the sense of Russell
(1905). In Example (9), the DP supports a weak definite reading. The weak definite
sentences were modeled on examples from Carlson & Sussman (2005); Carlson
et al. (2006; 2013) and Klein et al. (2013).

---

[7]Access on: https://www.mturk.com/mturk/welcome
[8]Access on: https://psiturk.org/

The 54 sentences were divided into 3 lists of 18 sentences, each list with six exemplars of each type: regular, generic and weak. The same noun was never repeated within a list. The same noun appeared in a different condition in each list. Each participant was presented with one of the lists.

We briefly describe each of the four experiments in the following subsections.

4.2 Experiment 1: Judgment

The first experiment used a judgment task in which the participants judged whether the DP referred to either an individual or a category. We reasoned that regular definite noun phrases would be rated as referring to individuals whereas generics would be rated as referring to categories. Finding this pattern would provide important evidence that we had successfully created a set of materials with regular reference and a set with generic reference. The critical question was whether weak definites would pattern with the generics, as suggested by the generic hypothesis, or with regular definites. Participants read one sentence on each trial and judged if the bold word (the target word in one of the readings) was either a *CATEGORY* or a *INDIVIDUAL*, using a continuous scale, ranging from 0 to 100 with the words *INDIVIDUAL* and *CATEGORY* as the endpoints. Whether the first endpoint was individual or category was balanced within lists, as showed in the Figure 3.

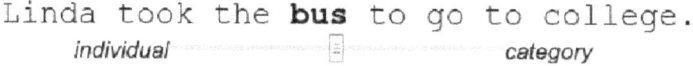

Linda took the **bus** to go to college.

Figure 3: Judgment task screen – Sentence with the word *bus* to be evaluated on a continuous scale (screenshot)

We expected that the noun with a regular reading would be judged as an *individual* while the generic would be evaluated as *category*. This pattern of results is necessary to validate the task. The generic hypothesis predicts that the weak definites should pattern with the generic definites, as we can see in Table 2.

Table 2: Judgment task – Hypothesis according to generic theory

Definite readings	Weak = Generic
Generic	*Category* judgment (uniqueness of a kind)
Regular	*Individual* judgment (uniqueness)
Weak	*Category* judgment (uniqueness of a kind)

4.2.1 Participants

90 workers (40 women) from MTurk (https://www.mturk.com/) participated for payment of US$0.30. All participants provided informed consent in this experiment and in all of the other experiments we report.

4.2.2 Results

We analyzed the data using a Linear mixed model fit by REML ['lmerMod']. Us-ing 0 as the individual endpoint and 100 as the category endpoint, regular defi-nites were rated as closest to individual endpoint (mean = 19.82), whereas gener-ics were rated as closest to the category endpoint (mean = 80.63). Weak definites were rated as closer to the individual endpoint (mean = 34.56). However, they fell between the regular and generics (Figure 4). Importantly, weak definites differed significantly from both the regular and generic noun phrases (Table 3).

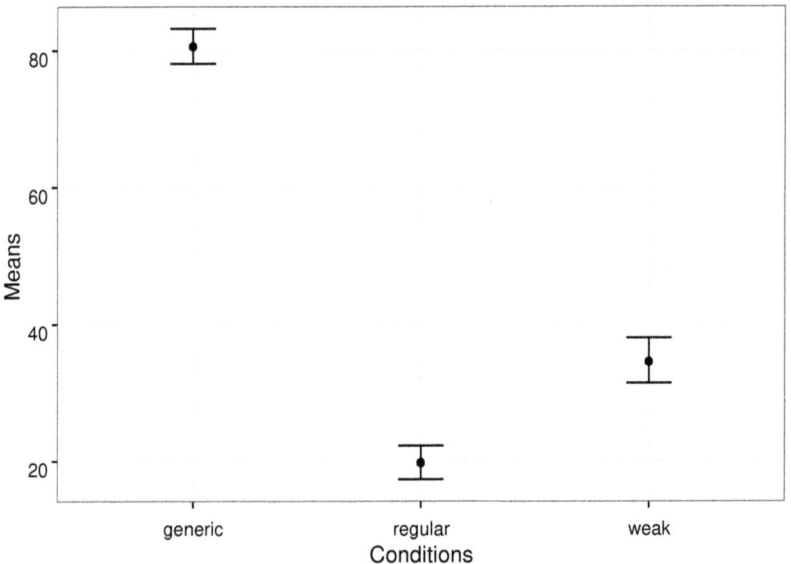

Figure 4: Judgment task – Judgment means (individual to category) by condition

Table 3: Judgment task – Statistics – Linear mixed model fit by REML ['lmerMod']

Formula:

`ScaledResponse ~ condition + (1 + condition | subject) + (1 | , item),`

Data:

`data, Control: lmerControl(optimizer = "bobyqa")`

	Estimate	Std. Error	t-value
(Intercept)	80.561	2.756	29.24
Regular condition	−60.719	4.501	−13.49
Weak condition	−46.133	4.134	−11.16

The results provide clear evidence that we successfully created two sets of sentences using the same nouns, that when used with a definite article in a DP, had a regular reading for one set and a generic reading for the second set. This serves as important validation for the materials. We also tested the prediction that if weak definites are, in fact, generics then they would show the same pat-tern. However, the sentences with weak definite noun phrases did not pattern with generic noun phrases and they were more similar to regular definite noun phrases than they were to generics. We note, however, because judgments of weak definites fell between the regular and the generics, one could argue that weak and generic definites are not different. One characteristic of noun phrases that have weak definite readings is that they can also be interpreted as regular definites. Therefore the results for the weak definites could, in principle, reflect a mix of regular and generic interpretations.

One way to assess the mixture possibility is to examine the distribution of responses to the three types of stimuli. If weak definites were a mix of regular and generics, we might expect to see a bimodal distribution, with an increased number of responses near the category endpoint. Figure 5 shows the distributions. Inspection of the patterns does not seem to support for the mixture hypothesis. Nonetheless this remains a possibility for results in which weak definites are intermediate between regulars and generics.

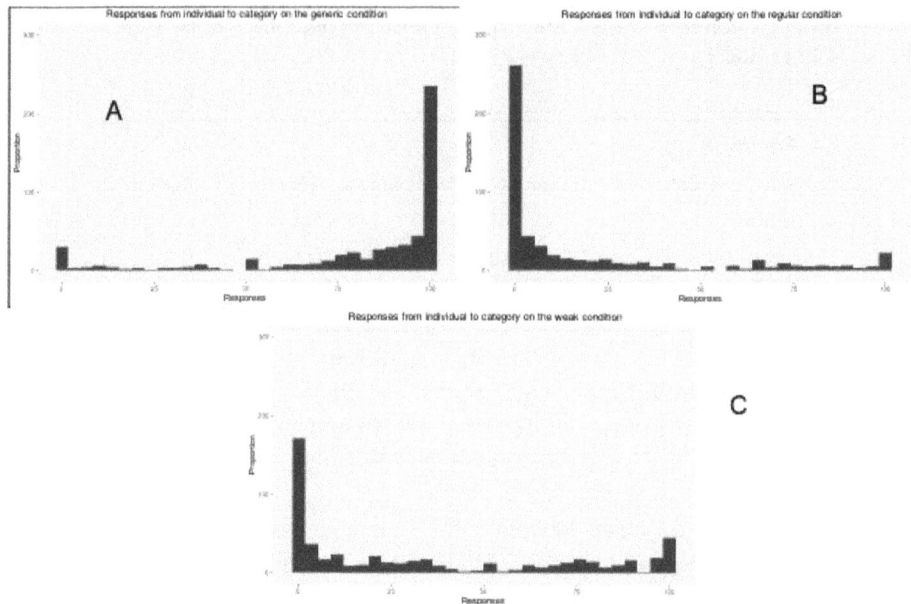

Figure 5: Judgment task – Condition histograms: (A) Generic distribution, (B) Regular distribution, (C) Weak distribution

4.3 Experiment 2: Forced choice

Our second experiment used a forced choice task, in which participants were presented with the same sentences as those use in the previous experiment. Participants were asked to choose between two possible noun phrases for a continuation sentence. One was a noun phrase that was anaphoric with the definite noun phrase in the preceding sentence (e.g. *That telephone...*). The other was a noun phrase that would introduce a new referent (e.g. *A telephone...*) (Figure 6).

Frank answers the telephone promptly.

A telephone...   That telephone...

Figure 6: Forced choice task screen

Our rationale was that regular definites would most likely be interpreted as referring to an individual, therefore licensing an anaphoric reference. In contrast the kind-reference supported by a generic would be more consistent with a continuation that introduced a novel referent. If weak definites are indeed a kind of generic, we would expect subjects to choose a new referent more often than the anaphoric continuation, i.e. weak definites would behave more like generic ones.

4.3.1 Participants

We again tested 90 workers (34 women) from MTurk for a payment of US$0.30, using the same lists as those created for Experiment 1.

4.3.2 Results

Figure 7 and Table 4 show the results. As we can observe, in sentences with the generic definite participants preferred a new referent (76.7%), while the regular reading showed the opposite preference, with 23.4% new referents. The weak definite did not pattern with the generic, participants chose a new referent only 42.9% (Table 5).

Results confirmed the expected pattern both for the clearly generic and regular expressions. Although the weak definites did not pattern with the generics, they showed fewer anaphoric choices than regular definites. This is not surprising because on the one hand, weak definites do not require a uniquely identifiable referent but, on the other hand, a weak definite noun phrase can easily be shifted to an interpretation with a uniquely identifiable referent.

Again however, one could argue that the results for weak definites could reflect a mix of generic and regular definites, In order to provide more nuanced evidence that did not require a meta-linguistic judgment with a binary choice, we conducted two production experiments.

4.4 Experiment 3: Free completion

In this experiment participants generated continuations for the sentences used in the previous experiments. No specific constraints were put on the form of the continuations except that participants should not use language that would upset their grandparents, as in Figure 8.

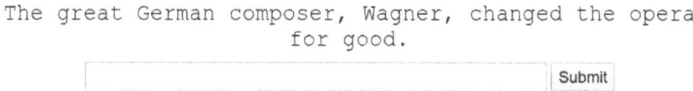

The great German composer, Wagner, changed the opera for good.

Figure 8: Free completion task screen

We analyzed the continuations to see if they repeated the definite expression. The logic of the analysis was based on the incorporation hypothesis by Carlson et al. (2013) and Klein et al. (2013). If weak definites are indeed part of incorporated structures, then the event would be more salient than an individual referent would be introduced by a regular definite noun phrase or a kind-reference as introduced by a generic.

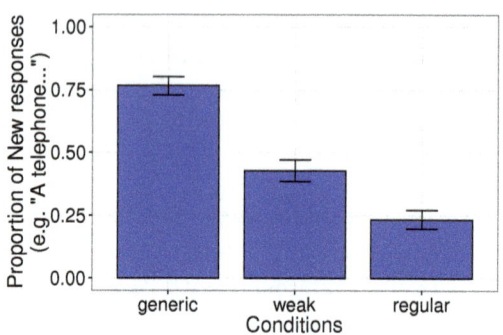

Figure 7: Forced choice task – Proportion of NEW by condition

Table 4: Forced choice task – Proportion of NEW and OLD by condition

Conditions	New (*A X...*)	Old (*That X...*)
Generic	0.767	0.233
Regular	0.234	0.767
Weak	0.429	0.571

Table 5: Forced choice task – Generalized linear mixed model fit by maximum likelihood (Laplace approximation) ['glmerMod']

Family:

```
binomial, ( logit )
```

Formula:

```
choice == "New" ~ condition + (1 + condition | subject) + (1 |,item),
```

Control:

```
glmerControl(optimizer = "bobyqa")
```

	Estimate	Std. Error	z-value	Pr(>|z|)	
(Intercept)	1.4719	0.2118	6.949	3.67×10^{-12}	***
Regular condition	−3.3248	0.3485	−9.540	$<2 \times 10^{-16}$	***
Weak condition	−1.9284	0.3130	−6.162	7.18×10^{-10}	***

4.4.1 Participants

90 workers (55 men) from MTurk participated for the payment of US$3.00.

4.4.2 Results

The frequency of repetition of the target word (e.g. *opera*) by condition was evaluated. The continuation in (10) is an example[9] of a situation which there was no target word repetition; the experimental sentence had the target word *opera* that was not used in the completion.

(10)   Experimental sentence: *The great German composer, Wagner, changed the opera for good.*
        Completion: *He was a beautiful person.*

We considered as repetition occurrences in which the target word was repeated in a pronoun form, as a DP (any kind of determiner + target word) or as a bare noun (only the target word, on in either plural or singular form). In Example (11), the repetition by a pronoun form (i.e. *it*) can be observed. In Example (12), the DP repetition occurred (i.e. *the opera*). The last example, (13), shows bare noun repetition (i.e. *operas*).

(11)   Experimental sentence: *The great German composer Wagner changed the opera for good.*
        Completion: *It is now much better then before.*

(12)   Experimental sentence: *The great German composer Wagner changed the opera for good.*
        Completion: *The opera is still a noble entertainment today.*

(13)   Experimental Sentence: *The great German composer Wagner changed the opera for good.*
        Completion: *Many later operas incorporated his changes.*

Table 6 and Figure 9 show that our hypothesis was confirmed, the weak definite was significantly less repeated (see Table 7 for stats) than the other definite conditions.

---

[9] All the following examples are from data.

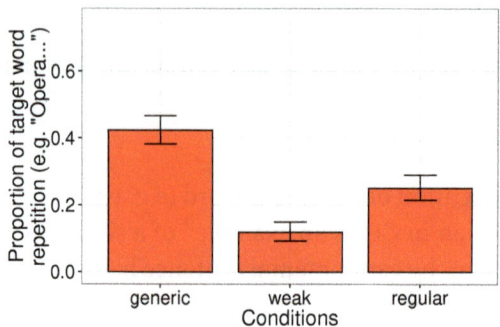

Figure 9: Free completion task – Proportion of target word repetition by condition

Table 6: Free completion task – Proportion of target word repetition (YES) and no-repetition (NO) by condition

Condition	NO	YES
Generic	0.576	0.424
Regular	0.750	0.250
Weak	0.881	0.119

Table 7: Free completion task – Generalized linear mixed model fit by maximum likelihood (Laplace Approximation) ['glmerMod']

Family:

```
binomial, ( logit )
```

Formula:

```
twr == "y" ~ condition + (1 | subject) + (1 |,item)
```

Data:

```
datac
```

Control:

```
glmerControl(optimizer = "bobyqa")
```

	Estimate	Std. Error	z-value	P(>|z|)	
(Intercept)	−2.3662	0.2654	−8.915	$<2 \quad \times 10^{-16}$	***
Weak condition	1.9978	0.3454	5.785	7.27×10^{-9}	***
Regular condition	1.0323	0.3487	2.960	0.00308	**

The results showed that the definite noun was more likely to be repeated in a continuation for the generic and regular sentences compared to sentences with weak interpretations. Unlike the previous studies where the weak definites fall somewhere between regular definites, the regular and generics were similar to one another with the weak definites showing the fewest repetitions.

Moreover, when participants chose continuations with repetitions they tended to use different morphosyntactic forms and they made different semantic choices. As we can see in the occurrence examples below, (14–16), the experimental sentence has its target word in the generic condition in which *opera* is a kind. When the subjects repeated *opera*, they used three different morphosyntactic forms, but they kept the kind reading.

(14)   Experimental sentence: *The great German composer Wagner changed the opera for good.*
       Completion: **It** *is now much better then before.*

(15)   Experimental sentence: *The great German composer Wagner changed the opera for good.*
       Completion: **The opera** *is still a noble entertainment today.*

(16)   Experimental sentence: The great German composer Wagner changed the opera for good.
       Completion: *Many later* **operas** *incorporated his changes.*

The morphosyntactic choices for generics was interesting, especially the use of bare noun forms, which have a generic reading. The final experiment used a forced completion task to investigate the forms that repetition would take.

4.5 Experiment 4: Forced completion

Another group of participants was asked to generate completions. In contrast to Experiment 3, participants were instructed to repeat the bolded noun used in the first sentence. However, they were not given any instructions about the form of the repetition.

The determiner choice (bare, definite, pronoun) was analyzed. We expected that, if in the first sentence there was a generic definite expression, then participants would be more likely to use the noun in a bare plural expression compared to a regular definite. Taken as a whole, the pattern of results from the previous experiments would suggest that weak definites would show similar patterns as regular definites, with minimal use of bare nouns.

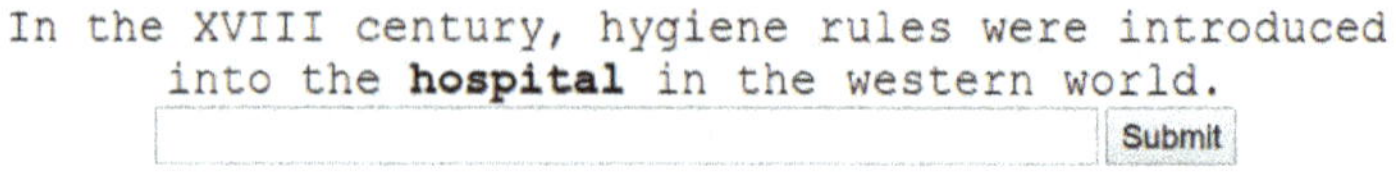

In the XVIII century, hygiene rules were introduced into the **hospital** in the western world.
[   ] Submit

Figure 10: Forced completion task screen

4.5.1 Participants

30 workers (16 men) from MTurk participated for the payment of US$3.00.

4.5.2 Results

In all conditions the definite article + noun ("dp" in Figure 11) was the most used form of repetition, as expected, both because the definite expression was used in the first sentence and because it is by most frequent kind of nominal phrase. However, bare plurals were sometimes used, but only in the generic condition ("bp" in Figure 11). In fact it was the the second most preferred repetition form for the continuations following generic sentences. Crucially bare plurals were never used in continuations that followed weak definites.

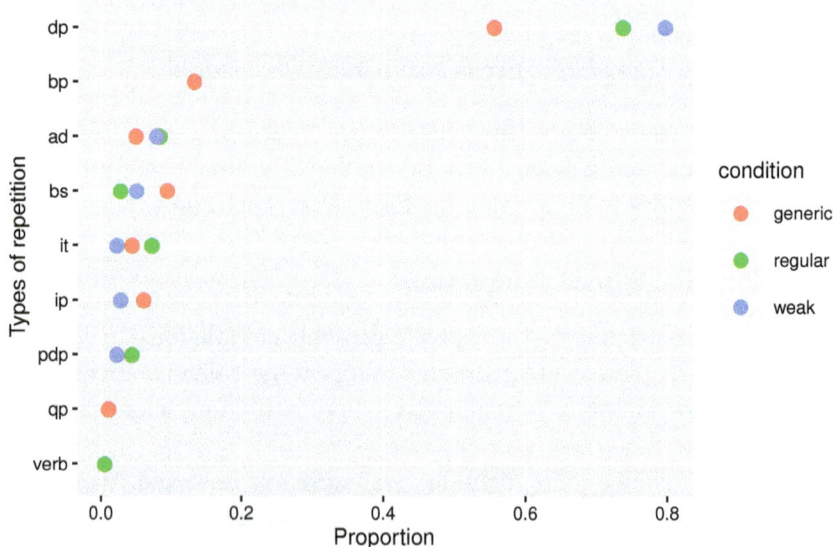

Figure 11: Forced completion – Types of repetition by condition

Below there are some completions and examples of some different morphological forms of repetition founded in our data. Example (17) is a "dp" (the+noun) occurrence; example (18) a "bp" (bare plural noun); example (19) an "ad" (noun transformed into an adjective); example (20) a "verb" (noun transformed into verb).

(17)   Experimental sentence: *In the XVIII century hygiene rules were introduced into the hospital in the Western world.*
       Completion: ***The hospital*** *was now a clean place.*

(18)   Experimental sentence: *In the XVIII century hygiene rules were introduced into the hospital in the Western world.*
       Completion: ***Hospitals*** *had never understood the importance of cleanliness.*

(19)   Experimental sentence: *In the XVIII century hygiene rules were introduced into the hospital in the Western world.*
       Completion: *The* ***hospital*** *industry is now one of the largest in the world.*

(20)   Experimental sentence: *In Medieval times merchants used the bank to deposit their credit.*
       Completion: *Merchants did a lot of* ***banking*** *and made money.*

Also in our data was the "bs" (bare noun singular), as Example (21); the pronoun (*it*), Example (22); the "ip" (noun determined by an indefinite article), Example (23); the "pdp" (noun determined by a pronoun), Example (24); the "qdp" (noun determined by a quantifier), Example (25).

(21)   Experimental sentence: *Most songwriters use the guitar when writing songs.*
       Completion: ***Guitar*** *is the perfect instrument to work out music.*

(22)   Experimental sentence: *Samuel sold the guitar last year.*[10]
       Completion: *He didn't want to sell* ***it*** *because it was his favorite guitar but he needed the money.*

---

[10] *Samuel vendeu a guitarra no ano passado.*

(23)   Experimental sentence: *Jimi Hendrix played the guitar better than anyone else.*
       Completion: *Nowadays **a guitar** that was played by him is worth very much.*

(24)   Experimental sentence: *Zack listens to the radio while he drives.*
       Completion: *His car **radio** is an aftermarket system.*

(25)   Experimental sentence: *In the XVIII century hygiene rules were introduced into the hospital in the Western world.*
       Completion: ***Every hospital** since then uses the same rules.*

The morphosyntactic repetition form was another interesting finding which distinguishes weak and generic definites. Bare plural nouns only happened in generic condition, behaving differently from weak definites once again.

4.6 Summary of experimental findings

In sum, we created a set of materials in which we would compare the properties of weak regular and generic sentences with object DP. Experiment 1 established that the regular and generic sentences showed the expected properties with regulars being judged as being about an individual and the generics as about a category. The weak definites behaved more similarly to the regular definites than the generics. In Experiment 2 we found that, as expected, regular definites licensed anaphoric completions, whereas generics encouraged interpretations that introduced new events. Again weak definites behaved more similarly to regulars compared to generics. Experiment 3 found similar results in a free completion task. Finally, Experiment 4 required participants to repeat the noun phrase in their completions, the distribution of the completions, suggested that generics behaved differently from both regular and weak definites.

5 Conclusions

In this chapter we presented new data from a corpus analysis and a set of experimental studies that examined properties of weak definites, regular definites and generics. The goal of this work was to provide additional evidence that could be used to evaluate the hypothesis that weak definite noun phrases are in fact generic DP.

In a corpus analysis we found that weak definites and generics are not in complementary distribution in either the syntactic environments in which they appear on the semantic types of events as indexed by the verb. Moreover, as predicted by the incorporation analysis, the majority of weak definites occurred in activity and telic clauses, while generic definites occurred more frequently in state and activity clauses. In a set of experiments we first created and validated properties of regular, generic and weak definites. We found that for the most part, weak definites behaved more like regular definites than generics. We also evaluated the possibility that the behavior of weak definites could be accounted for by the hypothesis that the behavior of weak definites reflected a mix of trials in which the weak definite was given a regular definite interpretation and trials in which it was given a generic interpretation. This type of model was, however, inconsistent with the results of several of the experiments. In sum, then, we found little evidence to support the hypotheses that weak definites showed similar properties to generics.

Our results are consistent with the incorporation hypothesis in that it assumes that the non-uniqueness of reference in weak definites does not arise because it is a form of generic. Therefore it would have been problematic for the incorporation hypothesis if weak definites had, in fact, patterned with generics in our studies. Further research will be necessary to determine whether the absence of generic-like behavior in these studies would be consistent with the type of analysis argued for in Aguilar-Guevara (2014), which accounts for non-uniqueness by assuming that weak definites derive their non-uniqueness of individual reference by virtue of their generic status and their eventive properties by virtue of the KLR rules, described in detail in Aguilar-Guevara (2014). Addressing these issues is beyond the scope of the current chapter.

Although the results we presented and the linguistic phenomena that we discussed lead us to conclude that the semantic incorporation hypothesis provides an account of the behavior of weak definites without assuming that they are generics, it is important to conclude with some caveats. First in the corpus analysis weak definites frequently appeared in subject position, which is unexpected in the incorporation analysis. Secondly, the conclusions from our experiments bring evidence to bear on the two analyses only insofar as we have been able to tap into the relevant referential behavior with our tasks. Third, there are properties of weak definites, in particular the parallel about restrictions on modifiers for weak definites and generics, that receive a straightforward account on the generic analysis developed by Aguilar-Guevara (2014), but require additional work to be explained by the incorporation analysis. Fourth, the arguments for the role of the definite article depend on the scoping analysis we presented, which has some precedents in the literature but is not addressed in these empirical studies. If this analysis proves problematic, it will be important to explore other alternatives. Finally, we want to emphasize a point that has emerged from the work that the authors have conducted in collaboration with each other and with other colleagues. For a phenomenon such as weak definites which involve subtle interactions between putative structures and conceptual representations, and for which the linguistic data is less than definitive, experimental studies that target particular hypotheses can prove to be an important complement to linguistic argumentation.

Acknowledgements

This research was partially supported by NIH sentence processing grant, NIH grant HD 27206.

Abbreviations

BP	Brazilian Portuguese	bs	bare singular noun
bp	bare plural noun	it	pronoun *it*
DP	Definite Phrase	ip	indefinite article (*a*/*an*) + noun
dp	definite article (*the*) + noun	pdp	noun determined by a pronoun
ad	noun transformed into an adjective	qp	noun determined by a quantifier
		verb	noun transformed into a verb

References

Aguilar-Guevara, Ana. 2014. *Weak definites: Semantics, lexicon and pragmatics* (LOT Dissertation Series 360). Utrecht: LOT.

Aguilar-Guevara, Ana & Joost Zwarts. 2011. Weak definites and reference to kinds. *Proceedings of SALT* 20. 179–196.

Aguilar-Guevara, Ana & Joost Zwarts. 2013. Weak definites refer to kinds. *Recherches linguistiques de Vincennes* 42. 33–60.

Carlson, Greg N. 2006. Generic reference. In Keith Brown (ed.), *Encyclopedia of language & linguistics*, 2nd edn., 14–18. Amsterdam: Elsevier.

Carlson, Greg N., Natalie M. Klein, Whitney Gegg-Harrison & Michael K. Tanenhaus. 2013. Weak definites as a form of definiteness: Experimental investigations. *Recherches linguistiques de Vincennes* 42. 11–32.

Carlson, Greg N. & Francis Jeffry Pelletier (eds.). 1995. *The generic book*. Chicago: University of Chicago Press.

Carlson, Greg N. & Rachel Shirley Sussman. 2005. Seemingly indefinite definites. In Stephan Kepser & Marga Reis (eds.), *Linguistic evidence: Empirical, theoretical and computational perspectives* (Studies in Generative Grammar 85), 71–86. Berlin: Mouton de Gruyter.

Carlson, Greg N., Rachel Shirley Sussman, Natalie M. Klein & Michael K. Tanenhaus. 2006. Weak definite noun phrases. *Proceedings of NELS* 36(1). 179–196.

Clark, Herbert H. & Catherine K. Marshall. 1981. Definite reference and mutual knowledge. In Aravind K. Joshi, Bonnie L. Webber & Ivan A. Sag (eds.), *Elements of discourse understanding*, 10–63. Cambridge: Cambridge University Press.

de Sá, Thaís Maíra Machado, Maria Emília Saramago & Maria Luiza Cunha Lima. 2016. A corpus data of weak definites in Brazilian Portuguese. *Revista da ABRALIN* 15(1). 101–120.

Donnellan, Keith. 1966. Reference and definite descriptions. *The Philosophical Review* 75(3). 281–304.

Dowty, David R. 1979. *Word meaning and Montague grammar: The semantics of verbs and times in generative semantics and in Montague's PTQ*. Boston: Reidel.

Heim, Irene. 1982. *The semantics of definite and indefinite noun phrases*. Amherst: University of Massachusetts. (Doctoral dissertation).

Klein, Natalie M., Whitney Gegg-Harrison, Greg N. Carlson & Michael K. Tanenhaus. 2013. Experimental investigations of weak definite and weak indefinite noun phrases. *Cognition* 128(2). 187–213.

Mason, Winter & Siddharth Suri. 2012. Conducting behavioral research on Amazon's Mechanical Turk. *Behav Res Methods* 44(1). 1–23.

Paolacci, Gabriele, Jesse Chandler & Panagiotis G. Ipeirotis. 2010. Running experiments on Amazon Mechanical Turk. *Judgment and Decision Making* 5(5). 411–419.

Poesio, Massimo. 1994. Weak definites. *Proceedings of SALT* 4. 282–299.

Russell, Bertrand. 1905. On denoting. *Mind* 14(56). 479–493.

Strawson, Peter F. 1950. On referring. *Mind* 59(235). 320–344.

Vendler, Zeno. 1957. Verbs and times. *The Philosophical Review* 66(2). 143–160.

Wachowicz, Teresa Cristina & Maria José Foltran. 2006. Sobre a noção de aspecto. *Cadernos de Estudos Llingüísticos* 48(2). 211–232.

6

Definiteness in Russian bare nominal kinds

Olga Borik
Universidad Nacional de Educación a Distancia

M.-Teresa Espinal
Universitat Autònoma de Barcelona

In the literature on generic nominal reference, it is usually pointed out that in Russian, both singular and plural nominal expressions can have a generic reference (Chierchia 1998; Doron 2003; Dayal 2004). The main contribution of this article is to propose an explicit analysis for composing definite kinds from bare nominals in this language. We provide independent empirical support for the definiteness of apparent bare nominals in argument position of kind-level predicates and argue that definiteness is to be associated with a null D(eterminer), interpreted as the iota operator. The general hypothesis we defend is that definite kinds, even in a language without articles such as Russian, encode definiteness semantically and syntactically.

1 Introduction

In the literature on generic nominal reference it is usually pointed out that in Russian, a language without articles, both bare singular and bare plural nominal expressions can have a generic reference (Chierchia 1998; Doron 2003; Dayal 2004). This is exemplified in (1), where nouns specified morphologically for singular (1a) and for plural (1b) occur in argument position of a k(ind)-level predicate.[1]

---

[1]In this paper, we assume a three-way classification of verbal predicates into k(ind)-level, i(ndividual)-level and s(tage)-level (Carlson 1977). While k-level predicates appear to form a scarce but stable class, it is well known that the division line between i- and s-level predi-

In this context both *panda* and *pandy* can be said to refer to kinds.

(1) a. *Panda*   *naxoditsja na grani isčeznovenija.*
         panda.NOM.SG is.found   on verge extinction.GEN

     b. *Pandy*   *naxodjatsja na grani isčeznovenija.*
         panda.NOM.PL are.found   on verge extinction.GEN

A common background assumption considers plural generics as more natural and preferable, so in a significant part of literature on genericity it is taken for granted that plurals (bare plurals in English) constitute the "default" way to refer to kinds.[2] Setting aside the question of what is the "default" way to express genericity in the nominal domain in Russian, we simply point out that, given that (1a) is grammatical and natural, an analysis of it is needed in the theory of grammar in any case.

In contrast to Russian, in a language with overt determiners, English for instance, the subject of a sentence corresponding to (1a) will be expressed by means of a definite generic (Carlson 1977) or the singular generic (Chierchia 1998) *the N* construction (i.e. *the panda*), as in (2a). On the other hand, English also allows bare plurals to refer to kinds, as illustrated in (2b).

(2) a. *The panda is on the verge of extinction.*

     b. *Pandas are on the verge of extinction.*

The correspondence between the so-called English definite generic and the Russian bare nominal with a kind reference interpretation in (1a) is usually assumed to hold merely on the basis of their singular number morphology (cf. Dayal 2004), so a reasonable expectation is that the analysis assumed for definite generics in English can also be extended to the corresponding Russian cases. This approach has to address at least the following issue. Any analysis of the English definite generic includes the iota operator (ι) in the semantic represen-

---

cates is not clearly marked. For instance, *fly* in (i.a) denotes an i-level property while in (i.b) it functions as an s-level predicate:

(i) a. *Hummingbirds fly backwards.*

     b. *Hummingbirds are flying over the lake.*

[2]See Ionin et al. (2011) for an experimental investigation on the expression of genericity in English, Spanish and Brazilian Portuguese.

tation (cf. Chierchia 1998, Dayal 2004), which is quite indisputable for English, given that these expressions appear with a definite article.[3]

More generally, a number of questions arise with respect to (2) if we take into account some cross-linguistic data. In Spanish, for instance, bare plurals do not have a generic reading (Laca 1990; Dobrovie-Sorin & Laca 1996; 2003), making them different from bare plurals in English (e.g. 2b), which are considered to be the genuine expression of kind reference in that language (Longobardi 1994; 2001; 2005; Chierchia 1998; Dayal 2004, i.a.). By contrast, the default way to refer to kinds in Spanish is by means of a (non-plural) common noun preceded by a definite article (Borik & Espinal 2015). The question is then how to derive a kind reference for languages like Spanish and English keeping in mind these crucial differences concerning the interpretation of bare plurals. A look at languages like Russian makes the issue even more complex: Russian, does not have any articles but clearly possesses the means to make reference to kinds, as shown in (1). Does this mean that the same type of analysis as for English and Spanish could or should be extended to Russian despite the observed superficial differences in the syntax of nominal phrases?[4]

This paper aims at contributing to an understanding of kind expressions of the type exemplified in (1a). We provide independent empirical support for the definiteness of the subject in (1a), and argue that it is to be associated with a null D(eterminer), interpreted as ι. We postulate the structure in (3a) for definite kind arguments in languages with and without articles (e.g. Germanic, Romance, Slavic), the meaning of which is represented in (3b).

(3)   a. $[_{DP}D[_{NP}N]]$

   b. $[\![\text{Def N}]\!] = \iota x^k[P(x^k)]$

   where P corresponds to the descriptive content of a noun N, and $x^k \in K$ (i.e. the domain of kinds)

Although we do not deal with plural kind expressions exemplified in (1b) in this paper, we would like to point out that they do not constitute a counterexample to our analysis for (1a). We assume that a different syntactic and semantic

---

[3] Although see Coppock & Beaver (2015), who argue that definiteness as encoded by the definite article must be distinguished from determinacy, which consists in denoting an individual. Should this claim also be adopted for Russian, it would need an independent motivation, since Russian does not overtly express definiteness.

[4] See also Cyrino & Espinal (2015) for an analysis of definite kinds and definite plural generics within the NP/DP debate in Brazilian Portuguese, a language that allows the omission of the article in all argument positions.

composition is to be associated with the generic (bare) plural in (1b). In particular, the analysis proposed in (Chierchia 1998), in which plural kind nominals are semantically derived by the down operator $\cap$ that applies to plural properties, could be adopted to account for plural generics in Russian. Our hypothesis (which we will not defend or justify further in this paper) with respect to plural kind nominals in Russian is, therefore, that these expressions are, indeed, derived from pluralities and are specified for Number, namely, for plural. Their structural representation would then look like in (4).

(4) $\cap[_{\text{NumP}}\text{Num}_{+pl}[_{\text{NP}}\text{N}]]$

The differences between (3a), the structure that we adopt for definite kinds, and (4), the structure that we would hypothesize for generic plurals, are obvious. First of all, definite kinds are syntactically and semantically definite and hence are structurally represented as full DPs, whereas there is no a priori evidence to suggest that the same holds for generic plurals.[5] Secondly, only in the structure for generic plurals Number is present.[6] We will not deal specifically with the syntax and semantics for Number in this paper, but in general, we assume that definite kinds are syntactically and semantically numberless, at least in those languages where nominals inflect for number (see Borik & Espinal 2015 for details).

The paper is organized as follows. §2 presents the theoretical framework that constitutes the basis for our analysis. We will introduce the fundamental theoretical claims regarding the composition of definite kinds, focusing, in turn, on the meaning of Ns (properties of kinds) and the meaning of the definite article (ι). In §3 we will present our analysis of definite kinds in Russian. With this aim in mind we will provide both semantic arguments for definiteness and syntactic arguments for a DP structure with a null D (translated as ι). This section will close with an account of modified definite kinds. §4 will conclude the paper.

---

[5] This matter, however, deserves a full and thorough investigation, which falls outside the scope of this paper.

[6] We differentiate between morphophonological number, on the one hand, and syntactic Number, which is always interpreted semantically, on the other. In Russian, any nominal expression is marked for number and case and these two specifications come as a cluster. In other words, it is impossible to determine which part of a cluster encodes number and which part encodes case, which is a standard feature of a language with synthetic morphology. We assume that this cluster does not necessarily correspond to a syntactic Number projection, which has to have a semantic effect, and yield either a singular or a plural interpretation for a nominal phrase (cf. Ionin & Matushansky 2006; Pereltsvaig 2013 for similar claims).

2 Theoretical background

In this section we will briefly summarize the theoretical assumptions or postulates underlying our account of definite kinds in natural languages.

We assume that definite kinds express D-genericity (cf. Krifka et al. 1995) and argue that they are composed by applying ι, which is encoded by the definite article, to the denotation of a common noun, which denotes properties of kinds. This proposal is conceived as a universal principle, no matter whether the languages considered have overt articles (such as English) or not (such as Russian).

We start this section by discussing the meaning of common nouns. We argue that they denote properties of kinds (Espinal & McNally 2007a,b; Dobrovie-Sorin & Pires de Oliveira 2008; Espinal 2010; Espinal & McNally 2011). Next, we discuss the meaning of the definite article, conceived as a maximality operator (Sharvy 1980), and the composition of a definite kind reading.

2.1 Theoretical postulate 1: Root common nouns denote properties of kinds

Kind reference in natural language is quite often assumed to be a special type of reference contrasted with the reference to objects. In other words, if objects are standard entities of the semantic ontology, so are kinds. This theoretical hypothesis can be traced back to at least Carlson (1977), who distinguished between three types of entities relevant for natural language semantics: kinds, that is, the denotation of *the panda* and *pandas* in (2); objects, that is, the denotation of proper names and common noun phrases; and stages, i.e. the denotation of the last type of nominal expressions in combination with stage-level predicates. Kinds and objects, in Carlson's typology, are abstract entities and together they form a class of "individuals", whereas stages are concrete spatio-temporal realizations of abstract entities.

In less fine-grained classifications of entities, only two types are recognized: kinds and objects (cf. Zamparelli 1995).[7] This is the ontology assumed here as well: we distinguish between kinds, or abstract entities, and objects, or particular entities, although we do not agree with Carlson (1977), Zamparelli (1995), and many others after them, for whom the denotation of a common noun is a kind entity.

---

[7]In a different terminological tradition (e.g. Vergnaud & Zubizarreta 1992) this distinction corresponds to types vs. tokens.

Under a different approach it is claimed in the semantic literature that common nouns denote properties, rather than entities (Chierchia 1984; 1998; Partee 1986 among many others), that is, common nouns are lexical predicates.

In this paper, we adopt a third alternative and postulate that common nouns denote properties of kinds.[8] This alternative has been empirically motivated in a number of recent proposals, including Dobrovie-Sorin & Pires de Oliveira's (2008) work on bare nouns in Brazilian Portuguese, McNally & Boleda's (2004) analysis of relational adjectives, and Espinal's (2010) and Espinal & McNally's (2007b; 2011) semantic description of the meaning of bare nouns in object position in Catalan and Spanish. The arguments supporting the hypothesis that common nouns denote descriptions of kinds are based on pronominalization, number neutral interpretation and adjective modification. The reasoning is the following:

(i) A common noun (a real bare nominal) cannot be taken to refer to individual object-entities because the anaphoric pronoun that it licenses (in some Romance languages) is not compatible with an object/token interpretation (cf. the difference between Catalan *en* lit. 'one', referring to properties, and *el/la/els/les* lit. 3RD.ACC.SG/PL.MASC/FEM 'it/them'); if it cannot denote an entity, it must denote a property.

(ii) If a common noun has a property denotation, it has no inherent number information, and therefore it has a number neutral interpretation (i.e. it is compatible with atomicity and non-atomicity entailments, Farkas & de Swart 2003); by contrast, nouns specified syntactically for Number refer either to atomic or non-atomic sums.

(iii) If a common noun had an individual property denotation, it would be expected to easily combine with any kind of modifier, but this is not the case. Bare nouns in syntactic positions that allow bare nominals (e.g. in object position of a restricted class of predicates (Espinal & McNally 2007b; 2011) and in predicate position of copular sentences (de Swart et al. 2007; Zamparelli 2008)) can only combine with classifying adjectives, and this restriction can be explained only if both expressions are taken to denote properties of kinds or if the appropriate adjectives are kind modifiers.

We thus conclude that it is highly plausible to assume the denotation of a common noun to be a property of a kind.[9]

---

[8]We adopt this hypothesis for all types of nouns, i.e. count, mass and abstract nouns.

[9]This view should be contrasted with those in which the interpretation of a nominal root is equivalent to that of a mass noun (Borer 2005; Rothstein 2010), and with those that derive taxonomic kinds in the lexicon by a direct application of the MASS operation to a N_{root} (Pires de Oliveira & Rothstein 2011; Trugman 2013).

Now, what precisely does it mean to say that common nouns denote properties of kinds? We assume that there are two domains in our semantic ontology, the domain of objects and the domain of kinds. Under a standard view, the denotation of the predicate with the descriptive content P is the set of objects that share property P. Thus, the denotation of the noun *boy* in the domain of objects is a set of objects that have the boy-property. Note, however, that in our world some nouns can denote singleton sets (e.g. *sun* or *moon*). Without challenging the process described above, we propose that instead of the domain of objects, common nouns range over kinds, conceived as integral entities. Thus, the same noun *boy* in our proposal looks for entities that share a boy-property but in the domain of kinds rather than objects.

In accordance with what we have just said the meaning of a common noun should have the logical representation in (5), where P stands for a property corresponding to the descriptive content of N, and x^k a kind entity, such that the property P applies to x^k.

(5) $[\![N]\!] = \lambda x^k[P(x^k)]$

Having given a formal definition of the denotation of a common noun, we will now briefly clarify our more general assumptions about kinds, although we do not pretend to give a full justified answer to the question of what type of entities kinds essentially are. Following Borik & Espinal (2015), we adopt the claim that kinds are not sets of subkinds, but are instead perceived as integral, undivided entities with no internal structure, which means that kinds do not form part of a standard quantificational domain for individuals represented by a lattice structure (Link 1983). We also share the view of Mueller-Reichau (2011), according to whom kinds are, in essence, abstract sortal concepts. Sortal concepts are mental representations that are used to "categorize and individuate objects" (Mueller-Reichau 2011: 21). Thus, kinds are entities, but their (mental) representations are obtained by abstraction over a number of individual objects that share certain relevant properties. This, however, does not necessarily mean that linguistically, a kind should necessarily be construed as a set of representative objects, although conceptually it might be the case.

2.2 Theoretical postulate 2: The definite article corresponds to ι and expresses maximality

In Partee (1986), it is proposed that definite noun phrases are generated by a type shifting operator that maps a singleton property $\langle e, t \rangle$ onto an individual denotation of type $\langle e \rangle$. This type shifting operation is called *iota*. In this sense, the meaning of the definite article is to map a property onto the maximal/unique individual having that property.[10]

(6) $[\![D_{DEF}]\!] = P \rightarrow \iota x[P(x)]$

When the definite article applies to a noun that denotes a property of a kind, the iota operator yields a maximal/unique kind entity. This is how definite kind expressions are derived. Crucially for our analysis, in the composition of definite kinds, there is no intervener between the iota operator, associated with the definite article (in languages with articles), and the noun. We illustrate this derivation in example (7).

(7)   a. ***The panda*** *is on the verge of extinction.*
       b. [$_{DP}$ *the* [$_{NP}$ *panda*]]
       c. $[\![the\ panda]\!] = \iota x^k[panda(x^k)]$

The subject of (7a), repeated from (2a), is a definite kind expression derived by applying the iota operator to the noun *panda*. Its syntactic structure is given in (7b), and the semantic composition associated with this expression is provided in (7c).[11] This is the essence of our analysis of definite kinds, which we would like to extend to Russian. In this section, we have presented the fundamental theoretical postulates on which we base our analysis of reference to kinds in natural languages. We now address the main issue of this paper, namely, the question of whether Russian has definite kinds, in spite of the fact that it has no overt articles, and which are the arguments that support the existence of definite kinds in this language.

3 Definite kinds in Russian

As we pointed out in §1, the correspondence between the English definite kind expression in (2a) and the Russian bare nominal in (1a) (repeated in 8) with a kind reference is usually assumed to hold, and a reasonable expectation is that the analysis adopted for definite kinds in English can also be extended to Russian cases.

---

[10] The terms *maximal* and *unique* are used in this paper in the sense of Sharvy (1980) and Link (1983), who provide a unified semantics for definiteness, independently of whether the definite article combines with a singular or a plural expression. Thus, these terms should not be confused or even associated with plural and singular number, respectively.

[11] Once again, we propose this derivation for all types of nouns, i.e. count, mass and abstract nouns. See Borik & Espinal (2015) for details.

(8) *Panda   naxoditsja na grani isčeznovenija.*
     panda.NOM.SG is.found   on verge extinction.GEN
     'The panda is on the verge of extinction.'

However, any analysis of English definite kinds includes at least the iota operator in the semantic representation (cf. Chierchia 1998, Dayal 2004). The iota operator is standardly assumed to correspond to the definite article, a claim that we do not want to challenge. However, in the absence of articles in Russian, we should be able to find other independent evidence that the iota operator is, indeed, present in the semantic representation of the subject argument in (8) and not merely assume that it is there due to an interpretation that corresponds to the English kind nominal. In §3.1 and §3.2 we provide independent empirical semantic and syntactic arguments for the definiteness of the subject in (8) and argue that it is to be associated with a null D(eterminer), interpreted as the iota operator.

3.1 Semantic definiteness of kind referring expressions

The core of the argument that we employ to prove that Russian definite kinds are really semantically definite is based on the use and interpretation of these expressions in a context that requires definiteness. The following context can show that kind-referring expressions behave like proper definites.

(9) Context: In a biology lesson, the teacher explains various things about mammals. She explains that there are many endangered species in the world, then says the following:
     The whale, *for instance, is on the verge of extinction.*

Note first that in English, the only morphologically singular expression that can refer to the species itself, and not to a subkind or an individual whale, is the definite one, i.e. *the whale* (Jespersen 1927), which we claim to be unspecified for Number. A DP with a demonstrative or a numeral, as illustrated in (10), will not get the same interpretation as the definite kind expression in (9).

(10) a. **This whale,** *for instance, is on the verge of extinction.*
      b. **One whale,** *for instance, is on the verge of extinction.*

(10a) with the demonstrative can only be acceptable if the teacher points directly to a picture of a representative instance of the corresponding type of whale (say, a blue whale), and thus, refers to a subkind via a representative, and (10b) can only refer to a subkind of whale as well.

In Russian, in the context of (9), the only expression that can be used is the bare noun *kit*, as illustrated in (11). *Kit* in (11) has exactly the same interpretation as the overt DP *the whale* in English, and cannot get an interpretation comparable to (10a) or (10b). This strongly suggests that *kit* in (11) corresponds to a *definite* kind referring expression.

(11)   **Kit,**   *naprimer,*   *naxoditsja na grani isčeznovenija.*
       whale.NOM. for.instance is.found   on verge extinction.GEN.

       'The whale, for instance, is on the verge of extinction.'

Note, however, that theoretically, there could still be an option that while in English the kind referring DP has to be definite, in Russian it might be indefinite. Next, we will discuss why this is not the case.

Even though it is commonly believed that with k-level predicates indefinite DPs can only be interpreted taxonomically, i.e. as referring to a subkind rather than to a kind (see Mueller-Reichau 2011 and references therein), Dayal's (2004) examples like *to invent a pumpkin crusher* challenge this standard assumption. In this paper, we follow Mueller-Reichau who argues that there is a fundamental difference between k-level predicates like *to be extinct* and the ones like *to invent*. Only the latter allow for reference to novel (non-familiar) kinds, whereas the former impose a familiarity condition on the argument. This is why, by default, *A blue whale is in danger of extinction* can only be interpreted as referring to a subkind of the blue whale, whereas *Fred invented a pumpkin crusher* can be interpreted as referring to the kind pumpkin crusher, as well as to a subkind of crusher.[12] This distinction between different types of k-level predicates is both empirically motivated by the examples just given and by our intuition: it is difficult for something that has not existed before to become extinct, therefore, *to be extinct* requires familiar entities. By contrast, it is expected that if someone invents something, they will invent novel entities.

We observe similar effects in Russian with the same type of predicates: in (12a) an indefinite description can only refer to a subkind of whale, but the nominal in

---

[12]We thank an anonymous reviewer for the observation that *Fred invented a pumpkin crusher* allows for two interpretations: the kind 'pumpkin crusher' and a subkind of 'crusher'. Our intuition is that this is due to the fact that the object NP contains a modified noun. Thus, if we consider a non-modified NP, as in *Steve Jobs invented an i-pod* only the subkind reading is salient.

object position in (12b) can refer, indeed, to a new kind of artifact, a 'mechanical calculator', as well as to a subkind of 'calculator'.[13]

(12)   a. ***Odin kit***   *naxoditsja na grani isčeznovenija.*
          One whale.NOM.SG is.found   on verge extinction.GEN
          'One whale is in danger of extinction.'

       b. *Fred izobrel* ***odnu   sčetnuju   mašinu.***
          Fred invented one.ACC.SG calculating.ACC.SG machine.ACC.SG
          'Fred invented a mechanical calculator.'

Thus, we have all reasons to believe that the same distinction between different types of k-level predicates that Mueller-Reichau postulates for English also holds in Russian. Crucially, according to this view, with predicates of the *extinct*-type, "the speaker presupposes the existence of instances of the kind X as known to the hearer" (Mueller-Reichau 2011: 80). This lexical specification blocks reference to a kind for an indefinite expression in the context of *extinct*-type predicates.[14]

Let us now go back to our example (11). As has just been demonstrated in (12a), should the subject of (11) be indefinite, it would necessarily yield a subkind reading, which it does not. This allows us to conclude that the subject argument in (11) is indeed a definite expression and the semantic representation for this BN includes the iota operator, which "supplies" its definiteness, as shown in (13).

(13) $[\![kit]\!] = \iota x^k [kit(x^k)]$

The iota operator simply selects the unique entity that refers to the class itself (i.e. to the class described by the noun *kit*), but does not make the denotation restricted to a given world.

The next issue we need to address is what kind of syntactic structure corresponds to the semantic representation in (13).

---

[13]There are overt indefinite markers in Russian, although they are not articles. In (12) we use the unstressed version of *odin* 'one', which we take to be a specificity marker for indefinites in Russian (cf. Ionin 2013). If this marker bears stress, it is interpreted as a numeral. Note also that not all native speakers readily accept a subkind interpretation for examples like (12a). We have encountered judgments that vary from full rejection to full acceptance.

[14]Similarly, Stanković (2016) postulates a complex DP structure for Serbo-Croatian, which includes a kind-referring DP embedded under an individual referring DP. He argues that the kind-referring DP can only be definite, not indefinite in Serbo-Croatian.

3.2 Syntactic arguments for a DP structure

In example (7b) of §2 we already gave a syntactic structure for the definite kind expression in (7a), so it should be clear by now that the general syntactic structure associated with definite kinds should look like (14).

(14) $[_{DP}D[_{NP}N]]$

Syntactically, we defend the claim that definite kinds in Russian are DPs, that is, the D-layer is present in the syntactic representation of definite kind arguments even though there is no overt realization of the D-projection.

Before we discuss this analysis, let us point out that we assume a strict correspondence between syntactic and semantic representations at the syntax-semantic interface as a null hypothesis. This view on the syntax-semantics interface by default requires a consistent syntactic representation for each particular semantic operation. In the case of definite kinds, the operator that turns the meaning of a common noun (i.e. a property of kinds; see §2) into a kind expression is the iota operator, which needs to be represented syntactically, unless we assume that all nouns are structurally ambiguous and one and the same expression can be associated with various syntactic structures. Since there is ample cross-linguistic evidence that the iota operator is syntactically represented by the definite article (consider, for example, the situation in Germanic and Romance), we should conclude that we need a D projection even for article-less languages where iota is not lexicalized. Making this proposal, we follow the insights of Longobardi (1994; 2001; 2005), who claims that semantic referentiality (i.e. being a referring expression) is associated with a particular syntactic position, namely, the head of the DP. This claim could be considered one of the strongest mapping principles between the syntax and semantics of natural languages, and it fits neatly with the syntax-semantics correspondence that we are assuming in this paper.

As for Russian, proposals that provide a similar semantic motivation for the DP projection with a null D have been made, for instance, by Ramchand & Svenonius (2008) who argue that the D head in Russian is needed for reasons of semantic uniformity: this is the head that turns nominal expressions, which are originally of property-type $\langle e, t \rangle$, to arguments, i.e. expressions of type $\langle e \rangle$. They further suggest that the D head in Russian should be underspecified for features like (in)definiteness, (un)specificity, etc., which are determined contextually. This means that DPs in Russian can represent definite or indefinite (specific and non-specific) arguments, the hypothesis that we adopt in here as well.

However, the strict syntax-semantic correspondence is a working hypothesis that, in and by itself, cannot be taken as an argument for the presence of the DP layer in the syntactic representation of definite kinds in Russian. A well-known debate in the literature on languages with and without articles is the discussion between the Universal-DP hypothesis (Longobardi 1994; Cinque 2005; Pereltsvaig 2007) and the Parametrized-DP hypothesis (Bošković 2005; 2008; Bošković & Gajewski 2008; Bošković 2009). According to the former, languages with or without articles would have all nominal arguments projected as full DPs and would allow null Ds. According to the second hypothesis, however, there exist two types of languages, those with articles (like English and Modern French), which project arguments as DPs, and those without articles (like Serbo-Croatian and Russian), which are postulated to project NPs.[15]

We adopt the view advocated by Pereltsvaig (2006), according to which nominal arguments can differ in "size", i.e. have different types of syntactic structure in argument position, both across languages and language internally. Thus, in both Russian and, for instance, English or Spanish, we can find nominal arguments that syntactically correspond to either full DPs or smaller nominals: NPs, NumPs or QPs.[16] In Russian, nominal arguments associated with different syntactic structures exhibit a number of different properties and have a different semantic interpretation as well. In particular, DP subjects obligatorily agree with the verbal predicate, whereas small nominals do not. Agreeing subjects allow an individuated / specific interpretation, a non-isomorphic wide scope reading, they may control PRO and be antecedents of anaphors, whereas non-agreeing subjects do not.[17] To illustrate this difference between agreeing and non-agreeing nominal subjects, consider the minimal pair in (15) (from Pereltsvaig 2006: 438–9, ex. 3). Example (15a) exhibits number agreement between *pjat' izvestnyx aktërov* 'five famous actors' and the verb, and this agreement is supposed to correlate with the distributive individuated interpretation of the subject, in the sense that each one of the famous actors played a role in the film. By contrast, in example (15b) there is no number agreement between the subject and the verb, the latter being in the third person singular neuter default form.[18] Lack of syntactic agreement

---

[15]The Parametrized-DP hypothesis is given extensive empirical motivation in the literature. However, the arguments for the DP/NP split between languages, to the best of our knowledge, are purely syntactic (e.g. left-branch extraction, negative raising, superiority effects, etc.; e.g. Bošković 2008). The proponents of the Parametrized-DP hypothesis usually do not take into account the semantic functions attributed to the DP projection as we do in this paper.

[16]For similar claims in Romance languages see Schmitt & Munn (1999; 2003), Munn & Schmitt (2005), Dobrovie-Sorin et al. (2006), Cyrino & Espinal (2015), among others.

[17]For details, see Pereltsvaig (2006: 447).

[18]Pereltsvaig (2006) does not indicate SG, but only NEUT, in the gloss for the verb in this example, because nouns, verbs, adjectives and various agreeing elements can express gender only in singular. We modified the gloss to include the number specification on the verb plus the number and case on the noun for the sake of explicitness.

correlates with a group interpretation of the nominal expression. This means that the subject argument *pjat' izvestnyx aktërov* 'five famous actors' is attributed a full DP structure with a null D in (15a) but a QP with a numeral in (15b).

(15) a. *V ètom fil'me igrali*   [*pjat' izvestnyx aktërov*].
          in this film   played.PL five famous   actors.PL.GEN
          'Five famous actors played in this film.'

  b. *V ètom fil'me igralo*   [*pjat' izvestnyx aktërov*].
          in this film   played.SG.NEUT five famous   actors.PL.GEN
          'Five famous actors played in this film.'

We find Pereltsvaig's proposal that in Russian some nominals are DPs but small nominals can be found in the same syntactic position as DPs very plausible, and thus we adopt the claim that in all languages, including Russian, there can be nominal arguments of different "size", that is, involving a different "amount" of functional structure on top of the minimal NP projection, the highest projection that a nominal argument can have being a DP.

Let us now go back to definite kinds and test how arguments of k- and i-level predicates behave with respect to some properties listed in Pereltsvaig (2006). Note that only some of the properties this author lists can be tested for definite kinds. The reason for this is that the majority of Pereltsvaig's arguments are built for nominal phrases with various types of modifiers (numerals, adjectives, etc.), but kind expressions almost never accept regular modifiers.[19] We thus focus on the following properties that kind arguments can be tested for: control of PRO, licensing of anaphors, substitution by pronominal elements and presence of non-restrictive relative clauses. We show that all these properties support an analysis of definite kinds in Russian as full DPs.

3.2.1 Control of PRO

Non-agreeing subjects cannot be controllers for PRO in infinitival clauses, while agreeing subjects, being full DPs, can. The contrast is exemplified in (16) (Pereltsvaig 2006: 444, ex. 10a).

(16) [*Pjat' banditov*]$_i$ *pytalis'* / **pytalos'*   [PRO$_i$ *ubit' Džemsa Bonda*].
       five thugs.PL.GEN tried.PL / tried.SG.NEUT PRO to.kill James Bond
       'Five thugs tried to kill James Bond.'

---

[19] See, however, §3.3 below.

Let us now look at definite kinds. As shown in (17), definite kind subjects can control PRO of a purpose clause and, hence, pattern with agreeing subjects. Since agreeing subjects are argued to be full DPs, we can conclude that the same syntactic category should be attributed to definite kinds.

(17) **Panda**$_i$ *imeet neobyčnye perednije lapy čtoby*   PRO$_i$
      panda.SG.NOM has.SG unusual   front   paws in.order.to PRO
      uderživat' stebli bambuka.
      hold   stems bamboo
      'The panda has unusual front paws to hold bamboo stems.'

3.2.2 Antecedents of reflexive pronouns

Our next piece of evidence in favour of the DP status of definite kinds is that these expressions can be antecedents of a reflexive pronoun. We start by illustrating the contrast between agreeing and non-agreeing subjects with respect to their ability to license reflexive pronouns (Pereltsvaig 2006: 455, ex. 11a): only agreeing subjects can license reflexive pronouns.

(18) [*Pjat banditov*]$_i$ *prikryvali / *prikryvalo   sebja*$_i$ *ot   pul'*
      five thugs.PL.GEN shielded.PL / shielded.SG.NEUT self   from bullets
      Džemsa Bonda.
      James   Bond
      'Five thugs shielded themselves from James Bond's bullets.'

As (19) illustrates, definite kinds pattern likewise.

(19) **Tigr**$_i$ *znaet   kak zaščitit'* **sebja**$_i$ *ot   napadenija.*
      tiger.SG.NOM knows.SG how defend   self   from attacks
      'The/a tiger knows how to protect itself from being attacked.'

This example shows that, according to the test, the antecedent of the reflexive must be a DP. This DP may be devoid of Number, as in the structure (14) above (i.e. the structure postulated for definite kinds), or may have Number. In the latter situation, the D can be either definite or indefinite, and either singular or plural.

3.2.3 Pronominal substitution

Finally, a pronominal substitution test also shows that definite kinds behave like DPs rather than other, "smaller" types of arguments. The test as used in Pereltsvaig (2006) shows that third person pronouns can be used to substitute full DPs, but not QPs or NPs, which can only be substituted by other (quantificational and/or pronominal) elements. The example below (based on Pereltsvaig 2006: 446, ex. 15a) shows that the pronominal subject of (20b) can only substitute the agreeing subject of (20a).

(20) a. *Pjat' par   tancevali / tancevalo   tango.*
         five couples.PL.GEN danced.PL / danced.SG.NEUT tango
         'Five couples danced tango.'

    b. *Oni   tancevali / *tancevalo   tango.*
         they.PL.NOM danced.PL / danced.SG.NEUT tango
         'They danced a tango.'

Coming back to definite kinds, it can be easily shown that the definite kind agreeing subject in (21a) can only be replaced by a third person pronoun *ona* 'she', thus supporting the claim that definite kinds are DPs.

(21) a. **Panda**   *naxoditsja na grani isčeznovenija.*
         panda.SG.NOM is.found.SG on verge extinction.GEN

    b. **Ona**   *naxoditsja na grani isčeznovenija.*
         she.SG.NOM is.found.SG on verge extinction.GEN
         'The panda/She is on the verge of extinction.'

The three arguments just given, which are based on the syntactic tests proposed in Pereltsvaig (2006) for differentiating between DP arguments and arguments associated with a "smaller" syntactic structure, all support the claim that definite kinds in Russian are syntactically DPs.

Let us add one more observation to the arguments given above.

3.2.4 Distribution of relative clauses

There is a limited number of constructions in Russian where a nominal argument seems to have the status of a real bare NP and be associated with a minimal possible NP structure with no additional functional layers. A couple of relevant examples from Russian is given in (22) (22b is from Borik et al. 2012: ex. 8).

(22) a. *Petja xodit v galstuke, (*kotoryj vsegda nravitsja ego žene).*
         Petja goes in tie.SG.OBL   which always likes   his wife
         'Petja is a tie-wearer, (*which his wife always likes).'

b. *Katya nosit*   *jubku,*   (**kotoruju ona vsegda pokupaet sama*).
   Katya wear.IMP skirt.SG.ACC which   she always buys.IMP self
   'Katya is a skirt-wearer, (*which she always buys).'

The objects *galstuke* 'tie' and *jubku* 'skirt', despite being morphologically mark-ed as singular, have a number neutral interpretation (i.e. one or more tie, one or more skirt), that is, can denote either an atomic or a plural entity satisfying the description of the nominal.[20] Number neutrality is a hallmark of bare nominals in various languages (cf. Farkas & de Swart 2003 for Hungarian; Dayal 2004 for Hindi; Espinal & McNally 2011 for Spanish and Catalan, etc.), so this is a good reason to assume that the objects in (22), despite being morphologically singular, are "true" bare nominals unspecified for syntactic and semantic Number.

Note, however, that neither *galstuke* 'tie' nor *jubku* 'skirt' in this interpretation can be modified by a relative clause.[21] We suggest that a reason for blocking a relative clause in (22) is that in a real NP structure there is no room for descriptive but only for classifying modifiers (which is in accordance with our theoretical postulate 1, see §2.1). A classifying modifier but not a restrictive relative clause is allowed in (23), under the intended reading that Katya is a skirt-wearer.

(23)   *Katya nosit*   *mini-jubku,*   (**kotoruju ona vsegda pokupaet sama*).
      Katya wear.IMP mini-skirt.SG.ACC   which   she always buys.IMP self
      'Katya is a mini-skirt wearer, (*which she always buys).'

Consider now an example with a definite kind expression:

(24)   a.   *Amurskij tigr, kotoryj očen' opasen,*   *obitaet na jugo-vostoke*
          Siberian tiger which very dangerous lives   on south-east
          Rossii.
          Russia.

          'The Siberian tiger, which is extremely dangerous, lives in the south-east part of Russia.'

---

[20] See Kagan & Pereltsvaig (2011) and Pereltsvaig (2013) for other types of number neutral argu-ments in Russian. In these papers, it is argued that semantically number neutral nominals are plural in Russian. We agree with this claim, but we think that Russian also has morphologically singular nominals with a number neutral interpretation.

[21] This is also a property of bare nominals in the same syntactic position in Romance languages, such as Catalan and Spanish. See Espinal & McNally (2011).

b. # *Amurskij tigr, kotoryj rodilsja   v našem zooparke, obitaet na*
   Siberian tiger which was.born in our   zoo   live   on
   jugo-vostoke Rossii.
   south-east   Russia

'The Siberian tiger that was born in our zoo lives in the south-east
part of Russia.'

As can be seen in (24a), definite kinds allow subsequent modification by a non-restrictive relative clause. Non-restrictive (or appositive) relative clauses do not restrict the (set of) referents denoted by the nominal phrase, they just provide *additional* information about an already established referent. By contrast, as the example (24b) illustrates, a relative clause that can only be interpreted restrictively, imposes an individual (as opposed to a kind) interpretation on the subject of the clause, which is then difficult to combine with the verbal predicate *obitaet* 'to live' that normally selects for kinds.[22]

Let us now go back to the claim that we made at the beginning of the section, namely, that the incompatibility of restrictive relative clauses with definite kinds can be seen as an additional argument for the DP status of the kind nominal. We now explain why it should be so.

Semantically, non-restrictive relative clauses are not interpreted in the scope of the determiner, as the following examples from English illustrate:

(25)   a. [[*The public transport*], [*which is state-owned*]], *is fast, clean and reliable.*

b. [*The* [*public transport which is state-owned*]] *is fast, clean and reliable.*

The example in (25a), which is interpreted non-restrictively, can be rephrased as a conjunction: 'the public transport is fast, clean and reliable and it is state-owned'. It does not imply (in fact, it cannot imply) that there is any other public transport except for the state-owned. The example in (25b), on the other hand, implies that not all the public transport is owned by the state and it is clear that the definite determiner *the* in (25b) has the whole nominal phrase, including the relative clause, in its scope.

Jackendoff (1977) suggested that the difference between restrictive and non-restrictive relative clauses should be reflected in their syntactic configuration, in

---

[22]Two notes are in order here. First of all, Russian has several verbs that can be translated as 'to live', and the one used in example (24) is often used with kind nominals since its lexical meaning is closer to 'to live permanently, to inhabit'. Secondly, the # sign in front of (24b) means that the subject can, in principle, be interpreted as referring to an individual tiger, although it takes a certain effort to get this interpretation, at least for one of the authors of this paper, and the intuition is that this interpretation is an effect of coercion.

the sense that the latter adjoin higher in the structure than the former. Demirdache (1991) specifically proposed that non-restrictive relatives are adjoined to
DP, although only at LF. De Vries (2006) postulates that appositive relative
clauses should be represented as a coordination of DPs, an appositive relative as
a specifying conjunct to the visible antecedent. Arsenijević & Gračanin-Yuksek
(2016) also argued that the configurational differences between restrictive and
non-restric-tive relative clauses should be reflected in overt syntax on the basis of agreement facts in Bosnian/Serbian/Croatian. Generalizing over these and
many more works on relative clauses, we can say that the main idea is that non-
restrictive relatives can only have a DP as an antecedent. There is no a priori
reason to believe that Russian non-restrictive clauses would be different in their
syntax and semantics. Therefore, we take (24a) to be another piece of evidence
in favor of the DP status of definite kind expressions.

The discussion of relative clauses once again supports the point made by Pereltsvaig (2006): we should allow for different structures to be associated with
nominals in argument position. (24a) above indicates that definite kinds cannot
be NPs, as we have seen that true bare NPs do not take relative clauses, restrictive or non-restrictive. If we consider the empirical contrast between (23) and
(24a), together with Pereltsvaig's arguments discussed earlier in this section, the
conclusion that we logically arrive at is the same: definite kinds in Russian are
DPs.

This conclusion allows us to preserve the correspondence between the presence of D projection and the contribution of the iota operator, which, as we have
seen above, is realized as a definite article in languages with articles. Our claim
for an article-less language like Russian is, thus, that the syntactic representation
of definite kinds involves a null D, which is translated as the iota operator, too.

3.3 Modified definite kinds

In §3.2 we have provided syntactic arguments for a DP structure. Still, a question
that remains to be answered is whether definite kinds allow any sort of modification inside the DP. We think that the answer to this question is positive, and,
following Borik & Espinal (2015) for Spanish, we show in this section that Russian
has kind expressions with modifiers, which we call modified kinds.

Modified kinds are ind-referring expressions composed by a noun and a modifier, normally expressed by an adjective, provide an additional semantic argument for the definiteness of Russian bare nominal kinds. Consider the data in
(26).

(26) a. ***Amurskij tigr*** *zanesen   v Krasnuju knigu.*
      Siberian   tiger registered in Red   book
      'The Siberian tiger is registered in the IUCN Red list.'

   b. ***Mavrikijskij dront*** *izvesten tol'ko po   izobraženijam i*
      Mauritius   dodo known only from drawings   and
      pis'mennym istočnikam XVII veka.
      written   sources   XVII century
      'The dodo of the Mauritius island is only known from drawings and written sources of the XVII century.'

The modified DPs in subject position in (26), similarly to the corresponding non-modified versions, denote kinds. However, in comparison to the non-modified counterparts (e.g. *tigr* 'tiger'), modified kinds (e.g. *amurskij tigr* 'Siberian tiger') are semantically more restricted. We suggest that modified kinds, composed by a noun preceded or followed by an adjective within a DP structure, are built by applying kind modifiers (of type $\langle\langle e^k, t\rangle, \langle e^k, t\rangle\rangle$) to properties of kinds (of type $\langle e^k, t\rangle$). The formal representation for the modified kind in (26) is given in (27).

(27) a. $[_{DP}D[_{NP}(A) N (A)]]$
   b. $[\![amurskij\ tigr]\!] = \iota x^k[(amurskij(tigr))(x^k)]$

A question that arises at this point is what kind of adjective can appear in a modified kind expression. We think that potentially any adjective can modify a kind although the whole expression is subject to an additional pragmatic constraint, known as the well-established kind restriction (cf. Krifka et al. 1995).

The well-established kind restriction has been widely discussed in the literature for English and other languages as applying to definite generics (cf. Vergnaud & Zubizarreta 1992, Krifka et al. 1995, Dayal 2004 and many others). If the well-established kind restriction is pragmatic in nature, it is expected that an appropriate contextual modification could make a definite kind reading in (28a) plausible. This is, indeed, the case. If there are only two relevant classes of tigers, wounded tigers and hungry tigers, (28b) becomes a perfectly acceptable characterization of the first class. In this case, the interpretation that should be attributed to the subject of (28b) is the one characteristic of a definite kind.

(28) a. *Ranenyj tigr opasen.*
      wounded tiger dangerous
      'A wounded tiger is dangerous.'

    b. *Ranenyj   tigr, kak vid, opasen.*
       wounded tiger as   type dangerous
       'The wounded tiger, as a kind, is dangerous.'

We propose that the well-established kind restriction can block a kind interpretation for modified nominal expressions at a pragmatic level, but this is not a grammatical constraint (for similar observations see Dayal 1992; Krifka et al. 1995: 69; Dayal 2004: footnote 30). Rather, it is our world knowledge and accessible encyclopedic information that determines which expression can correspond to a known or established kind in the actual world. Note, furthermore, that this information can change, and hence, relevant contextual or extra-linguistic factors can have a strong influence on the interpretation of nominal expressions.

4 Conclusions

In this paper we have provided an analysis of definite kinds in Russian at the syntax-semantics interface. We have presented arguments for the semantic definiteness of bare nominal kinds, and syntactic arguments for a null D. We have argued that definite kinds are compositionally built by applying the iota operator corresponding to a (covert) definite D to the property of kinds denoted by the N, and we have extended this analysis to modified definite kinds. The analysis we propose applies to one specific type of expressions which refer to kinds, the one that corresponds to English definite kinds. In Russian, as in many other languages, there is a range of other expressions which plausibly encode D-genericity, notably, plural generics. We see it as one of the main questions for future research to complement our proposal by an analysis of other types of nominal generics in Russian and an account of similarities and differences in the meaning and use of various kind referring expressions.

Acknowledgements

We would like to thank the editors of the book and the reviewers of this paper, as well as the audience of the conference *Definiteness across languages* (Ciudad de México, 2016) for their comments. This research was supported by the Spanish MICINN (grants FFI2014-52015-P and FFI2017-82547-P) and the Catalan Government (grants 2014SGR2013 and 2017SGR634). The second author also acknowledges an ICREA Academia award.

Abbreviations

GEN	genitive	MASC	masculine
ACC	accusative	FEM	feminine
OBL	oblique	NEUT	neuter
SG	singular	IMP	imperfective
PL	plural		

References

Arsenijević, Boban & Martina Gračanin-Yuksek. 2016. Agreement and the structure of relative clauses. *Glossa: A journal of general linguistics* 1(1). 17.

Borer, Hagit. 2005. *Structuring sense: Vol. I: In name only.* Oxford: Oxford University Press.

Borik, Olga, Sonia Cyrino & M.-Teresa Espinal. 2012. On determiners in languages with and without articles. (Paper presented at the Workshop on Languages with and without Articles. Paris: CNRS, Université Paris-8, 2012).

Borik, Olga & M.-Teresa Espinal. 2015. Reference to kinds and to other generic expressions in Spanish: Definiteness and number. *The Linguistic Review* 32(2). 167–225.

Bošković, Željko. 2005. On the locality of left branch extraction and the structure of NP. *Studia Linguistica* 59(1). 1–45.

Bošković, Željko. 2008. What will you have, DP or NP? *Proceedings of NELS* 37(1). 101–114.

Bošković, Željko. 2009. More on the no-DP analysis of article-less languages. *Studia Linguistica* 63(2). 187–203.

Bošković, Željko & Jon Gajewski. 2008. Semantic correlates of the NP/DP parameter. (Paper presented at the 39th Meeting of the North East Linguistic Society. Ithaca: Cornell University, November 7-9, 2008).

Carlson, Greg N. 1977. *Reference to kinds in English.* Amherst: University of Massachusetts. (Doctoral dissertation).

Chierchia, Gennaro. 1984. *Topics in the syntax and semantics of infinitives and gerunds.* Amherst: University of Massachusetts. (Doctoral dissertation).

Chierchia, Gennaro. 1998. Reference to kinds across languages. *Natural Language Semantics* 6(4). 339–405.

Cinque, Guglielmo. 2005. Deriving Greenberg's Universal 20 and its exceptions. *Linguistic Inquiry* 36(3). 315–332.

Coppock, Elizabeth & David Beaver. 2015. Definiteness and determinacy. *Linguistics and Philosophy* 38(5). 377–435.

Cyrino, Sonia & M.-Teresa Espinal. 2015. Bare nominals in Brazilian Portuguese: More on the DP/NP. *Natural Language and Linguistic Theory* 33(2). 471–521.

Dayal, Veneeta. 1992. The singular-plural distinction in Hindi generics. In Chris Barker & David Dowty (eds.), *Salt II: Proceedings from the Second Conference on Semantics and Linguistic Theory* (Ohio State University Working Papers in Linguistics 40), 39–58. Columbus, OH: Ohio State University.

Dayal, Veneeta. 2004. Number marking and (in)definiteness in kind terms. *Linguistics and Philosophy* 27(4). 393–450.

de Swart, Henriëtte, Yoad Winter & Joost Zwarts. 2007. Bare nominals and reference to capacities. *Natural Language and Linguistic Theory* 25(1). 195–222.

de Vries, Mark. 2006. The syntax of appositive relativization: On specifying coordination, false free relatives, and promotion. *Linguistic Inquiry* 37(2). 229–270.

Demirdache, Hamida. 1991. *Resumptive chains in restrictive relatives, appositives and dislocation structures.* Cambridge: Massachusetts Institute of Technology. (Doctoral dissertation).

Dobrovie-Sorin, Carmen, Tonia Bleam & M.-Teresa Espinal. 2006. Bare nouns, number and types of incorporation. In Liliane Tasmowski & Svetlana Vogeleer (eds.), *Non-definiteness and plurality* (Linguistik Aktuell/Linguistics Today 95), 51–79. Amsterdam: John Benjamins.

Dobrovie-Sorin, Carmen & Brenda Laca. 1996. Generic BNPs. (Paris VII/University of Strasbourg. Unpublished manuscript).

Dobrovie-Sorin, Carmen & Brenda Laca. 2003. Les noms sans déterminants dans les langues romanes. In Danièle Godard (ed.), *Les langues romanes: Problèmes de la phrase simple*, 235–281. Paris: Les Èditions du CNRS.

Dobrovie-Sorin, Carmen & Roberta Pires de Oliveira. 2008. Reference to kinds in Brazilian Portuguese: Definite singulars vs. bare singulars. In Atle Grønn (ed.), *Proceedings of Sinn und Bedeutung (SuB) 12*, 107–121. Oslo: ILOS.

Doron, Edit. 2003. Agency and voice: The semantics of the Semitic template. *Natural Language Semantics* 11(1). 1–67.

Espinal, M.-Teresa. 2010. Bare nominals in Catalan and Spanish: Their structure and meaning. *Lingua* 120(4). 984–1009.

Espinal, M.-Teresa & Louise McNally. 2007a. Bare singular nominals and incorporating verbs. In Georg Kaiser & Manuel Leonetti (eds.), *Proceedings of the workshop "Definiteness, Specificity and Animacy in Ibero-Romance Languages"*

(Arbeitspapiere / Fachbereich Sprachwissenschaft 122), 45–62. Konstanz: Fachbereich Sprachwissenschaft der Univ. Konstanz.

Espinal, M.-Teresa & Louise McNally. 2007b. Bare singulars: Variation at the syntax-semantics interface. (Paper presented at the Workshop on Bare nouns and Nominalizations. Stuttgart: University of Stuttgart, 2007).

Espinal, M.-Teresa & Louise McNally. 2011. Bare singular nominals and incorporating verbs in Spanish and Catalan. *Journal of Linguistics* 47(1). 87–128.

Farkas, Donka F. & Henriëtte de Swart. 2003. *The semantics of incorporation: From argument structure to discourse transparency*. Stanford: CSLI Publications.

Ionin, Tania. 2013. Pragmatic variation among specificity markers. In Stefan Hinterwimmer & Cornelia Ebert (eds.), *Different kinds of specificity across languages* (Studies in Linguistics and Philosophy 92), 75–103. Berlin: Springer.

Ionin, Tania & Ora Matushansky. 2006. The composition of complex cardinals. *Journal of Semantics* 23(4). 315–360.

Ionin, Tania, Silvina Montrul & Hélade Santos. 2011. An experimental investigation of the expression of genericity in English, Spanish and Brazilian Portuguese. *Lingua* 121(5). 963–985.

Jackendoff, Ray. 1977. *X-Bar syntax: A study of phrase structure* (Linguistic Inquiry Monographs 2). Cambridge: MIT Press.

Jespersen, Otto. 1927. *A modern English grammar on historical principles*. London: Allen & Unwin.

Kagan, Olga & Asya Pereltsvaig. 2011. Syntax and semantics of bare NPs: Objects of intensive reflexive verbs in Russian. In Olivier Bonami & Patricia Cabredo Hofherr (eds.), *Empirical Issues in Syntax and Semantics 8 (Proceedings of CSSP 8)*, 221–238. Paris: CNRS.

Krifka, Manfred, Francis Jeffry Pelletier, Greg N. Carlson, Alice ter Meulen, Gennaro Chierchia & Godehard Link. 1995. Genericity: An introduction. In Greg N. Carlson & Francis Jeffry Pelletier (eds.), *The generic book*, 1–125. Chicago: University of Chicago Press.

Laca, Brenda. 1990. Generic objects: Some more pieces of the puzzle. *Lingua* 81(1). 25–46.

Link, Godehard. 1983. The logical analysis of plurals and mass terms: A lattice-theoretical approach. In Rainer Bäuerle, Christoph Schwartze & Arnim von Stechow (eds.), *Meaning, use, and interpretation of language* (Grundlagen der Kommunikation und Kognition / Foundations of Communication and Cognition), 302–323. Berlin: de Gruyter.

Longobardi, Giuseppe. 1994. Reference and proper names: A theory of N-movement in syntax and logical form. *Linguistic Inquiry* 25(4). 609–665.

Longobardi, Giuseppe. 2001. How comparative is semantics? A unified parametric theory of bare nouns and proper names. *Natural Language Semantics* 9(4). 335–369.

Longobardi, Giuseppe. 2005. Toward a unified grammar of reference. *Zeitschrift für Sprachwissenschaft* 24. 5–44.

McNally, Louise & Gemma Boleda. 2004. Relational adjectives as properties of kinds. In Olivier Bonami & Patricia Cabredo Hofherr (eds.), *Empirical Issues in Formal Syntax and Semantics 5. Papers from CSSP 2003*, 179–196. Paris: CNRS.

Mueller-Reichau, Olav. 2011. *Sorting the world: On the relevance of the kind-level/object-level distinction to referential semantics*. Heusenstamm: Ontos Verlag.

Munn, Alan & Cristina Schmitt. 2005. Number and indefinites. *Lingua* 115(6). 821–855.

Partee, Barbara H. 1986. Noun phrase interpretation and type-shifting principles. In Jeroen Groenendijk, Dick de Jongh & Martin Stokhof (eds.), *Studies in discourse representation theory and the theory of generalized quantifiers*, 115–143. Dordrecht: Foris.

Pereltsvaig, Asya. 2006. Small nominals. *Natural Language and Linguistic Theory* 24(2). 433–500.

Pereltsvaig, Asya. 2007. The universality of DP: A view from Russian. *Studia Linguistica* 61(1). 59–94.

Pereltsvaig, Asya. 2013. On number and numberlessness in languages without articles. In Chundra Cathcart, Hsuan Chen, Greg Finley, Shinae Kang, Clare S. Sandy & Elise Stickles (eds.), *Proceedings of the 37th Annual Meeting of the Berkeley Linguistics Society (BLS)*, 300–314. Berkeley, CA: Berkeley Linguistics Society.

Pires de Oliveira, Roberta & Susan Rothstein. 2011. Bare singular noun phrases are mass in Brazilian Portuguese. *Lingua* 121(15). 2153–2175.

Ramchand, Gillian C. & Peter Svenonius. 2008. Mapping a parochial lexicon onto a universal semantics. In Theresa Biberauer (ed.), *The limits of syntactic variation* (Linguistik Aktuell/Linguistics Today 132), 219–245. Amsterdam: John Benjamins.

Rothstein, Susan. 2010. Counting and the count-mass distinction. *Journal of Semantics* 27(3). 343–397.

Schmitt, Cristina & Alan Munn. 1999. Against the nominal mapping parameter: Bare nouns in Brazilian Portuguese. *Proceedings of NELS* 29. 339–353.

Schmitt, Cristina & Alan Munn. 2003. The syntax and semantics of bare arguments in Brazilian Portuguese. In Pierre Pica (ed.), *Linguistic variation yearbook*, vol. 2, 185–216. Amsterdam: John Benjamins.

Sharvy, Richard. 1980. A more general theory of definite descriptions. *The Philosophical Review* 89(4). 607–624.

Stanković, Branimir. 2016. DP in a language without articles – Case of Serbo-Croatian adjectives. (Paper presented at the Workshop on the Semantic Contribution of Det and Num: (In)definiteness, genericity and referentiality, Universitat Autònoma de Barcelona, Barcelona).

Trugman, Helen. 2013. Naturally-atomic singular NA kinds in Russian as lexically derived. In Uwe Junghanns, Dorothee Fehrmann, Denisa Lenertová & Hagen Pitsch (eds.), *Formal Description of Slavic Languages: The Ninth Conference. Proceedings of FDSL 9, Göttingen 2011*, 325–348. Frankfurt: Peter Lang.

Vergnaud, Jean-Roger & María Luisa Zubizarreta. 1992. The definite determiner and the inalienable constructions in French and in English. *Linguistic Inquiry* 23(4). 595–652.

Zamparelli, Roberto. 1995. *Layers in the determiner phrase.* Rochester: University of Rochester. (Doctoral dissertation).

Zamparelli, Roberto. 2008. Bare predicate nominals in Romance languages. In Alex Klinge & Henrik H. Müller (eds.), *Essays on nominal determination: From morphology to discourse management* (Studies in Language Companion Series 99), 101–130. Amsterdam: John Benjamins.

Permissions

All chapters in this book were first published in DAL, by Language Science Press; hereby published with permission under the Creative Commons Attribution License or equivalent. Every chapter published in this book has been scrutinized by our experts. Their significance has been extensively debated. The topics covered herein carry significant information for a comprehensive understanding. They may even be implemented as practical applications or may be referred to as a beginning point for further studies.

The contributors of this book come from diverse backgrounds, making this book a truly international effort. We would like to thank all the contributing authors for lending their expertise to make the book truly unique. They have played a crucial role in the development of this book. Without their invaluable contributions this book wouldn't have been possible. They have made vital efforts to compile up to date information on the varied aspects of this subject to make this book a valuable addition to the collection of many professionals and students.

This book was conceptualized with the vision of imparting up-to-date and integrated information in this field. To ensure the same, a matchless editorial board was set up. Every individual on the board went through rigorous rounds of assessment to prove their worth. After which they invested a large part of their time researching and compiling the most relevant data for our readers.

The editorial board has been involved in producing this book since its inception. They have spent rigorous hours researching and exploring the diverse topics which have resulted in the successful publishing of this book. They have passed on their knowledge of decades through this book. To expedite this challenging task, the publisher supported the team at every step. A small team of assistant editors was also appointed to further simplify the editing procedure and attain best results for the readers.

Apart from the editorial board, the designing team has also invested a significant amount of their time in understanding the subject and creating the most relevant covers. They scrutinized every image to scout for the most suitable representation of the subject and create an appropriate cover for the book.

The publishing team has been an ardent support to the editorial, designing and production team. Their endless efforts to recruit the best for this project, has resulted in the accomplishment of this book. They are a veteran in the field of academics and their pool of knowledge is as vast as their experience in printing. Their expertise and guidance has proved useful at every step. Their uncompromising quality standards have made this book an exceptional effort. Their encouragement from time to time has been an inspiration for everyone.

The publisher and the editorial board hope that this book will prove to be a valuable piece of knowledge for students, practitioners and scholars across the globe.

List of Contributors

Adina Williams
New York University

Urtzi Etxeberria
CNRS-IKER

Anastasia Giannakidou
University of Chicago

Miloje Despić
Cornell University

Elizabeth Coppock
Boston University
University of Gothenburg

Linnea Strand
University of Gothenburg

Thaís Maíra Machado de Sá
Universidade Federal de Minas Gerais

Greg N. Carlson
University of Rochester

Maria Luiza Cunha Lima
Universidade Federal de Minas Gerais

Michael K. Tanenhaus
University of Rochester
Nanjing Normal University

Olga Borik
Universidad Nacional de Educación a Distancia

M.-Teresa Espinal
Universitat Autònoma de Barcelona

Index